Praise for *Scr...*

"Harvey is a master storyteller with a passion for creating inspiring films and television programs. He's driven by his love of helping others tell their own stories, so if you have one to tell, *Scratching the Surface* is an invaluable resource and a great guide to unleashing your own creativity."

—Bill Pace, television and feature film producer on *A League of Their Own*; HBO's *A Private Matter*; PBS's *LateNight America*; and movies for CBS, ABC, NBC, and *Hallmark Hall of Fame*

"Utilizing his unique ability to depict life experiences in a way that captivates and informs, Harvey brings his own human adventure into focus when conveying the important role that storytelling plays in our society."

—Aaron Dworkin, author of *The Entrepreneurial Artist: Lessons from Highly Successful Creatives* and professor of Arts Leadership and Entrepreneurship, University of Michigan

"A thoughtful exploration into the life of a passionate storyteller. From the moment I met Harvey, I felt his unmatched enthusiasm to share stories and inspire greatness. *Scratching the Surface* is a must read for anyone interested in the art of sharing stories."

—Scott Bogoniewski, former chair of entertainment arts at College for Creative Studies and technical director in the entertainment industry

"Leave it to Harvey Ovshinsky to create a new genre, the biotext, where memoir meets textbook. With its mix of life struggles, creative escapades, and production war stories, *Scratching the Surface* reads like a fireside chat with a storytelling sage. I'll be keeping this trove of inspiration and concrete advice on my writing desk for years to come."

—Desiree Cooper, author, filmmaker, Kresge Artist Fellow, and Pulitzer Prize–nominated journalist

"I love the journey in this book. Whether it's in Harvey's documentaries, screenplays, or his own backstory, *Scratching the Surface* reminds us what it takes to make our work 'stronger, tighter, deeper.' And it's about so much more that makes this book such a wonderful read. It's about not being afraid to go past our own boundaries to be creative and fresh and innovative."

—Linda Seger, author of *Advanced Screenwriting*, *Making a Good Script Great*, and *Making a Good Writer Great*

"In this master class for filmmakers and journalists, Mr. O (as his former students call him) slyly teaches storytelling through the action of showing, instead of telling. His light touch allows for deep dives with a killer sense of humor, personal vulnerability, and profound poetry. I have a renewed understanding of my beloved city's roots, gained a unique insight into story *crafting*, and am inspired to reimagine my next film project by scratching its surface."

—Lara Sfire, filmmaker and co-owner/founder/ executive director of the Film Lab

Scratching the Surface

(Photo by John Sobczak. Courtesy of Motor City Memoirs.)

Scratching the Surface

Adventures in Storytelling

A Memoir by
Harvey Ovshinsky

Foreword by Don Gonyea

A Painted Turtle Book
Detroit, Michigan

ISBN 978-0-8143-4474-3 (paperback)
ISBN 978-0-8143-4475-0 (e-book)

Library of Congress Control Number: 2020938999

Wayne State University Press
Leonard N. Simons Building
4809 Woodward Avenue
Detroit, Michigan 48201-1309

Visit us online at wsupress.wayne.edu

For Catherine, because every ship needs a harbor.
And for my children, Sasha and Noah,
who each in their own way continues to amaze and inspire.

There is an undercurrent, the real life beneath all appearances everywhere . . . It is this sense of the persistent life force back of things which makes the eye see and the hand move in ways that result in true masterpieces.

Robert Henri, *The Art Spirit*

Contents

Part 4. Impossible Is Hard

Foreword

Harvey Ovshinsky has been a guiding force in my career, and he doesn't even know it.

Yes, we've known each other for more than thirty years. And yes, in that time we've had occasion to share a coffee or a beer and talk about the news of the day or projects we're working on. But it hasn't been a regular occurrence, especially since 2001 when my job at NPR took me away from Detroit to Washington and the national politics beat.

As a young reporter—even before I knew him personally—the Ovshinsky touch was something that I recognized in stories that stood out for me while watching the news on TV in Detroit or listening to him host a talk show on the radio.

The stories Harvey has told over the years have consistently done the very thing that I strive for every day as a journalist. That is to connect the stories that dominate the news at any given moment with the lives of individual readers and viewers.

In short, a Harvey Ovshinsky story is about the humanity behind the headline. He finds the person who will make me care. And he gets them to tell their story in an honest, compelling fashion, utterly without artifice.

It always feels authentic, for one simple reason—because it is.

When Harvey sits an interview subject in front of the camera, he makes them so comfortable that they seem to be talking to me and me alone. As someone who spends his life with a microphone in hand, interviewing people in diners and union halls, at community gatherings and political rallies, I can assure you that this is no easy feat. So often the camera and the microphone can get in the way of realistic, human storytelling. The mere presence of the technology will alter the moment so that the interviewee is "performing" or thinking about how this will all look on the screen (TV, computer, smartphone, tablet—pick a format). That doesn't happen with a story that Harvey has put together.

The camera disappears—and we get to the essence of the story. The heart of it. The humanity of it.

Early in my career, while still learning my craft as a journalist, I saw it in his stories about the razing of a Detroit neighborhood to make room for GM's Poletown plant. I spotted it in his tales of now legendary Detroit street artist Tyree Guyton and his internationally known blocks-long explosion of color and folk art known as Heidelberg Street. And it was the centerpiece of the heartbreaking story of Tammy Boccomino and her son's battle with AIDS.

As I got to know Harvey personally over the years, I learned after the fact that many of the most memorable profiles of Detroiters—artists, musicians, civil rights leaders—that I had seen on WXYZ or WDIV television had been his. I wasn't surprised.

Go through his entire history, and even as his work evolved from his youthful days at the *Fifth Estate* underground newspaper and at the pioneering free-form FM radio station WABX in Detroit, through the challenges of TV and film, to the classrooms where he spends much of his time, teaching others how to get inside the art of storytelling, and you'll always recognize what is the essence of a Harvey Ovshinsky story.

So now Harvey turns the focus on himself with this memoir. In it he searches for answers within himself—extracting the same kind of honest, human observations that he has long worked to coax out of others.

But the book isn't just about him and his work. It's also about a place, the city of Detroit. The city that we've all seen struggle in our lifetimes, a place that's currently going through a revival that those of us who love the place hope truly takes hold. Harvey's work and stories are so rooted in Detroit that the book also serves as a reminder of stories and people who are part of the fabric of the city's history.

You'll see what I mean in the pages that follow.

Trust me when I tell you that Harvey will be an able and worthy guide.

Don Gonyea
Washington, DC

Preface

At the MacArthur Foundation, they call it "the big C," but you don't have to be a genius to be creative. "In this era of mindfulness, and today's preoccupation with pursuing a meaningful life," the *New York Times* reported, creativity has become "a new antidote . . . to cure the doldrums of midlife." As the author points out, "Who needs a Ferrari when you can pick up a paintbrush?"

Or find the words to tell our stories.

In retrospect, it makes perfect sense that I found my words early on, first in 1965 when, at age seventeen, I started one of the country's original sixties-era underground papers, and then in 1970, when I became news director of WABX-FM, Detroit's notorious progressive rock underground radio station.

For me, these were not hard choices. I have always enjoyed creating under the radar and scratching below the surface.

"What's this?" I used to ask my young creative writing students at the Grosse Pointe Academy when I drew a scraggly line across the chalkboard. "It's a line," they observed correctly. "A straight line!"

So far, so good.

"It's also a metaphor. It may look like a line," I told them, "but it also represents the surface. And here's the problem," I continued, drawing several vertical arrowheads above the surface, each pointing upward. "This is your enemy, your nemesis. There's nothing new above the surface. We can't *learn* anything up here. There are no surprises, no bombshells. We've seen and heard it all before."

I ignored the blank stares and proceeded to scrawl a raggedy circle a few inches below the scraggly line. And inside the circle I wrote three words: *The Good Stuff.*

"This is why we're here," I explained, pointing to the circle. "This is our soft spot; it's who we are below our surface. Our Good Stuff is private, it's personal. It's what we think and how we feel *inside*." It's what's important to us and what matters to us the most.

"The question is how do we break through the surface, this hardened protective shell of ours, so we can get to this best part of ourselves? And share it with others?"

Silence.

"I'll give you a hint." And, without warning, I took my fingernails and scratched the surface of the chalkboard as hard as I could, running them past the scraggly line, all the way down until they landed on the raggedy circle where, I told them, their Good Stuff was hiding.

But some surfaces are harder to scratch than others.

In 2004, the Detroit Docs International Film Festival honored me with a Lifetime Achievement Award, the *Detroit Metro Times* generously describing my work in print, radio, and television as a "colorful and fantastic voyage, at times brave and visionary." But I knew that wasn't the full story. Although I had a knack, a gift even, for asking questions that got to the heart of a story, after so many years of spinning my yarns with other people's threads, I was beginning to feel something was missing, a voice long absent from my storytelling.

My own.

There's an irony here. I have always lived my creative life in italics—my outside voice brave, bold, energetic, and passionate—but when it came to sharing my inside voice with anyone other than my family and a few close friends, for the longest time, I clammed up.

"Welcome to the club," my painter friend Arthur Schneider tried to console me whenever I whined about my discomfort with kibitzing and socializing with the people I worked with. "But then, I let myself off the hook by telling myself that whatever I have to say, I'm saving for the canvas."

I liked the sound of that, even though there were times when covering my tracks did little to advance my career prospects. "Harvey's a decent enough director and producer," a local television station executive once remarked about the distance I tended to keep between myself and my coworkers, especially my bosses, "but really, have you ever tried *talking* to him?"

I'm sure it was all very confusing for my colleagues, especially considering how perfectly comfortable I felt in front of a mic or behind the camera talking to complete strangers and inviting them to sit down with me and spill their innermost beans. *Show me yours*, was my mantra, *just don't expect me to show you mine.*

On one level, I get it. Truth-telling isn't for the reticent or the timid. It's one reason why writers call their first attempts "rough drafts"; filmmakers, "rough cuts"; and my fourth-grade writing students, "sloppy copies." And why, in Shakespeare's *The Tempest*, the sorcerer Prospero described his magical, transformative powers as his "potent art" and "this rough magic." The work can be that difficult, feel that impossible. Even when you're good at it.

Especially if you're good at it. But you don't have to be a writer, an artist, or even especially creative to take the plunge. You just have to feel strongly about something or have something important to say or get off your chest. And then you have to find the courage to scratch your own surface and share your Good Stuff with others.

Even when you think nobody wants to hear it.

In addition to my own story *Scratching the Surface* also recalls the adventures of more than a dozen other rough magicians, who, each in their own way, helped inspire and shape my hometown of Detroit, a city where resistance has always been fertile and our rough magic topsy-turvy.

Because in this town, now you *don't* see it, now you *do*.

A few words about accuracy: Writing this memoir reminded me there is more than one way to tell a true story. In reporting on the Watergate scandal for the *Washington Post*, journalist Bob Woodward explained that his goal in his work with his partner, Carl Bernstein, was to obtain "the most obtainable version of the truth." That was always my goal, but in writing my own exposé, I found myself having to serve two masters. Which is why, although the stories in this book are true, others may recall certain incidents I've described and the dialogue I've recalled and re-created differently. And from their perspective, they may be right, considering that in my attempt to share both the emotional and literal truths of my life's story it was necessary to compress and composite certain characters, situations, and events. For the documentarian in me, that was an especially hard surface to crack.

Difficult, but not impossible.

Part 1

My First Childhood

1

Shouts and Whispers

In 2006, three years after Fred Rogers died of stomach cancer, his production company, Family Communications, Inc. (now called Fred Rogers Productions), was desperate to find a new series to replace *Mister Rogers' Neighborhood*. PBS had already decided to discontinue airing reruns of the beloved children's program, and time was running out for the company to create a replacement show.

Many in the industry deemed the challenge an existential dilemma of the highest order, what Mister Rogers might have called a "pickle." Without its creator, star performer, head script- and songwriter, and lead producer, what was his production company to do?

What *could* it do?

Rolling over and accepting its fate as a one-trick (albeit glorious) pony was one possibility but a horrific option for the award-winning team that produced *Mister Rogers' Neighborhood*. FCI's mission impossible? To find a way to save the Fred Rogers brand and build a new children's franchise based on the Neighborhood's guiding principles of kindness and caring, and their goal of nurturing the emotional, intellectual, and creative development of children and families.

That's where I came in. In 2007, myself and my best friend and production partner, Bill Pace, were invited by Family Communications, along with two other production companies, to help save the Mister Rogers franchise. Our proposal, *The Playful Universe of the Mighty Hubble*, featured the adventures of a high-spirited, fun-loving, intergalactic space child who travels to Earth for the sole purpose of learning how to learn through play.

Poor Hubble. It wasn't his fault he was clueless about how to have fun; nobody ever taught him how. On his home planet, children were exceedingly

*The Mighty Hubble, "just burstin'" to take off for his next adventure.
(Courtesy of Family Communications, Inc. and Play Shop Productions.
Character design by Paul Andrejco, Puppet Heap Studios.)*

well educated and well behaved beyond their years, but they didn't have time in their busy and overscheduled lives to simply enjoy themselves and "just be kids."

I loved Hubble, and creating him with Bill was a highlight of my several careers, even though we ended up losing the bake-off to a worthy competitor, the amazing Angela Santomero, who went on to produce *Daniel Tiger's*

Neighborhood. What I loved most about our interstellar Pinocchio was his *exuberance.* The eternal optimist, the Mighty Hubble had more enthusiasm and gusto than he knew what to do with. "I'm just burstin'!" was one of his favorite expressions, and he'd say it beaming with the joy of both discovery and mastery that came from playing with and learning with others.

In other words, in his bravery and his courage, his cheerfulness and his unbridled lust for life and learning, the Mighty Hubble was everything, as a child, I was not.

I'm a Machinist, Not a Mechanic

In the 1940s and '50s my father was a machinist and a budding inventor, a Sacco and Vanzetti, Eugene Victor Debs socialist married to his high school sweetheart, Norma Rifkin, an Adlai Stevenson, Hubert Humphrey Democrat. According to family lore, Mom's family warned her against marrying Dad because he was a radical and worse. According to Lillian Hoddeson and Peter Garrett's brilliant biography, *The Man Who Saw Tomorrow: The Life and Inventions of Stanford R. Ovshinsky,* he was "a troublemaker who carried a lunch pail."

Mom was beautiful, artistic, and intensely devoted to her husband and her three children. Although they had their differences, it didn't hurt that both my parents were very physical people, and their sexual attraction to each other was as immediate as it was mutual.

Unfortunately, when it came to Dad's other passions, what he called his "creative urges" and his "advanced methods" of tool making and machine building, my father came to bitterly resent what he saw as my mother's lack of understanding and appreciation for his work.

There were bumps in the relationship almost immediately. The most obvious hurdle, at least from my father's perspective, was that Mom didn't share his passion for radical politics.

Or, in my father's opinion, much of anything else.

"I tried to teach her how to love me," Dad recalled years later, "but she didn't know what I was talking about."

"I'm a machinist, not a mechanic," he implored, looking for the words that would explain to her why he was always so preoccupied and wrapped up with his efforts to make his lathes, milling machines, and other shop tools work faster, harder, *smarter.* "Machines," he wrote to her, "are always to me what

My mother and father in happier days.
(Photo by Herb Ovshinsky. Courtesy of the Ovshinsky family and Bentley
Historical Library.)

writing [*is*] to a poet, painting is to an artist. That's what I mean by sounding stilted, but so help me, it's the key to what's happening to me . . . I feel my personality being gripped by it."

Mom was sympathetic and tried to understand what Dad was trying to tell her, but, in the end, she couldn't get past what she considered my father's grandiosity and inflated sense of self, once described even by his own mother as "Stan's big headedness."

"One of the reasons I didn't want to talk machines with you," he struck back at my mother in one of his letters, "is that you, too, doubt. You're thinking like a wife and a mother about the future & what's going to happen without money, etc. etc. Your fatal error is that you think it is a business to me; I guess everyone does, but it isn't & never will be [*for me*]."

Eventually, my father's festering unhappiness took its toll, and not only on their relationship. "Please come home. Or at least write," Mom wrote during one

My father (third from the left) with one of his first inventions, the Benjamin center-drive lathe, named after his father.
(Courtesy of the Ovshinsky family and Bentley Historical Library.)

of his many business trips, when I was about four years old. "Harvey is having a rough time of it. Benjie gets so much attention since he goes to school. If you were here one of us could preoccupy Harvey while Benjie talks about his school. He hasn't napped even once since Benjie started and he cries a lot."

Dad attempted to comply. At least on paper: "Dear Harv, I wanted to write to you to tell you how much I miss you—I know that you are taking good care of mommy, especially when Benjie's at school. When I come home, I would like to tell you all about the interesting machines I work with here—and maybe I will draw you a picture of the shop, too. Keep on being a good boy—and look after Dale for me. Love, Your Daddy."

Although my father may have felt some guilt over his being away so much of the time, he was adamant about what he believed were the roots of the problem. What "the boys"—my older brother, Benjie, and my younger brother, Dale—*really* needed, he scolded my mother, was a father who was happy and *wanted* to be home. "Will you be a good girl?" he wrote to my mother. "Try to be happy & helpful and make me happy like the devoted wife you are."

Well, that explains a lot, I thought, reading these letters many years later. Even when he was home, it often felt like Dad wasn't there. *Where do you go when you're with me?* I used to wonder when I would talk to him and he would not respond, his "advanced thinking" and "creative urges" taking him a million miles away from me.

I missed my father whenever he left, and years later, when I was writing guest columns for the *Detroit Free Press* and in my early days of parenting, I imagined how his frequent departures might have impacted my own relationship with my two children, Natasha (Sasha) and Noah. Although I love my work, I have always considered the relationship I have with my wife and children to be my most satisfying and proudest of my accomplishments. And yet . . . "Dads don't stay," I wrote in the *Free Press*, second-guessing myself. "Noah, my ten-year-old, is convinced that when it comes to tucking him in and saying goodnight at the end of a hard, grueling day in the fourth grade, his mother is really the expert. Mom cuddles. Mom crawls into bed. Mom pays attention. She talks and listens.

"And stays."

No Noise

Dad's space travels were compounded by the fact that when he was around, he was often so angry. Mom tried to keep the peace. She swore Dinah Shore

Dad with Benjie, me, and Dale on our way to "church" at the Cranbrook Institute of Science.
(Photo by Norma Ovshinsky. Courtesy of the Ovshinsky family and Bentley Historical Library.)

Mom with "the boys."
(Courtesy of the Ovshinsky family and Bentley Historical Library.)

was Jewish; it was a game she enjoyed playing with me when we watched TV together. She loved identifying celebrities she insisted were of the tribe even if they were not. Sammy Davis Jr., OK. Charlton Heston? I don't think so.

My father, on the other hand, did not share her sense of child's play, especially when he was tired. On one of his rare return visits home, he expressly warned her to keep the boys quiet so he could sleep in. My poor mother even failed at that. That morning my brother Ben and I were playing in his bedroom with our pet parakeet. Petey was a gift from my mother, her way of trying to calm things down in the house and give the boys something of our own to care for and, I suspect, in lieu of our father, to play with.

Suddenly, the door of our bedroom burst open, and Dad was no longer in lieu. His teeth were clenched, his fist raised. "I *told* you," he screamed in a high-pitched rage. "No noise!" He reached out to push me against the wall, but I ducked, the blow striking and killing poor Petey, who was resting on my shoulders, trembling and every bit as terrified as we were.

I don't remember an apology, but I will never forget the chilling look in my father's eyes when my mother walked into the room. *How many times do I have to tell you?* He wasn't talking to me, but I got the message.

No noise.

The World Situation Is Looking Kind of Bad

It wasn't all doom and gloom.

One of my favorite memories as a child was when Dad agreed to join us for a week at Camp Tanuga, an overnight secular Jewish summer camp for kids and their families. I appreciated Tanuga's intention to, as it promised in one of its brochures, "give youngsters a chance to explore the great outdoors and to learn a little about themselves," but what I *really* loved about the place, and for which I will forever be grateful to my mother, was how, even though by then she knew Dad was having an affair and deeply involved with another woman, these overnights at Tanuga gave my brothers and me a rare opportunity to spend quality time with our parents.

Both of them, in the same cabin. As if we were a family.

What I remember most about that summer was that for the first time in the longest time, I realized I wasn't afraid or worried about the world situation. Like so many of my generation, I grew up in the 1950s convinced that if

Family time at Camp Tanuga.
(Courtesy of Harvey Ovshinsky and Bentley Historical Library.)

a thermonuclear war with Russia or Red China didn't kill me, surely the fallout from the nuclear testing in the atmosphere would, or at the least, I would succumb to that strontium-90 in my Twin Pines and Borden's milk.

"The world situation is looking kind of bad," Dad wrote to me when I was later shipped off to another summer camp for several weeks of R&R. "You're lucky being in camp where there are no newspapers."

Well, almost none. In 1961, my father sent me a newspaper article reporting on the brutal beatings endured by our family friend, Dr. Walter Bergman, who, along with his wife Frances and fellow Freedom Riders, was set upon by a mob of white racists during protests challenging state laws that made it illegal for Blacks and whites to cross state lines in the same buses or trains. "Less than two weeks later," reported the *New York Times*, "Dr. Bergman suffered a severe stroke. He retained most of his speech but had to learn to write and feed himself again. He never regained the ability to walk."

Still, my father tried to lighten things up.

In his own way.

While other kids were tucked in at night, serenaded with fairy tales and tender lullabies, Dad's idea of quality time was to call a meeting to order, during which he crooned old labor and union songs and what were then called Negro spirituals like the ones his own father, a fellow socialist active in radical and Jewish causes, sang to him.

My grandfather, Benjamin Ovshinsky, was a scrap collector, what my father called a scrap "picker-upper." ("He wasn't a *dealer*," Dad insisted. "He had no interest in that sort of thing.")

In the 1930s Grandpa, who immigrated to the United States from a shtetl on the East Prussian border of Lithuania, rode his horse-driven cart, often with his middle child, Stanford, through the cobble streets of Akron, Ohio, in search of any discarded car batteries or scraps of sheet metal, iron, or steel. That's what my grandfather did for a living, but his soul was elsewhere. "He loved listening to the radio, especially opera broadcast and news programs," Dad recalled. "He could speak intelligently on many subjects and wrote columns for radical Yiddish newspapers."

Much to the chagrin of my Orthodox grandmother, Grandpa and my father were practicing atheists. "All thinking men are," my father would insist, recalling a line from Hemingway's *A Farewell to Arms*. Still, they were both orthodox in their commitment to the idea and values of Judaism, especially as practiced by the Akron chapter of the Workmen's Circle, a self-described "social and cultural Jewish labor fraternal order founded . . . to support the labor and socialist movements of the world."

Father and son shared Workmen's Circle's core philosophy of *un besser, shayne velt* (a better, beautiful world), the belief that every Jew, every *person*, has the duty to help make the world a better place. Although they were atheists, that was their goal, their shared religion.

In that way, and so many others, Ben and Stan Ovshinsky were not only father and son, they were each other's best friends, comrades and soulmates who, when they weren't attending labor union meetings, made a point of calling their own to order.

Our own meetings produced their share of heated debates. Once, when I told Dad I wanted to join the Cub Scouts, my father was impressed with my argument, but refused to budge, mainly for the same reason he wouldn't let us watch the popular World War II TV series *Victory at Sea*: it was too violent and glorified war. In Dad's worldview, the Cub Scouts' navy-blue uniforms with the accompanying badges, patches, and neck scarfs were too militaristic and, in his mind, reminiscent of Hitler's infamous youth league, a paramilitary fascist organization.

My mother intervened when she could. "Why don't you become a safety patrol boy instead, and help the younger children cross the street? It's a good compromise," she assured me, aware of my father's adamant feelings on the subject. "After all," she offered with a tender and, as I recall, satisfied smile, "a belt is not a uniform."

I thought of my mother's efforts on my behalf when, years later, I partnered with two local television stations to produce a half-hour screenplay of mine, a Chanukah/Christmas/Kwanzaa special I called *Max Maxwell's Miracle*. The feedback from the stations after they read my third first draft was grueling and prompted my interns, Jeff Caruana and Dee Mazurak, to ask, considering the number of notes and "fixes" being requested of me, why I didn't just quit the project and just walk away.

"Not yet," I told them. "When I lose the oranges and walnuts, that's when I'm gone."

They knew what I was talking about. One of my favorite scenes in the script was inspired by a tradition started by my mother at the very beginning of what I later came to call the Seven-Year War between my parents. Max Maxwell is a grumpy, aging widower seeking solace on a Christmas Eve that also coincides with his first night of Chanukah since his wife died. On his way to the downtown synagogue where they were married, taking the Detroit People Mover tram, Max meets a fellow passenger, an off-duty department store Santa Claus with whom he shares a story of about how, even though they were Jewish, every Christmas Eve, his beloved Rose insisted on filling each of their sons' stockings with oranges and walnuts.

"From Florida," the lovely Rose Maxwell told her grateful children, knowing how much they would appreciate the splurge.

"They can request all the changes they want," I told my interns. "As long as I get to keep my oranges and walnuts."

Both Barrels

Juggling my parents' priorities with my own was always a tightrope act, especially when it came to balancing my lack of interest in politics with my father's passion for his. Once, when I resisted joining him on a picket line, Dad gave me both barrels: "Do you think it's *right* that Woolworths refuses to serve Negroes? Or hire them? Is that something you're *proud* of?"

And that was just his opening argument.

"But rather mourn the apathetic throng, the cowed and the meek," he made me read aloud from a poem written by socialist and labor activist Ralph Chaplin, "who see the world's great anguish and its wrong. And dare not speak."

I tried to meet my father halfway. Growing up in the 1950s, I thought, because the actors were all Negroes, I could score points by telling him how much I enjoyed watching the *Amos 'n' Andy* TV series, but Dad wouldn't hear of it, insisting the series was racist and demeaning to Black people. Which of course it was, but for this ten- or eleven-year-old white kid who knew nothing of such things, it was all very confusing. And besides, I knew my father would be impressed that summer when he saw my performance as Al Jolson at the Camp Tamarack talent show. Surely my singing "Swanee" in blackface would show my solidarity with the oppressed.

He was not amused. And once again, I was clueless. "But Dad," I insisted, grabbing at straws, "it's Jolson. He's *Jewish!*"

It didn't matter. My father was an absolutist in many things and, like his father, especially when it came to his politics and commitment to peace and social justice. In Stan's world, his right was right, everybody else's wrong was wrong, and there was little space for middle ground, which, I'm sure to my dad's utter dismay and disappointment, was my favorite part of the road.

Although, I did try taking a stand once. In 1962, the Teen News and Views page of the *Detroit News* paid me ten dollars to write an editorial for its Student Soapbox column.

It was my first paying job as a journalist. As a fourteen-year-old tenth grader, my political consciousness was still in its latency stage, so I thought long and hard about what I could protest against. Finally, I chose a subject that would allow me to draw on my own experience and expertise.

And my politics at the time. Which is why the headline of my Student Soapbox was "Most Boys Mannerly; Others are Lost Cause."

"Some boys are not chivalrous, some boys are not even polite," I wrote in response to a previous Soapbox that decried rudeness in today's teenagers, "but there are those of us—about four out of every five—who do have good manners.

"We of the 80 percent open doors for girls, walk on the correct side of the street and show signs of respect. We don't go around slaying dragons for ladies in distress, but that doesn't mean we aren't gentlemen."

My mother was impressed, both with the content of my writing and my being able to earn money at such a young age. "You're such an early bird," she said approvingly. I'm sure, in his own way, my father was proud, too, but I can only imagine his reaction to my being awarded, shortly after, the American Legion's Certificate of Distinguished Achievement for "the preservation and protection of the fundamental institutions of our government and the advancement of society."

It's Only a Squirrel. It's Not a Dragon.

It turned out my father was not the only source of tension in our home. Growing up, I always knew there was something wrong with my younger brother. Was Dale deaf? Was that why he couldn't talk? Or was he simply, as my mother tried to explain, delayed in his "cognitive and communicative skills"?

Whatever that meant.

And why did my brother seem so *frightened* all the time? At all hours of the day and night in the bedroom we shared, he would habitually turn the lights on and off, as if to ward off imaginary terrors. "It's only a squirrel," I tried to explain when we played outside together. "It's not a dragon."

In the 1950s, the autism spectrum wasn't really on anybody's radar, so when my older brother, Ben, and I were told Dale was aphasiac, at least my parents finally had something they could agree on. Unfortunately, between my father's frequent absences and his creative preoccupations at home, it fell to my mother to provide the 24/7 care and attention required to guide my younger brother through his turbulent childhood.

I tried to fulfill my role as the acquiescent middle child by doing whatever I could not to call attention to myself. The one time I did break character and decided to speak up for myself was when I told my mother how frightened I was of Dale's behavior. Mom tried to lend a sympathetic ear, but unfortunately, her weary response was less than comforting.

"Yes, but Harvey," she sighed, wetting her thumb to help try and rub away what she called the worry wrinkles from my forehead, "can you imagine how *he* must feel?"

Out of Sight, Out of Mind

As it turned out, Dale wasn't the only one in our family suffering from a disability. And because my wheel wasn't nearly as squeaky as my younger brother's, my subtle version of a language processing disorder went unnoticed. Or at least undiagnosed. Which explains why, growing up, I found it so difficult to receive, absorb, and retain spoken and verbal information. Whoever coined the expression "out of sight, out of mind" knows what I'm talking about. If I couldn't *see* what was being discussed or taught to me, it was almost impossible for me to adequately process and then understand what was being said.

Which explains why, for as long as I can remember, metaphors, similes, analogies, and idioms have always been my go-to figures of speech. "Strange words simply puzzle us," Aristotle said, explaining the critical role figurative language plays in our ability to absorb and express information. "Ordinary words convey only what we know already; it is from metaphor that we can best get hold of something fresh."

Aha! Now I know why, when my second-grade teacher, Miss Petrini, told me to open my desk, pull out my pencil case, open my workbook to page 15, and begin working on short division, I'd be lucky to remember even the part about the pencil case.

Looking back, it's ironic that story problems were my biggest nemesis. I barely understood the *instructions* to each problem, let alone the story.

"I know Harvey hasn't caught on to adding and subtraction," my fifth-grade teacher wrote in a letter to my mother. "I don't doubt that he could do better, but as you say, he doesn't listen all the time. However, I expect as he gets older, he will change and settle down to business." Hebrew school didn't help. Unless I wrote it down, or *drew* it, remembering any commandment after the first four was next to impossible. Poor Mrs. Gornbein. "Harvey has a great deal of energy," she wrote on my report card. "If *only* he could learn how to pay attention!"

In elementary school it didn't take long before I was off to the principal's office for disrupting the class with my increasingly frequent bursts of what would now be called "acting out," which my less sympathetic teachers called my "clowning around." Although really, in my mind, I was just rehearsing. Whenever Mom and I watched the handsome crooner Dean Martin and his spastic sidekick comic, Jerry Lewis, on TV, I *longed* to be Dean Martin and imagined I was, but in real life, that position was already filled by my older brother, Ben, who was, I was so frequently reminded, better looking and much smarter than I was. "And better behaved," my teachers reminded me at every turn.

I got the message. If Ben was the family's Moses, I was destined to be the designated Aaron.

2

The Two Mrs. Ovshinskys

In my old neighborhood of Forrer Street near Seven Mile and Greenfield in northwest Detroit, kids identified each other by religion, nationality, or our fathers' careers. On our block, which was largely Catholic, the Ovshinskys were the Jews; the Hagopians were the Armenians; Mr. Ewing and Mr. O'Mara were police officers; the Bielazcyks were Polish; the Catalanottis across the street were *very* Italian; and Mr. Buckner, my father would hiss, was a lobbyist, whatever that meant.

It was, as I recall, Kathy O'Mara who first blew the whistle on my parents. One day, when she was particularly upset with me about something, "Catholic" Kathy turned on me and blurted, "At least my parents aren't getting *divorced*!" I was shocked. What was she talking about? *Who* was she talking about? My parents weren't getting divorced; why should they? They barely *talked* to each other!

When I confronted Mom with Kathy's lie, she was upset but characteristically tried to put a happy face on the situation. "It won't be too different," she promised, holding back tears. "You know your dad has been spending a lot of time away from home."

"Sure, traveling because of work," I said, thinking I was stating the obvious. "You said he had a lot on his plate."

"That's right," my mother replied. "Because of work. And because of *her*."

The Monster in Me

"She's really very nice," Dad told us when, several days later, he called a meeting to explain to me and my brothers what was going on. "Iris is beautiful," he said,

18

Dad and Iris in love.
(Courtesy of the Ovshinsky family and Bentley Historical Library.)

trying to assure us, "she's smart and she can cook. I already told her about your favorite foods. And not just salmon patties," he added contemptuously, still smarting over my mother's apparent lack of gourmet cooking skills.

"But she's your mistress!" I heard the monster in me scream at him, not at all certain what the word even meant. I'm sure it killed him to hear my brothers and me talk like this about the new love of his life, but surprisingly and uncharacteristically, he managed to keep his composure while deciding what, under the circumstances, was the right and fair thing to say.

"That's your mother talking," he whispered, keeping a tight grip on his pipe.

If this were a screenplay, at this point I'd add what we call in the industry a "parenthetical action" to this dialogue. Directors and actors generally hate seeing these "beats" in their scripts because it suggests the screenwriter doesn't trust them to deliver the goods and make sure the audience gets the point:

```
                         STAN
          You're a writer, Harvey.
               (beat)
          Why don't you do your own research?
```

It wasn't easy. Mom's bitterness was compounded by the fact that she had spent so much of her married life apologizing to my father for her "failure" as a wife and not being able to live up to his expectations. Or his standards, she would later correct me, reminding me of the time Dad called her out for buying him the second edition of some book or another, and not the first. "I'm sorry," Mom responded, congratulating herself on the money she saved on the purchase. "I didn't think it would make a difference."

My poor mother. As the long-forgotten, much-maligned "first wife" in my father's narrative, Norma Rifkin Ovshinsky Marks endured as best she could her role as the designated footnote. Of course, my mother was more than that; in addition to being an accomplished artist, a photographer, and an art teacher in her later years, Mom was also the best wife and mother she knew how to be.

Under the circumstances.

Still, as resilient and creative as her survival skills were, for the longest time, my mother's bitterness and rage toward my father for leaving her and the boys often expressed itself at our expense.

And I have both the scars and the stories to show for it.

Suddenly, there were two Mrs. Ovshinskys. Although Dad and Iris weren't married yet, they were living together, and in the early days of my parents' separation, Mom and the other Mrs. Ovshinsky both shared J. L. Hudson department store credit cards. That hurt. I remember hearing my mother on the phone more than once, in tears, trying to explain to the department store who the "real" Mrs. Ovshinsky was. They didn't believe her. "You don't deserve this," my father's mother wrote her at the time. "You're the mother of his children and he should show some respect."

I felt bad for my mother and as the dutiful and compliant middle child empathized with her suffering. But eventually I decided to test the waters, and, following Dad's advice, I did my own research. It took a while, but in time I got to know the "other" Mrs. Ovshinsky, Iris Miroy Dibner, and her two beautiful young children, Robin and Steven. And when I saw how much my father seemed to *change* and mellow whenever he was with them, it became increasingly difficult for me to stay angry and unforgiving for long. A PhD biologist by education, Iris had an appreciation of and affection for all living things that was only matched by her kindness and the unfettered generosity of her free spirit. In Iris, my father found his catalyst, his sticky atom, a fellow lover of first editions and a brilliant, selfless collaborator who understood and embraced not only him but also, and especially, what his own mother called Dad's "big ideas" about how to use science and invention to help save the world.

And I wanted some of that.

Once, I broke ranks with my mother and told Iris how much I appreciated her correcting my spelling and typing up so many of my poems, short stories, and book reports. Iris thanked me back, assuring me it was no trouble, and then, with a wink and a half smile, she asked me if I could keep a secret.

"Don't tell your father I said this," she pretended to whisper as she covered her old IBM Selectric typewriter, "but it's such a *pleasure* to be able to type something other than scientific papers!"

My father and Iris collaborating in the early days of their company, Energy Conversion Devices.
(Courtesy of the Ovshinsky family and Bentley Historical Library.)

Years later, in my screenwriting and video production classes, my students would ask, when rewriting and reediting their stories, how could they know what to leave in and what to take out? In other words, what was essential? "One way," I explained, unable to resist yet another metaphor, "is to consider your stories a house of cards. If you pull a card out and the house stays upright, then you know you didn't need it in the first place. But if you pull a card out and the entire house falls apart on you, then voilà—you know what was essential. And what was not."

In my life, first as a child and later as an adult, Iris Miroy Ovshinsky was not only a beloved stepmother, she became one of my and my family's essentials.

Who Are You and What Have You Done with My Father?

For my brothers and me, my father's transformation during his separation from my mother was as striking as it was totally unexpected. Suddenly, Dad was *happy* like we had never seen before. And attentive! I was impressed but also confused. I remember thinking, *Who are you? And what have you done with my father?*

I knew my father's conversion was complete when, during one of our weekday nights together—"just the two of us"—we stopped by a record store and he bought me the soundtrack album to the Kirk Douglas movie *Spartacus*, and without complaint or criticism also offered to pay for another record I desperately wanted, the soundtrack to John Wayne's *The Alamo*.

Unfortunately, all this attention only added fuel to my mother's fury. Whenever any of the boys showed even the slightest signs of weakening in our resolve to resent my father and his new family, she would turn up the heat.

"He's trying to buy your love—you know that, don't you?" Mom railed at me, after I spent an otherwise perfect evening celebrating my thirteenth birthday with Dad, Iris, and Iris's children. What had made the evening especially satisfying was that, in lieu of a Bar Mitzvah, I was given thirteen birthday presents, each one, in my mind, more spectacular than the other.

"What am *I* supposed to do with *this*?" Mom fumed when I walked in the door, thrusting my new, used Nikon 35mm camera in front of my face. "How do you think this makes me feel?"

What to do? What could I possibly say to assuage her anger? *Happy for me,* I wanted to scream at the top of my lungs, but my outside voice took a different and, to my shame, painfully familiar tack.

"I'm sorry," I said, fighting back tears. "I'll call them and make them take it back."

3

The Magic in Me

It didn't help that my parents fought their battles on two fronts. Once, after Mom got a court order forbidding the boys to visit their home until Dad and Iris were married, my father couldn't resist informing me that my mother had once threatened to pay him back for his treachery by killing my brothers and me in our sleep. "She's a real Medea, your mother," he informed me. "And you wonder why I left?"

Fortunately, I developed an active fantasy life to help me escape the shelling, a knack I frequently called on in my later years, most recently when my creative and production partner Bill Pace and I imagined for Fred Rogers Productions that the Mighty Hubble and his play pals would use their imaginations, what they called their "pickle power," to resolve conflicts and solve problems.

As a child, I used my own pickle power to imagine Walt Disney, who in 1955 created the wildly popular children's television series *The Mickey Mouse Club*, was covertly recording my every move and that it was only a matter of time before one of his talent scouts would shine a spotlight on me and offer to fly me to Disneyland for an audition.

We've been keeping an eye out for you, Harvey, I fantasized Uncle Walt saying to me as he took me aside and wrapped a fatherly arm around my shoulder. *You're very talented, and I must say, we're impressed.*

Wait. There's more:

```
         WALT DISNEY (cont'd)
    Cubby is leaving the show, and we're looking
    for someone to replace him.
         (beat)
    Are you available?
```

Was I ever! "The sun is shining—the sun is shining. That is the magic," Miss Davidson, my elementary school librarian used to read aloud from *The Secret Garden*. I loved that book, hanging on to every word, desperately wanting to believe that what I was hearing was true. "The flowers are growing—the roots are stirring," we were assured. "That is the magic . . . The magic is in me—the magic is in me . . . It's in every one of us."

Well, almost everyone.

Each of us has defining moments, episodes from our childhood that foreshadow the central themes of our lives and help define our core personality and character traits. Family legend has it that when he was very young, my father and his mother were in a bakery and the man behind the counter offered him a cookie. "Stan," my grandmother said, admonishing my father for his rudeness, "what do you say when someone offers you a cookie?"

"More," my father said, licking his fingers.

Dad had his cookie; *Citizen Kane* had his sled. My Rosebud of choice was a carrot sprout.

When I was in second grade, my older brother, Ben, brought home a carrot plant he was attempting to grow in class. "We have to be patient," my mother tried to explain when I complained I couldn't see any sign of a plant growing in the dirt-filled Styrofoam cup. "Just wait for a few days, it'll come," she promised.

I gave it a try, but not for very long. I wanted to watch the carrot grow. Now.

So, I decided to take matters into my own hands. Literally. After my mother left the room, I gripped the tiny speck of sprout and tugged on it. Hard. In my mind, I thought I was doing the carrot a favor. I just wanted to help make the poor sprout grow.

Of course, my childhood attempt at magical thinking failed, and much to my brother's dismay, I ended up killing his carrot. I was crushed but, truthfully, more surprised than anything. I was certain my shortcut would do the trick. In his own limited vocabulary, my younger brother, Dale, tried to console me. *Don't worry*, I imagined him saying, *I would have done the same thing*.

Unfortunately, my skills as a wishful thinker did not improve with age.

Several years later, when I was about to be harassed by a neighborhood bully, my outside voice, as was its nature, chose not to engage with the enemy. But my inside voice was more than happy to pipe in with a splendid, albeit silent curse. When neither approach worked and my nemesis, his fists clenched, continued to march in my direction, I decided it was time to rethink my defense strategy.

So, I ran home with both my voices tucked between my legs.

That's when I decided magic was no longer an option for me, that if I had any hope of surviving the blitz that was my childhood, the only magic I could count on was not the words I kept to myself, but the ones I said out loud.

At least on paper.

4

Cub Reporter

When Boris Karloff said of his Frankenstein's creature, "My dear old monster. He was the best friend I ever had," I knew the feeling. In real life I may have been a speechless, frightened worrywart, but when I picked up my mother's movie camera and made my 8mm monster movies or put on my favorite monster makeup or mask, I knew no fear.

When my best friend Bobby Hagopian and I weren't cavorting on his grandparents' property, the original Hagopian & Sons Carpet Cleaners on Eight Mile Road, we would spend our Saturday afternoons at the old Mercury and Royal movie theaters gorging on double-bill matinees featuring classic B movies about monsters like *Attack of the Crab Monsters*, *Creature from the Black Lagoon*, and *The Thing*.

I especially identified with one of the main characters in *The Creeping Unknown*, an obscure English horror movie about an astronaut who, after he returns to Earth from outer space, finds himself transformed into a creature who is mute and unable to communicate.

Recently, Bob, with whom I have kept in contact over the years, made a gift to me of some of the original movie ads we cut out and collected in our scrapbooks. "Konga—Not since King Kong has the screen exploded with such fury and spectacle!" And what twelve-year-old, hormonally challenged boy could resist the heaving, bosomy charms of *The Wasp Woman*, "A beautiful woman by day, a lusting queen by night!"

Start the Presses

It was my passion for horror and monster movies that sparked my interest in journalism. In 1961, the movie magazine *Fantastic Monsters of the Films* (not to be

26

confused with the more popular *Famous Monsters of Filmland*) announced that my four-page, mimeographed *Transylvanian Newsletter*, "a small newspaper-like publication. . . . intended to report the latest news in the horror world," was available to its readers at an introductory subscription rate of six issues for thirty cents.

Publishing the *Transylvanian Newsletter* with Bobby was significant in my development as a journalist, not only because I was so young, and my paper was a national publication; it also marked the beginning of my friendship with Skip Williamson and Jay Lynch, two best friends who later became popular cartoonists both in the underground press and in men's magazines like *Playboy*. Skip and Jay were among my first subscribers, and despite our age differences both were extremely generous in their praise of my efforts. "Monsters are cool, Harvey," Jay wrote to me. "But let us know when you want to write funny."

I did try funny once, but with only limited success. "Vote for me, or you won't sleep tonight," promised a cutout of Bela Lugosi's *Dracula* on the campaign poster I created when I ran for a seat on the Coffey Junior High student council. "I have my eye on you," warned another poster featuring the cyclops from Ray Harryhausen's *The 7th Voyage of Sinbad*. "So, you better vote for Harvey for class president."

My attempts at humor were cute and clever but, in the end, met with mixed results. "Very original," one of my teachers congratulated me after a particularly bruising campaign. "Sorry you lost."

Although it was only a mimeographed fanzine, by eighth-grade standards, the *Transylvanian Newsletter* looked professional, but then only compared to my first attempt at publishing several years earlier. The *Creative Boys Club Newspaper* was a typed-up, carbon-copied neighborhood gossip sheet paper Bobby and I published for our friends. I didn't mind that our club didn't have any members or that we held very few meetings, I just wanted to publish my own paper. "Butch Ewing's club seems to have a nice meeting place," I wrote in one of my first-ever editorials. "They talk, look at maps and a microscope. [*But*] if you look at our last issue, you will see that everything they do, we have done before."

Ah, the monster in me. I never knew when it was going to come out. For me, reporting on other people's activities, snooping on their lives, and using my words to tell their stories was my way of coping, of at least *pretending* I had control over my environment. Putting words on paper was my flight plan, and it didn't take long for me to discover that, when I took off, like Icarus I could use my winged words to get high.

Without ever leaving the ground.

What Joy, What a Relief!

My mother encouraged my writing early on by buying me a diary. "That way, you won't forget what happens," she told me. I was grateful for her support, but by then I was already talking to myself big-time; I didn't feel the need to transcribe the conversations, too.

It was my father who introduced me to my favorite writing toy. When the microscopes and chemistry sets didn't take, he relented and bought me a child's printing press with large block letters embedded on pink rubber stamps. What joy, what a relief! Now with my very own printing press, like Ralph Waldo Emerson, when I dipped my pen in the blackest ink, I was not afraid to fall in the ink pot.

It didn't take long for me to spread the word, *my* word, with poems, short stories, and, before long, theatrical productions Bobby and I would perform in our backyards. "*My Spirit Shall Rise* by Harvey Ovshinsky will be put on to any non-members who wish to see it," I announced in the *Creative Boys Club Newspaper*. "The play starts out in a Japanese Army Post with three men. One man is to die as a court martial punishment. He vows to rise and stick a grenade down the throat of the man who convicted him."

My mother, who had long sacrificed her own creative streak to accommodate my father's and to provide the round-the-clock attention Dale required, loved watching our backyard productions and pitching in by making the costumes. Dad, on the other hand, because he wasn't around very much, was more a fan of my short stories, especially "Pardon Me, Are You Human?" It was a *Twilight Zone* knockoff about a man who, according to the story's narrator, was "an inventor, doctor, writer, and just about everything else in the English dictionary. His work involves chemicals, microscopes, telescopes, electricity and things like that."

Writing "Pardon Me" was fun. In those days it was easier to write fictional stories about what my father did for a living than try to explain his career choice to my friends and teachers. Bobby's father was a TV repairman, Ray Bielazcyk's father was a fireman, Vince Catalanotti's father worked on the line at Ford; everybody knew what their fathers did for a living. But I wasn't sure. Once, when one of my teachers asked the class to write personal essays about our fathers' jobs, I struggled. After all, Dad wasn't a "real" inventor, not like the usual suspects, Alexander Graham Bell or Thomas Edison. "I'll make it easy for you," he told me in a fatherly attempt to let me off the hook. "Just tell them I'm an engineer. Everybody knows what they do."

But Dad, Clark Kent Is a Journalist!

Although I loved the pure pleasure of writing for its own sake, it didn't take long for me to discover there was added value in the effort, and that, when chosen carefully, what the poet Samuel Taylor Coleridge called "best words, best order" could also be used to bend others to my will. I had a chance to test my newfound powers of persuasion when, after being held back in elementary school for "not reading to my potential," my father threatened to take away my beloved comic book collection.

I was sad and furious, crazy with grief, but no amount of crying or cajoling would change Dad's mind. "Reading comics is a waste of your time, Harvey," he insisted, "because it's not *real* reading."

What? Not *real* reading? Didn't he know that, as much as I was a fan of *Superman* and respected his awesome superpowers, it was his alter ego, Clark Kent, who spoke to me. *Kal-El of Krypton may be the strongest man on the planet,* I thought, *but Clark Kent is even more powerful.*

After all, he was a writer—he was a journalist!

But Dad wasn't convinced. Other than his politics and his passion for science and social justice, reading was his heart's desire and his most fervent pastime. He devoured books, magazines, newspapers, scientific journals—everything he could get his hands on—and frequently read more than one publication at a time. "It's how I learn," he told me years later. "I've always studied. One of my fondest memories was when I was eight years old; I staggered out of the library with a stack of a books piled high in my arms. I was reading everything from poetry, science, philosophy, history, politics. I remember once the librarian said, 'Oh, Stanford, what's going to happen when you grow up? You'll have read all the books!'"

But that was my father's story, not mine. "Dear Daddy," I wrote to him in a frantic burst of creative energy, "I know reding [*sic*] is important to you and I'm sorry I'm not better at it. But I feel good when I read my comics and trade them with Bobby. Can we negoshiate [*sic*] this? How about a copramise [*sic*]?"

Whether it was my debating skills or my mother once again intervening on my behalf, Dad never followed through on his threat. We agreed I could keep my *Lois Lane* and *Superman* comics, but only after I promised to add to my collection *Classics Illustrated* versions of Homer's *The Iliad*, Alexandre Dumas's *The Count of Monte Cristo*, and adaptions of *The War of the Worlds* by H. G. Wells and Jack London's *Call of the Wild*. They were, after all, two of Dad's favorite authors when he was growing up.

I Enter Another Dimension

I've always been a fan of my fellow Detroiter Lily Tomlin, who with her partner, Jane Wagner, in their hit Broadway show, *The Search for Signs of Intelligent Life in the Universe*, observed that reality was the leading cause of stress among those of us in touch with it.

Which is why, in the mid-1980s, although I enjoyed Steven Spielberg's science fiction and fantasy series *Amazing Stories*, really, only one episode held my attention. After returning from a mission, the crew of a World War II B-17 Flying Fortress finds their landing gear hopelessly damaged. Although they just barely manage to make it back to base, they realized that without functioning wheels they were certain to face a fiery death upon landing.

All hope is lost until Kiefer Sutherland, a young bombardier (who also happens to be a cartoonist), picks up a pencil and feverously doodles two enormous inflatable, balloon-like tires to bring the plane and its crew home safely.

That's how I have always felt about writing. It's not about the words. It's about the tires.

Still, although I basked in my little victory during the comic book wars, I felt something was missing, a gap in my early education that school couldn't fill or satisfy. My poems, plays, and parental plea bargains were a start, but it didn't take long before I felt the need to up the ante and take what the German-Swiss poet Herman Hesse called his "blood whisper" and Jack London his "wolf cry" to the next level.

The problem was, at age thirteen, I knew I didn't just want to write, I wanted to be good at it, which is why, in 1961, not long after the blowout with my mother over Dad and Iris's thirteen gifts, I gave myself my own Bar Mitzvah present by writing to my favorite writer, Rod Serling, the creator of *The Twilight Zone*, who was, according to the *L.A. Times*, "a master storyteller and dreamer" and "one of the best known and most honored writers in television."

What was his secret? How did he become a writer? And why? And, most importantly, I asked him, did he have any trade secrets he could pass along that might be able to accelerate my dream of becoming a professional storyteller like him?

My hero wrote back within weeks:

Dear Harvey,

Thank you for your letter. I am always reluctant to advise young people on their writing careers because there aren't any magic rules to follow to ensure success. But I will gladly answer your questions.

I learned how to write by writing, writing, writing. To become a good writer, you must practice your craft diligently. Writing involves rigid discipline. The novice must not only possess a basic talent but must have a sincere desire to write.

There are several disadvantages to writing. Practically every writer has a period of rejections which can be terribly disappointing and frustrating. Many writers and other creatives go through a stale period when ideas just don't come to them, plots go wrong, etc.

I think the main advantage to writing is its creative aspect. To a writer, nothing is more rewarding than seeing his name in print. It is a thrill and a sense of accomplishment that has never paled for me.

The main thing to remember is that writing mirrors life which encompasses so many things; therefore, the standard rule to observe when you begin your education is to consider a "whole" education. Don't limit yourself in the subjects you take. Don't simply take "writing" per se, because you don't just write about writing, you write about the world and everyone in it. Cram every bit of knowledge into your head. Ultimately it will be grist for your writing mill.

Much good luck to you, and I hoped this has helped you.

Sincerely,

Rod Serling

His letter *did* help me and still does. There is rarely a class I teach, a workshop I facilitate, or a speech I give to young or aspiring writers, directors, or producers during which I don't reference or quote from Rod Serling's wise counsel. For this bumbling boy wizard, Rod Serling was my first Dumbledore.

But if he was the first, Norean Martin was my second.

A Glass-Walled Sanctuary in Room 204

Technically, Mrs. Martin was my English teacher at Coffey Junior High School, but her real role, her gift to me was inviting me to write for the school paper, the *Coffey Crusader*, and to join what years later I fondly referred to as her "Purple Gang," so-called, not in deference to Detroit's infamous gang of Jewish mobsters, but because purple was the color of the ink our ditto machine used to print the school's unofficial, satirical yearbook, which we called the *Coffey Coloring Book*.

Working with Mrs. Martin and my fellow Purple Gangers, I discovered that my restlessness, or what my Jewish grandmother often referred to as my *shpilkes*, wasn't getting in the way of my learning. Combined with my love of writing, and the control and *power* I felt when I expressed myself with words on paper, my work with Mrs. Martin and my fellow Crusaders made me feel like my shpilkes *was* my way of learning.

"Once upon a time, there were three little pigs," I wrote in an early front-page editorial raging against students who were "soaping windows, molesting innocent bulletin boards and dropping trash in the drinking fountains."

"It's time the wolf knocked at their door," I ranted at these infidels. "Let's blow their thatched hut houses down and send them back to their make-believe world. They don't belong in junior high."

I loved Mrs. Martin. Well, not literally, but I did have a crush on her. And I wasn't alone. In those days, seventh- and eighth-grade girls wanted to *be* her, and the boys, me included, wanted to *date* her. Still, in room 204, a glass-walled sanctuary, a playground both she and I called our "second home," Mrs. Martin managed to wield her own form of rough magic to keep us at bay.

And keep our words flowing.

She was highly motivated. Although I didn't know it at the time, Coffey was her first teaching assignment. She had cut her teeth as a summer camp counselor and had been eager to teach children the basics of reporting and writing in order to publish a camp newsletter. "The children's response," she later wrote to me,

The Coffey Crusader

VOL. III No. 3 Coffey Jr. High School, 19330 Lindsay, Detroit 35, Mich. December 1961

9A Fund Expands

Tuesday, Dec. 19th, the 9A's found time in their extremely busy schedule to organize another successful bake sale. Students and teachers alike ate their quota with the thought in their minds of how unselfishly they had helped the 9A's increase the amount of money in their class fund. This fund now totals far over one hundred dollars and all 9A's hope their conference teacher has put the money in a safe place.

A committee of eight students was chosen by Mr. McLaughlin, their sponsor, to take suggestions from fellow students, make posters, and to organize a system by which they could sell their wares. The members of the committee

Front: Martha Claus, Mrs. Martin, Diane Akers Second: Ellen Farber, Larry Boxer, Jon Jaffa, John Kauppila, Rosalind Moore Third: Larry Bernstein, Harvey Ovshinsky

TEEN PANEL THEME
GETTING ALONG WITH PARENTS

"To be a perfect parent you'd have to have a perfect

Areas of Conflict?"
The panel was composed of 7th, 8th, and 9th graders, Diane Akers, Harvey Ovshinsky, Martha Claus, Larry Bernstein, Larry Boxer, John Kauppila, Jon Jaffa, Ellen Farber, and

Mrs. Martin and her Crusaders.
(Courtesy of Norean Martin, Harvey Ovshinsky, and Bentley Historical Library.)

"and the joy they took in their publication confirmed my belief that the opportunity to give voice to ideas and feelings is liberating."

Was she reading my mind? To both student and teacher writing wasn't, in her words, "just in the service of communication and self-expression," it also, and mainly, enabled students "to become empowered."

I liked the sound of that. And if I was really good at it, one day, I vowed, like Rod Serling, I would even get paid for writing professionally.

But, as it turned out, not right away.

Not long after I joined the Purple Gang, my father enrolled me in a special summer camp for junior high school journalism students facilitated by the University of Michigan's award-winning Department of Journalism. Although it was an unfamiliar feeling for me, I allowed myself to actually get excited about my first big chance to learn real journalism from real journalists!

Except that it never happened.

At the last minute, my mother canceled the trip. I was stunned. Why? How could this have happened? What crime could I have possibly committed that was so unforgivable that my mother should pull the rug out so harshly?

"It's not you, Harvey," she said, insisting I look directly into her eyes to make absolutely sure I got the message.

```
                    MOM (cont'd)
    This is your father's fault. Next time he'll
    talk to me first.
          (beat)
    And ask permission.
```

Part 2

Sixties Going on Seventies

5

My Whisper Becomes a Roar

I knew the Seven-Year War was officially over when Mom started dating and eventually met and married Adolph Marks, a record distributor, who, until he met my mother, was an older, confirmed bachelor with little interest in starting a family of his own. *No problem*, I imagine Mom assuring him. *I have more than enough family for both of us.*

Actually, my mother had started her healing process years earlier, when she enrolled in Detroit's Mercy College and earned her bachelor's degree in art education. In addition to her interest in becoming an art teacher, I think she also wanted to go on record: *Your father's not the only creative person in this family.*

I was happy for her on both counts. Adolph adored her and, in his abiding love for my battle-fatigued mother, delivered on his promise to bring little drama or angst to the relationship.

For me, their marriage and her resulting happiness was a welcome respite from the crossfire and barrage of paybacks and parental reprisals I was used to. Plus, Adolph had a delicious habit of providing me with promotional copies of original cast recordings of my favorite Broadway musicals; listening to them remains to this day one of my all-time not-so-guilty pleasures. I devoured original Broadway cast albums of shows like *West Side Story*, *Camelot*, and *Funny Girl*. But it was my passion for *How to Succeed in Business Without Really Trying*, with J. Pierrepont Finch's penchant for self-talk, that made it that much easier for me to embrace my mother's marriage to her new husband.

Mumford Music

As grateful as I was to my new stepfather for expanding my record collection, his and Mom's greatest gift to me was their decision to move out of my childhood home to a new, swankier address several miles away in another school district. The move was a welcome change, not only because it meant I would now have my own room, but also, and mainly, because it enabled me, in the tenth grade, to transfer high schools.

Before it was embossed on Eddie Murphy's T-shirt in *Beverly Hills Cop*, Samuel C. Mumford was one of this country's most famous high schools, whose graduates included an entire generation of American baby boomers who, collectively, had an unprecedented impact on local, national, and international culture.

In the 1960s, Mumford was a hothouse of intellectual and artistic freedom and self-expression. TV and movie producers Jerry Bruckheimer and Bob Shaye were part of what was later affectionately referred to by expats in New York and L.A. as "the Mumford Mafia." Gilda Radner went to Mumford for a brief while, as did *Ghost* screenwriter Bruce Joel Rubin; *Ordinary People* author Judith Guest; Allee Willis, the Grammy-winning songwriter who wrote the theme song to *Friends* and the Broadway musical *The Color Purple*; famed jazz guitarist Earl Klugh; and gospel greats the Winans and the Clark Sisters.

And, in 1963, me.

Right away I knew I wasn't in Kansas anymore.

After transferring from Detroit's spanking-new Henry Ford High School, I remember being shocked to discover that at Mumford the boys swam in the nude. At least that's what I called it. "Naked," one of my gym teachers corrected me. "I don't know what they taught you at Henry frigging Ford, Mr. Ovshinsky, but at this school we swim butt naked."

Somebody once said home is any place where you feel like you belong. I didn't feel that way at Henry Ford, where, even as a freshman, my reputation as "Ben's brother" was starting to wear on me. But Mumford was a different story, literally a horse of a different color. As soon as I walked into the ancient maroon-and-powder-blue building on Wyoming Avenue, I knew I was exactly where I belonged.

And not just me. "Every time I stepped into the building," Allee Willis later told the Detroit Public Schools Foundation, "I was very aware how happy the burst of color made me." A passionate but unschooled musician, driven by what she called her "spirit and guts," she always credited the education she received at Mumford and other Detroit public schools with supporting her need for artistic expression from an early age.

Bobby Hagopian and my childhood friends from the old neighborhood didn't get it. I don't blame them; I was probably the only white kid who ever left the all-white Henry Ford to attend the infamous integrated but increasingly "changing" Mumford, where, rumor had it, all the Jewish kids were snobs and wore cashmere sweaters and roving bands of Black students beat you up and flushed you down the toilet for your lunch money.

"You're like a fireman, always going in the opposite direction," a therapist friend once told me. "Most people *leave* burning buildings, they don't rush in."

The irony was I heard a similar refrain when I arrived at Mumford. "Oh, Harvey," one of my teachers confided in me. "You should have been here five years ago, when Mumford was *Mumford*." This, of course, was her way of saying before the school became too Black.

Mumford may have started to "turn" by time I got there, but for every rumor about Black kids "beating you up for a dime," there were other stories that drew me to my new home. One of my favorites was how, several years earlier, Mumford seniors were booked at a posh Washington, DC, hotel but when they arrived, the African American students were not allowed to register. The solution? The entire class boycotted both the hotel and the special event that was scheduled there that night.

While many of the Jewish kids hung out at neighborhood delicatessens like Fredson's and Moishe Pipik's on Wyoming, rumor was Mumford's African American students mainly congregated at Cupid's Bow restaurant on Six Mile. It may not have been entirely true, but in my mind, it felt like it was only at Adolph's neighborhood record store, Boulevard Records, once called Mumford Music, where students from both cultures hung out together, kibitzed, and grooved to each other's jams.

I Will Roar. Let Him Roar Again.

Within a year of my arrival at my new school, I was invited by several of my classmates to join an off-site, after-school Yiddish youth chorus specializing in Eastern European songs made popular by the oppressed residents of the Jewish ghettos and in the factories and sweatshops where they labored.

The invitation surprised me.

"I know you're eager to participate, Harvey," one of my elementary school music teachers once told me, after I began singing at the top of my lungs. "But you're not contributing."

It didn't take long before I discovered politics, and I became an activist in Mumford's student council and president of the school's Human Relations Club, which collected food and raised money for young civil rights activists in the student-led voter registration drives down south. I also discovered a love for performing, eventually scoring leads in two school plays, including my favorite role as Bottom, the weaver-turned-donkey in *A Midsummer Night's Dream*. "Let me play the lion too," Bottom bellowed. "I will roar, that I will do any man's heart good to hear me. I will roar, that I will make the duke say, 'Let him roar again. Let him roar again.'"

It didn't take long for me to assemble a Purple Gang of my own, publishing, with the help of my fellow Mustangs, the *IDiom*, an independent, alternative literary and visual arts magazine. Unfortunately, our first issue scratched the wrong surface.

It was a surreal experience when my counselor called me into her office and, shoving an issue of the *IDiom* in my face, demanded to know "since when do we permit pornography in this school?" I was *very* confused. When I denied doing any such thing, she opened my magazine and pointed to one page in particular. "Then what do you call *this*?" "It's a charcoal sketch," I responded, not quite believing my ears. "Of a Hiroshima survivor," I lied. "Her flesh has been burned off, and she's reaching to the sky as if to ask God, entreating him, 'Why?'" I was on a roll. "'How could you let this happen to me and my family?'"

I thought I made a convincing argument, but apparently, not very. "That may be," my counselor insisted. "But she's a woman and she's *still* naked."

It wasn't the first time I attracted the attention of one of the more conservative school administrators. Months earlier, during the height of the civil rights movement, I was stopped in the hall and challenged by a teacher for wearing a button with what he called a "political statement" embedded on it. "It's not a statement," I pronounced, "it's an equal sign," I lied, not wanting to admit I purchased the button at the recent Fight for Freedom Fund dinner held annually by the NAACP's Detroit branch.

"It's for math club."

He Was This Close

One of my favorite *Peanuts* comic strips is the one where Charlie Brown is about to break the tie and kick the game-winning field goal. He was *this* close, until

Helping heal the world in the Mumford Human Relations Club.
(Courtesy of Harvey Ovshinsky, Mumford's Capri yearbook, and Bentley
Historical Library.)

at the very last second, just before his foot is about to make contact with the football, Lucy jerks it away.

Which was exactly how I felt in 1965 when, in my last year of high school, my mother informed me of her intention to leave Detroit with Adolph and "make a fresh start" in Los Angeles. And take me with them.

Six months before my graduation in January.

What? This made no sense at all. Where was this coming from? What was the mad rush? I tried to negotiate with my mother. Couldn't I at least live with Dad until I graduated in January and *then* join her in Los Angeles? Absolutely not. How about a compromise; until then, how about I live with my best friend and next-door neighbor, Lanny Lesser, and his parents? At least that way, I argued, I'd still have a chance of being elected president of the Mumford student council and maybe even president of my senior class. Not to mention possibly being offered the lead in the drama club's next production, Thornton Wilder's apocalyptic morality play, *The Skin of Our Teeth.*

My suffering was compounded by the fact this wasn't the first time my mother had pulled my rug out. And I'm not counting the episode with my thirteenth-birthday presents or even my aborted attempt at attending the U of M journalism camp. Before Mom married Adolph, when she announced her intention to pick up stakes and start anew with my brothers and me in Los Angeles, I actually welcomed the idea. It would be a reprieve, I remember thinking, and a relief to be bivouacked so far away from the front lines of my parents' Seven-Year War.

But as much as I looked forward to my new adventure, the downside was that I would have to leave Coffey's Purple Gang, and that meant surrendering the opportunity to become the next editor of the *Crusader*.

But all that changed when, out of the blue, Adolph proposed, and my mother decided she and her new husband could make their fresh start in Detroit after all. It was good news for her but a crushing blow for me because when I returned to

Trying to put on a happy face for my graduation from summer school.
(Courtesy of Harvey Ovshinsky and Bentley Historical Library.)

room 204 to tell Mrs. Martin I was staying, she apologized but said because I had already taken myself out of the running—she had already offered the *Crusader's* editorship to someone else.

Flash-forward to years later, when, in 1965, my mother decided yet again to move to California, only this time, she meant it. By now, my younger brother had been sent to a school in Arizona, where Dale became an avid reader and, after taking a Rorschach test administered by the school psychologist, was delighted to discover he had a knack for creative thinking. Or as Max Powell, a family friend, told Lillian Hoddeson and Peter Garrett in *The Man Who Saw Tomorrow: The Life and Inventions of Stanford R. Ovshinsky*, "I always thought Dale was the *other* genius in the family."

So, while Dale was flourishing and Ben was away at college, with my short straw in one hand and my meaningless summer school diploma in the other, my only hope, my only consolation was that at least I would not have to face my exile to Los Angeles alone.

And that I could take my creativity, my karma, and my Mumford Music with me.

6

In L.A. I Promise Not to Tell

So much for magical thinking.

At Mumford I was the biblical Joseph thriving in Egypt, but in Los Angeles I felt abandoned and lost among the Philistines, an exiled *Juif errant* condemned to roam the Sunset Strip at all hours in search of someone — *anyone* — who would take pity on this desperately homesick, seventeen-year-old Motown fish out of water. "Like an arsonist looking for wood," I wrote in one of my several poems describing the depth of my despair, "all I wanted was to talk to this beautiful girl with the black boots and long blond hair."

> She was sitting on a concrete
> wedge-like thing but as
> I walked to her she told
> her friend that I walked
> funny and she stuck her foot
> out to trip me
> I went back to the car
> And I wished she had

Ouch. It also didn't help that the temporary apartment my mother and Adolph found for us was on a street called Detroit. The night we arrived, my mother and Adolph tried to cheer me up by taking me out to eat at a nearby delicatessen. But I was so depressed and so angry I refused to eat at the same table. Or anywhere near them.

Even the specialty of the house, the popular Hank Greenburger, couldn't lift my spirits. Although I did try to like the organic tea and cold "hot cider" served at the area clubs and coffeehouses later made famous by Frank Zappa's "Freak Out Hot Spots" guide to Beat hangouts like the Blue Grotto and Pandora's Box, but that didn't work. Nothing did. "There's literally nothing for me in this town," I lamented in one of my less depressing journal entries, "as far as the eye can see. This is not my idea of home."

> In the Plush Pup
> I paid 90 cents for a pink lemonade
> because they were out of milkshakes

This was *not* how my mother imagined her "fresh start." We eventually reached an armistice when she reluctantly offered to send me home on the condition that I try Los Angeles out for a year. But there was a catch: she would only agree not to fight my return to Detroit if I promised to keep my true feelings to myself and, for the entire year, not tell anyone how I really felt about the move. Especially my father and Iris.

Got it, I reminded myself. Check.

No noise.

Mom was convinced my mood would improve once I enrolled in college. Unfortunately, the only school that would accept me on such short notice and with such terrible grades was East Los Angeles College, where in my phys ed class I studied rope climbing and in my journalism 101 class we probed the origins of the Gutenberg Bible and the history of photo offset printing—"everything but journalism," I whined in my journal.

My only relief came when I discovered the late-night screenings of experimental and "underground" 16mm films showing at the Sunset Strip's famed Fifth Estate coffeehouse, described by the locals as a "bohemian gashouse." There, I wrote in my journal, "the Beats were plucking funny sounds with their guitars and singing Sonny and Cher and I just sat there and played with my ice." In the language of its patrons, I "dug" all the films shown there and especially grooved on my favorite, *Black Orpheus*. I tried getting off on Luis Buñuel's *The Exterminating Angel*, a surreal tale of several aristocrats inexplicably unable to leave their dinner party who end up turning on each other, but that flick hit a little too close to home.

Bummer. Growing up, one of my favorite *Classics Illustrated* comics was no. 108, *Knights of the Round Table*. I was hooked on the story of young Arthur, the lowly orphaned squire, and how he pulled out Excalibur, an enchanted sword the wizard Merlin stuck in a large stone to test Arthur's powers as the future king of England. Marooned in Los Angeles in the late summer of 1965, that's exactly how I felt, only unlike Arthur I had no Merlin to show me the ropes.

Until I met Arthur Kunkin and joined the staff of his *L.A. Free Press*.

It Was a Zoo, but It Was My Kind of Zoo

Before discovering the *Freep*, I had all but given up hope. "I nearly flipped," I wrote in my journal after buying my first issue at a local newsstand. "It was like reading a hip *Coffey Crusader*" with "articles about Vietnam and long-haired people. And even a dirty word or picture or two."

Like my father, thirty-five-year-old Kunkin was a one-time machinist, a secular Jew, and a socialist. In 1964, he started his alternative newspaper, a weekly tabloid newspaper originally known as *The Faire Free Press* because it was sold exclusively at the popular Los Angeles Renaissance Pleasure Faire.

I owe my first meeting with him to insomnia. One restless night I tried to induce sleep by turning on a late-night television talk show, *The Joe Pyne Show*, "almost a *Tonight* type of format," I wrote my Mumford girlfriend, Susan De Gracia, "except anyone can go on [*and*] talk about anything."

Well, almost anything. Pyne was a hostile, argumentative, and confrontational host who was constantly complaining about the "tennis shoe-wearing demonstrators," whom he attacked for destroying the country by "playing into the grubby hands of the commies." When irritated or upset about a remark made by one of his guests, it was not uncommon for Pyne to invite him (or her) to "go gargle with razor blades." After the 1965 Watts riots, he became especially notorious when he interrogated a controversial Black Power activist. The exchange became heated, and the exasperated host tried to shock his guest by revealing he was carrying a handgun. But the activist didn't flinch. Instead, he opened his own coat and showed he, too, was packing.

The soft-spoken, chain-smoking Kunkin was a guest on the night I was watching. I don't recall the details of their conversation, but I do remember Kunkin infuriating Pyne with his paper's coverage of the increasing number of student and antiwar protests on the Sunset Strip.

Who was this guy? What fourth dimension was this? In the early and mid-sixties, unless they were in trouble, front-page news reports about teenagers and

Black people were infrequent in the *Detroit News* and *Detroit Free Press*, lead stories about the civil rights and burgeoning peace movement were all but invisible, and articles about women's issues were often quarantined to the Society or Features sections. And growing up, the only weekly newspapers I ever heard of were the *National Enquirer* and the locally published *Northwest Detroiter*, featuring the latest Hollywood entertainment news reported by the young and up-and-coming Shirley Eder, who went on to write for the *Detroit Free Press*. Years later, when we became friends, I told Shirley I used to cut out her columns from the *Northwest Detroiter* and paste them, along with my own movie and record reviews, in an imagined version of my own newspaper. "All I wanted to do," I gushed, "was grow up and be like you."

The day after Kunkin's interview with Pyne, I skipped my rope-climbing class and drove to the offices of the *L.A. Free Press*, which were literally underground, in the basement of the Fifth Estate coffeehouse. The atmosphere in the *Freep*'s digs was later best described by a reporter for *Esquire*: "Kids, dogs, cats, barefoot waifs, teeny-boppers in see-through blouses, assorted losers, strangers, Indian chiefs wander in and out, while somewhere a radio plays endless rock music and people are loudly paged over an intercom system. It's all very friendly and rather charming and ferociously informal."

It was a zoo. But it was *my* kind of zoo, and for the first time since being yanked away from the mother planet, I finally felt like I was home. Not *at* home exactly, but under the circumstances, close enough. In Kunkin, this Joseph had finally found his pharaoh, someone to whom I could offer my services and with whom I could share my powers.

When I introduced myself, Art seemed genuinely happy to see me. Apparently, the paper was in need of an additional layout assistant, and he needed all the help he could get to prepare the next issue for its press run. I was put right to work, typing up copy on the *Freep*'s ancient Vari-typer machine, making up clever headlines for the reporters' stories and helping with layout and pasting up pages for the photo offset printer.

Although I hadn't smoked marijuana yet, I remember thinking nothing could compete with the natural high I was getting from the *Freep*'s own stash, the fresh aroma of the photo-printing chemicals emanating from the Vari-typer and dried-out cans of Best-Test rubber cement.

The staff embraced me. I developed a tremendous crush on Eve Babitz, who was an up-and-coming writer and artist but who was equally well known for her

LOS ANGELES FREE PRESS

75 PLACES TO GO THIS WEEK - PAGE 8

LETTERS AND REVIEWS
ON CURRENT THEATRE, BOOKS,
MOVIES, ART, MUSIC.

CUMMINGS: The City Elections Cometh
METZGER: V. Woolf Revisited

THE NEW WEEKLY 10¢

VOL. 2, No. 1   FRIDAY, JANUARY 1, 1965   10¢
(15¢ outside of Los Angeles)

SAVIO ON FREE SPEECH:
Issues Behind The Student Protest

One of the most unusual protest demonstrations of 1964 took place in front of the South African Tourist Corporation in Beverly Hills from December 15th to 18th. Featuring a "cell" in which Martin Legassick endured a 90 hour hunger strike as well as a picket line, the vigil was designed to inform the public of the tyranny existing in South Africa.

The 2500 leaflets distributed during the demonstration told of the 5,000 political prisoners in the jails of South Africa, the repressive laws maintaining white supremacy, and the tortures practiced in the prisons.

The leaflet called upon the public to boycott the products of South Africa and for support of the United Nations in its call for economic sanctions against the South African government.

The demonstration was sponsored by the South African Freedom Action Committee (SAFAC) of 11650 Gotham Pl. Los Angeles. SAFAC has asked that interested persons contact them by telephone at 474-0628.

Mario Savio was interviewed by Claude Hayward of KPFK News on December 25. The following are excerpts from the tape of that interview, transcribed and edited by Carol Hampton and Claude Hayward.

MARIO SAVIO: (Student Leader)

It's not so much a student uprising that we want to cause...we simply want our constitutional rights. The San Francisco Chronicle referred to "their most outrageous demand." What they were talking about was our demand that only the courts regulate the content of our speech. They didn't include the demand in their editorial because it would look rather silly.

There is nothing outrageous about it at all. We are asking for very elementary things; we're asking for some of those basic First Amendment rights and the administration has not seen fit to give them to us. We're not going to stand for that kind of abridgement of very fundamental rights. That's what we want.

We also want a hand in deciding the form of political expression. We make the distinction between the content and the form...It's a distinction in constitutional law...with a long history. There is a lot of case law built up around it.

The content must be protected in ways that the form is not. Restrictions of the form cannot be used as a means, either directly or indirectly, to restrict the content.

The faculty should likewise have a hand in deciding what the form should be. It shouldn't be fiat of the administration. But in the question of content, the administration should have no say at all.

Regarding the form, we recognize the need for reasonable regulations...We've held that the university can make no regulation governing the content. Concerning the form, we've held that the regulation should be in accordance with two principles: first, that the form of political expression should be conducive to political expression; second, that form of political expression should be so regulated that the political expression not interfere with the regular educational functions of the university.

We hold that you can't use regulations of a form to throttle people as far as the content is concerned.

There is a rule you have to obtain permission for off-campus speakers 72 hours in advance. First of all, what right has the university to give you permission to have someone off-campus speak to you. We hold that at the most, they are entitled to notification that someone is using their grounds, at most. And that they certainly don't need 72 hours. So that is an example of using the form to regulate the content.

So our complaints are twofold...one, that the university wants to regulate the contents in certain ways and, two, that its regulations on the form are harassing regulations, rather than regulations essential to the normal function of the university. The third thing is, that we want a voice in deciding what the regulations on the form should be.

We want the faculty to have a voice. Had the regulations been reasonable from the start, we would never have asked for that voice. But, the administration has shown itself to be so arbitrary in its interpretation and enforcement of its regulations that we've come to the conclusion that unless we've a voice in the enactment and enforcement along with the faculty and the administration we are not going to get a fair break. The faculty has agreed in a vote of 824 to 115. They voted to take the matter entirely out of the hands of the administration and decide it themselves. I prefer that to a tripartite. I've had my experience with tripartite boards... and I would be more than happy to have the faculty do the thing

(Continued on Page 3)

I find a lifeline at the L.A. Free Press.
(Courtesy of Los Angeles Free Press and https://losangelesfreepress.com/.)

romantic escapades with local musicians and movie stars. I admit my infatuation with Eve may have also been influenced by the now infamous nude portrait by Julian Wasser of her playing chess with a much older artist and chess master, Marcel Duchamp. Needless to say, I left out any mention of my crush on Eve in my letters to Susan De Gracia.

Harvey Who?

Someone once famously said, "You don't drown by falling in the water; you drown by staying there." As lifesaving as my work at the *Free Press* was, I knew it wasn't enough to keep me in L.A.; I missed my friends too much; I missed Dad and Iris. And I missed my pond, my big little Detroit life where I could share my stories with the people I loved and with whom I had history and a *connection*. "All I want," I wrote Sue, is to "leave here and buy a warm winter jacket, some heavy shoes without laces . . . save my money for a new Volkswagen, play my stereo . . . [*and*] play Buffy [*Sainte-Marie*] and Judy Collins and the [*new*] Dylan album."

For as long as I could, I tried to keep the promise I made to my mother, to stick it out and maintain a vow of silence. "Only you must know how I really feel," I warned Sue. "My father must know I'm having a wonderful time and really enjoying myself."

But I couldn't keep it up. In the end, my body betrayed me, and I started to get headaches and severe stomach cramps. I lost sleep and ate my way through what I'm now sure was clinical depression. Sadly, there was nothing "post" about my traumatic stress.

I knew what to do about it, I just didn't know if I had the courage to do it. After all my mother endured when my father abandoned her, it was a tape I was not looking forward to replaying by returning to Detroit. "If I do this, I screw my mother," I wrote to Sue. "If I don't, I end up screwing myself." And yet, only when I allowed myself to entertain even the *possibility* of leaving L.A., "my dark clouds" of sadness and depression, as I called them at the time, all but evaporated.

I was so just tired of mouthing the words! And anyway, I convinced myself, in leaving Los Angeles, I wouldn't be running *away* from home as much as running *to* it. And I wouldn't be returning empty-handed. I wanted to publish my own newspaper, and in doing so bring back the best parts of what I had seen and learned in Los Angeles: the teeming antiwar and civil rights scenes, the vibrant youth and music culture. And above all, I wanted to bring back with me the freedom that *Free Press* writers and their readers had to speak out and express themselves. I wanted to know what that felt like. Again.

But where to begin? Years later, whenever my fourth- and fifth-grade creative writing students were stumped and struggled to solve a particularly difficult problem, I encouraged them to use one of my many soft, squishy, rubber hand toys I called "stumpers." That way, I promised them they could relieve some of the stress they felt from not knowing the answers.

In L.A. where were my stumpers when I needed them?

I started with what my father called a "war dance." Part manifesto, part a brainstorming to-do list, Dad's war dances were famous for envisioning new and exciting strategies to find scientific solutions to global problems like war and pollution. His war dances also came in especially handy whenever it was necessary (which was often) to rescue his alternative energy company, Energy Conversion Devices, from near-certain bankruptcy.

Over the years, I've discovered my father and I shared many traits, but none stronger than our abilities to imagine and visualize our way through a problem. At the patent office they called Dad "the man with the balls" because, in his mind, he always pictured things and then drew the things he imagined. Among his most prized possessions were the Styrofoam balls he created that represented atoms, which, under his control, could be manipulated to appear both aligned *and* disordered.

It didn't take long for me to envision the first issue of my new paper clearly in my head. Inspired by what independent filmmaker Jim Jarmusch later described in *MovieMaker* magazine as "authentic stealing," I forgave myself for my lack of originality. "Steal from anywhere," Jarmusch wrote, "that resonates with inspiration or fuels your imagination . . . Select only things to steal from that speak directly to your soul."

Which is why the original mockup of my first issue of my phantom newspaper looked so strikingly like the *L.A. Free Press*. For a while, I even christened my new paper *The Detroit IDiom* after my old Mumford literary magazine. But in the end, I settled on the *Fifth Estate*, not at all referring to the four pillars of democracy, but instead as an homage to the coffeehouse that helped save my life.

It was all very thrilling. Like Edmond Dantès, the wrongly imprisoned protagonist from my *Count of Monte Cristo* comic, I counted the moments before I could make good my escape.

An early pencil sketch of how I imagined the first issue of the Fifth Estate. *(Courtesy of Harvey Ovshinsky and Bentley Historical Library.)*

Leaving on a Jet Plane

Meanwhile, in the real world, I continued to attend classes and perform my duties at the *Free Press*, my mind racing all the while with new plans and new strategies for launching what eventually became the *Fifth Estate*. I didn't eat, I couldn't sleep, I was too excited imagining all the stories I would cram into the first issue of my paper: how a Detroit record store owner was being threatened with arrest for selling Lenny Bruce records; the reorganization of the city's Friends of the Student Nonviolent Coordinating Committee (SNCC) chapter; a review of the upcoming Bob Dylan concert at Masonic Temple; and the possible downtown reopening of the old Vanguard Theater, once home to actor and former Detroiter George C. Scott.

But first, I had to face my mother. And her music.

I knew introducing any thought of my returning to Detroit was out of the question. I'd tried that several times before and it hadn't worked. "You promised me a year, Harvey," she would remind me whenever I brought up the subject. *And you'll just have to do your time and serve your sentence*, I said, finishing her thought in my head.

In the end, I chickened out and left a note. The irony is that, for someone who prided himself on his writing, I could not find the words that would relieve my own suffering at the cost of adding gasoline to hers. What could I say? What *difference* would it possibly make? I knew Mom would be furious and feel deeply hurt by my infidelity. But I didn't care. I paid my dues; I made my deposits. I was done.

Now, I just wanted to go home.

"I'm writing this note," I informed her and Adolph in a hastily written letter I left for them, "to let you know that I am either in or on my way to Detroit. I don't like to cry when there are human beings around, especially to say good-bye. I thought an unplanned abrupt finish would be easier on you and better for me. I will write soon. Please don't feel badly—too much."

I called a cab and headed for the airport to grab a red-eye to Detroit paid for by Dad and Iris, with whom I had shared my plans. I had tried for so long to honor my mother's wishes and not share my unhappiness with them, but in the end, I couldn't continue the charade. I finally split the difference and tipped off my older brother, Ben, who then passed my note in a bottle to Dad and Iris. Once they were in on the conspiracy, they agreed to intervene on my behalf as soon as I gave the word.

I gave the word.

The take-off was a little bumpy, but otherwise the flight to Detroit was uneventful. I spent most of my time immersed in my war chest of assorted war dances, dummy articles, and mockups of what I fantasized the first issue of the *Fifth Estate* would look like.

And then something unexpected happened. As we made our descent over Detroit's Metro Airport, my mood suddenly shifted and I was overcome with a rush of intense and unexpected feelings. I was happy, of course, and excited.

But I was also sad. And scared. Especially scared. I had experienced each of these feelings before in my life but never all at once. What did this mean? What was going on?

And then I knew. The moment we touched down in Detroit, I understood *exactly* what was happening to me. And why.

This must be, I thought, *what graduation feels like*.

7

You Can't Print That! My Life in the Underground Press

It was not the reunion I expected.

When I returned to Mumford to visit my old friends from the Class of '66, it seemed like they didn't know what to do with me. Or what to say. They were too busy holding their student council elections and rehearsing their production of *The Skin of Our Teeth* and didn't seem to have the time or the interest to pick up where we left off.

When I pitched my former *IDiom* colleagues on the idea of writing for the *Fifth Estate*, they were eager to lend a hand, but were confused. Start your own newspaper? Who does *that*?

Dad and Iris welcomed me home with open arms. Once I settled into living with them in their Bloomfield Hills home, they agreed to loan me three hundred dollars to pay for the *Fifth Estate*'s first printing bill. Meanwhile, Iris's young children, Robin and Steven, volunteered to help me type up and lay out the first issue on Dad's desk in his lower-level home office.

One problem: as eager as I was to publish my alternative newspaper, first I had to come up with alternative news.

I began by knocking on the doors of the area's most prominent civil rights and antiwar organizations. Ernest Mazey, then executive director of the Michigan chapter of the American Civil Liberties Union, was extremely receptive, not only offering to supply stories for the paper but also subscribing on the spot. Other activists weren't sure what to make of my plans, but they were eager for the opportunity to have a newspaper, *any* newspaper that would print their press releases instead of simply tossing them in the wastebasket.

Unfortunately, not everyone was as eager to support our efforts.

The *Fifth Estate*'s first issue was delayed by several weeks when our printer refused to print our layout sheets because of what he called "unpatriotic" content. The front-page Jules Feiffer cartoon borrowed from the *L.A. Free Press* ridiculing President Lyndon Johnson wasn't the problem. The printer's primary objection was a political cartoon on page 2 that portrayed an American flag with rifles and bayonets in place of the stripes. "We don't print treason," he announced proudly.

That hurt, but the real problem was that he didn't *tell* us we weren't going to press. I thought he was just stalling, but finally my father insisted we "put an end to this bullshit" and find another printer.

It wasn't easy. In 1965, finding someone to print the first issue of an unpatriotic and treasonous newspaper like the *Fifth Estate* was like trying to pin down a priest or a rabbi to marry a "mixed" religious couple. Finally, the Reverend Albert Cleage Jr., a Black Nationalist minister, and his brother Henry, who published their own radical newspaper, agreed to print the paper, and in November of 1965, after a painful gestation in Los Angeles and a frustrating pregnancy in Detroit, the *Fifth Estate* was born.

A Flawed Masterpiece

I was a *very* proud father.

The first issue of the *Fifth Estate* featured a front-page story reviewing the Bob Dylan concert at the Masonic Temple auditorium. The writer, my high school buddy and *IDiom* cohort Steve Simons, loved Dylan but was confused by his "wielding an electric guitar surrounded by a rock and roll combo. Now Bob Dylan feels like he can 'make it' in rock and roll," Steve wrote. "Perhaps he can."

Oh well, we were journalists; we never said we were prophets.

Readers of that first issue were particularly impressed by the number of ads promoting local art movies like *The Pawnbroker* and *The Collector*, and hip concerts like Randy Sparks and the Back Porch Majority at the Masonic.

I accepted the compliments but told no one that I'd lifted every one of these display ads from the local aboveground papers; they weren't paid for, none of them.

The issue stood out for several other reasons. Where else could you find our "What's On" calendar, which informed readers about such lefty arts and cultural events as "A Second Night with the Wobblies" with folk singer Ellen Stekert, Edward Albee's controversial *Death of Bessie Smith* at the Kresge Court Theater, or the stunning new Sarkis Sarkisian exhibition at the Detroit Artists Market?

It was a far cry from so many of the front-page headlines *Detroit News* and *Detroit Free Press* readers were used to: "Police to Squelch Teen Party Raids—Hoodlums Harass Suburbs," "Along with New Weapon? Nagging Women!" and my all-time favorite, "Weird Way-Out World of Art 'springs' at Detroit."

As proud as I was of the *Fifth Estate*, the first issue was a flawed masterpiece. For one thing, each copy came with two blank pages. No one ever told me that when you lay out six pages of copy, tabloid newspapers can only print four pages at a time.

Still, we impressed. Because I was a newly enrolled student, Wayne State University's *Daily Collegian* newspaper wrote a glowing review, inviting readers to "look for something different in newspapers. Like to see topics treated from a new angle?" asked the article. "You might want to take a look at the *Fifth Estate*, a *Collegian*-size paper and a product of a university freshman, Harvey Ovshinsky.

"The austere, modest office might easily invoke an image to the romantic that, here, he will find an angry young man bent over a cluttered table, pen in hand lashing out at established institutions and the status quo."

The article helped, not just because it made me look the way I felt, but also because of the several new subscriptions we received from curious students and faculty members. "Good luck with your newspaper," one new subscriber wrote. "I'm enclosing a check to help pay for a dictionary. I'm no journalist but I do know the word publicity has two 'i's in it, not just one."

I've always been proud of having started the paper so young, but by the second issue, my youth and inexperience were starting to show in other ways. "*The Fifth Estate*, so far, isn't much more than a hick cut-and-paste job of pilfered materials," wrote *Playboy* in its reporting on the early days of the underground press. They called it "the shortest, most derivative and least professional-looking of the papers, replete with unreadable gray type, spelling mistakes and malapropism."

That hurt. What if my mother was right after all: instead of starting my own literary magazine at Mumford, I should have "buckled down" and joined the staff of a *real* magazine like the school's official literary magazine, the *Muse*. Or a real newspaper like the *Mumford Mercury*.

Maybe, probably, but then I took heart from a lesson I learned from my father during one of our many visits to the Henry Ford Museum and Greenfield Village to see the re-creation of Edison's Menlo Park laboratory. On our tours, Dad would often remind my brothers and me that for every one of Edison's early light bulbs that worked, there were hundreds, even thousands, that didn't.

THE FIFTH ESTATE

dedicated to norman r. morrison

THE MARCH ON WASHINGTON

THE FBI AND U of M

THE C.I.A. AND VIETNAM

REPORT FROM NATCHEZ, MISS.

DETROIT'S NEW PROGRESSIVE
BI-WEEKLY NEWSPAPER
November 19 - December 2
ISSUE NO. 1

10¢

Bob Dylan; In Memoriam

Detroit took its first glimpse at the "new" Bob Dylan in his concert at the Masonic Temple on Oct. 24. The first half of the spectacle was the traditional Dylan. Following the intermission, the audience was confronted by Dylan welding an electric guitar, surrounded by his rock & roll combo.

His first song, "Tombstone Blues", resulted in cries of "We want Dylan!" to which he replied, "Well, who'd ya come to see?" After a few unfavorable responses to his songs, he seated himself at the piano and sang, "Ballad of a Thin Man." The chorus is: "There's somethin' goin' on up here but you don't know what it is, do you, Mr. Jones?" The audience remained quiet for the remainder of the concert.

When the concert ended, those who had come not knowing the "new" Dylan were astonished and offended. Others merely shrugged their shoulders and left the auditorium. For most of the audience, the image of Bob Dylan, bard of young America, was crushed.

Detroit's reaction was not so radical or unusual. Dylan has met the same response throughout the United States.

The question which remains in the minds of many is simply "Why?" "why the change?" Dylan states, "I don't have to prove anything to anyone. Those people who dig me know where I'm at - I don't have to come on to them; I'm not a bathroom singer." Regarding those who dislike the rock & roll, he states, "I'm not interested in them. I'm not writing and singing for anybody, to tell the truth. Hey, really, I don't care what people say, I don't care what they tell other people I am."

Now Bob Dylan feels he can "make it" in rock & roll. Perhaps he can.....
STEVE SIMONS

JOE HILL;
A TRIBUTE

Labor History Archives of Wayne State of Wayne State University is commemorating the 50th anniversary of the execution of Joe Hill, America's most famous Wobblie and the "Man Who Never Died."

The program will be held at 8 p.m. Friday November 19, in the WSU McGregor Memorial Conference Center, Second at Ferry, and will highlight Hill's life in "living newspaper style." Further details about the event can be obtained by calling the University Archives office at TE 3-1400.

FEIFFER

ACLU BLASTS DRAFT AS PUNISHMENT

The American Civil Liberties Union of Michigan (ACLU) has condemned the announced intent of Colonel Arthur A. Holmes, state Selective Service Director to use the Selective Service Act "as a device to punish dissent".

Colonel Holmes was reported earlier as calling for "the immediate induction" of Vietnam war protestors who had violated Selective Service regulations or had caused any interruption of procedures.

Rolland O'Hare, Chairman of ACLU of Michigan, commented:

"Until now, no one in any position of responsibility in the government has suggested that the Selective Service Act may be used as a device to punish dissent. If young men who disagree with the government's policy in Vietnam may be singled out for discriminatory application of the Act today, who can say how the threat may be used to dragoon youth into conformity tomorrow?

"The selective service system which places awesome power in the hands of government administrators must, as a matter of law, treat all who come within its scope fairly and uniformly on the basis of reasonable classifications equally applied. The moment it is allowed to deviate from those limitations, we have placed the lives and liberties of a sizeable portion of the population of the United States at the unfettered whim of what this or that draft board or functionary considers the national interest to require.

"If any person in the course of his protest on the subject of Vietnam or

any other matter of public concern transgresses the law, he may obviously properly be made to answer in a court of law for his act and, if found guilty, be punished in accordance with the law. The Selective Service Act itself has provisions carrying criminal penalties which, however, are to be enforced by a court, not by a single administrative officer."

NEW
LEFT

A group has formed calling itself the Detroit Circle. Its purpose is to fill the void that exists among those who consider themselves part of the independent left. One of its spokesmen said this about the organization: "There is a need for new ideas, reevaluating the old ones, and fresh discussion among us who reject totalitarianism in any form. There is a need for the youth and the adults of this city not only to discuss in depth new concepts, but to reevaluate old ones. There is a need to have a forum for the community as a whole so that others who are contributing to creative thinking can be heard-people like Hal Draper, Erich Fromm, etc. We ought to set up a dialogue with the Detroit liberal and radical community with the purpose of helping, and even, when necessary, initiating actions concerning the problems and issues of peace and civil rights."

The first meetings were enthusiastically received. The group plans to meet every two weeks. Information concerning the next meeting, contact THE FIFTH ESTATE PO Box 303, Bloomfield Hills, Mich.

PRISON
NOTES

NATCHEZ, MISS.— Within the last month, more than 500 people have been arrested in the city of Natchez, Mississippi. Although news of the arrests received wide circulation, the brutality and the indignities which the prisoners were forced to endure during their stay in Parchman State Penitentiary has untilnow been kept secret. However, with the release of some of the arrested, the story is finally getting out. What follows is the report by two of those recently released:

James Herman Johnson, twenty-year old Alcorn College junior, states that upon arrival at Parchman, he was forced to disrobe and to allow his private parts to be examined by a police officer. Johnson was then pulled up by his beard so forcefully that some of the beard came off in the policeman's hand. Johnson said he thought the policeman to have been about six feet tall, weighing over 200 pounds.

Phil Latansky, 24 year old white PDP volunteer from Seattle, Washington gave this report of his arrest: "After our arrival at Parchman, we were admitted to the maximum security building where we were stripped of all our clothing. Each of were forced to swallow approximately eight ounces of laxatives. Naked we were
(continued on page 2)

DISCREDIT
WHO?

WASHINGTON, Oct. 20 (AP)— Senator Stephen M. Young, Democrat from Ohio, said Thursday that he had learned that the Central Intelligence Agency hired persons to disguise as Vietcong and discredit Communists in Vietnam by committing atrocities.

The C.I.A. and Representative Cornelius E. Gallagher, Democrat of New Jersey, said it was not so.

Thursday night Senator Young denied having said that the report came from a C.I.A. man, but he said that he got it from an American military officer whom he did not name.

Nevertheless, Mr. Young said, "I confirmed through the C.I.A. today that it employed some South Vietnamese nationals to pose as Vietcong—and I take a dim view of that."

Mr. Young who recently returned from Vietnam, had at first said to newsmen that a C.I.A. man told him the C.I.A. hired South Vietnamese who dresses as Vietcong, then committed such acts as killing men and raping women.

Mr. Young, a member of the Senate Armed Services Committee, said he would ask that group to investigate C.I.A. activities. Mr. Gallagher has also recently visited South Vietnam.

NOTE: The above article is reprinted exactly as it appeared on Friday, October 22 in The New York Times. Because of reproduction difficulties, the article has been retyped. Nothing has been changed or edited.

Start the presses: The first issue of the Fifth Estate, *November 1965.*
(Courtesy of Harvey Ovshinsky, the Fifth Estate, *and Bentley Historical Library.)*

At the time, I thought my father was talking about Edison. Years later, when I imagined he was thinking of his own failed experiments, he dismissed the very idea: "That's not how it works, Harvey. In science, there's no such thing as a failed experiment."

You Really Should Meet John Sinclair

It was my friend Jeffrey Feldman who told me about John Sinclair. Jeff was a fellow Mumford Mustang and one of the *Fifth Estate*'s first and most energetic and ardent supporters. Our mutual friend Marshall (Muzzy) Tate loved telling the story of how, in 1965, he went to a movie playing at the Wayne State University Cinema Guild and there was a guy selling the *Fifth Estate*. "One of the professors in the audience," Muzzy recalled, "said, 'I'll buy a paper if you can name the original Four Estates.' The guy," said Muzzy, "was Jeff, and of course he could."

Although originally from Flint, John Sinclair was known around the Wayne campus as an emerging poet who, along with his German-born wife, Leni, a photographer, cofounded the Detroit Artists Workshop, an arts collective providing public venues for concerts, poetry readings, gallery shows, publishing, and other cultural events.

When I called to arrange a meeting, John answered the phone. I was excited but also extremely anxious. In those early days of the paper, the word *hippie* wasn't yet an essential part of my vocabulary. I thought the Sinclairs were beatniks, and I was nervous about meeting my first ones.

"Thanks for seeing me," I heard myself tell John as he welcomed me into his off-campus apartment deep in the heart of the Warren-Forest area near the university. I remember Coltrane (or was it Ornette Coleman?) playing on the turntable, and even though I didn't know who they were, I was impressed by books by Ferlinghetti and Allen Ginsberg resting on top of the coffee table; Leni was in the kitchen, cooking up a pot of spaghetti and meatballs. "It's all I know how to cook," she said, unapologetically.

I had absolutely no idea how to behave. What if they offered me a joint? Or *LSD*? I knew nothing. It was one thing to seek the support of old-school politicos like Ernie Mazey; I could speak their language. But what did this clueless seventeen-year-old intellectual virgin know about art, poetry, and music—*real art, real poetry, and real music*?

Nothing. *And that*, I reminded myself, *was the point of the visit*.

Me and "Detroit's first hippie," Jerry Younkins.
(Photo by Leni Sinclair. Courtesy of Leni Sinclair, Harvey Ovshinsky, and
Bentley Historical Library.)

"We like what you're doing with the paper," John said, interrupting my conversation with myself. "How can we help?"

That was a new experience! Before John and Leni, I'd never met any adults, other than my father, Iris, and, of course, Mrs. Martin, my junior high school journalism teacher, who were so unconditionally supportive of my work.

And, as it turned out, invested in it!

Although we came from different planets, John, Leni, and I understood that in those days, Detroit-area artists, "longhairs," druggies, and politicos rarely communicated with each other. Nothing wrong with that, I argued, but considering each of these groups was harassed, under surveillance, and often arrested by the same police, why not connect the dots, seek out common ground, and create an opportunity for us to learn from each other, or at least *read* about what we were each up to?

I was on a roll. What was missing, I told John, and what the paper desperately needed, was an identity that reflected a shared sense of community. And with their help, that's exactly what we could become: a conduit, a bridge between the different factions of what eventually came to be called Detroit's counterculture.

I hoped I made an impression—I *thought* I did—but I wasn't at all certain until the end of the meeting when, as they were seeing me out, John and Leni said I could count on their support. As a result, the second issue of the *Fifth Estate* looked very little like the first. The front page was adorned with several stunning black-and-white photographs by Leni accompanied by her article about "The New Sound of Sound" being heard on campus.

"Very soon now," Leni wrote, "Wayne State University will finally become known across the country—not for its football team (I hope that will never happen), or for its student sit-ins (unfortunately, that will never happen either), but for the fine presentations of contemporary music sponsored by a small group of students known as the WSU Artists' Society."

Our glorious second issue also featured the debut of The Coat-Puller, John's new column about Detroit's alternative arts and culture scene: "It shouldn't be news to anyone—but it probably is—that the local gestapo is responsible for ending the performance of LeRoi Jones' *The Toilet* and *The Slave* at the now shutdown Concept East Theater.

"What amazes me," John continued, "is that this city's 'theater lovers' have kept entirely mute about [*this*] case and have allowed the 'authorities' to do whatever they want to with Detroit's small theaters. OK, now they have exactly what they deserve—the Fisher [*Theatre*], whose every production is for these ears, hopelessly obscene, i.e., totally devoid of any art or human use."

I wanted to tell John I actually *enjoyed* Sammy Davis Jr. in the Fisher Theatre's production of *Golden Boy*, but I resisted the urge.

Checkmate

We were "hip, exciting, angry . . . and intelligent," Chris Edwards and Elaine Weeks wrote about the *Fifth Estate* more than fifty years later in their immense coffee table book, *5000 Ways You Know You're from Detroit*. But all that came later. In 1966, very few people outside the Wayne State University campus had ever heard of us. And to correct the situation, I knew I would need help from the

Detroit poet John Sinclair and me being interviewed on The Lou Gordon
Program.
*(Photo by Leni Sinclair. Courtesy of Leni Sinclair, Harvey Ovshinsky, and
Bentley Historical Library.)*

Chess Mate, Detroit's legendary folk and blues cafe, which hosted acts like
the up-and-coming Chuck and Joni Mitchell; Linda Ronstadt and her band,
Stone Poneys; Tom Rush; Dave Van Ronk; the Siegel-Schwall Band; and James
Cotton.

Before he owned the Chess Mate, Morrie Widenbaum was a champion
speed chess player who, legend had it, once played Bobby Fischer. He was also,
in my experience, a total prick of the first order. When I stopped by the coffeehouse to see if he would consider selling the paper, Morrie agreed, but only if he
could keep the entire ten cents purchase price for each copy.

It was a tough call. I'd like to say this episode was a teaching moment for me,
an opportunity for this brash, young, crusading editor to tell the Morrie Widen-
baums of the world to go fuck themselves. Instead, I held my fire, and with Phil
Ochs singing "The Highwayman" in the background, I handed Widenbaum
my stack of *Fifth Estates*, silently cursing him under my breath and vowing that
someday I would make him pay.

Which is exactly what happened. Once the Chess Mate started feeling the heat from other coffeehouses like the Living End, the Poison Apple, and the Wisdom Tooth, I got a call from Morrie, who was "curious" about our latest advertising rates.

We're Like the Beatles, Only I'm Paul and You're John

As pleased as he was to have me back in Detroit, my father did not support the move unconditionally; I had to promise to return to college and complete my education. I reluctantly agreed, although I was confused. "You know, Dad," I reminded him, "you never went to college. And you turned out pretty well."

I tried to get into several local universities, but apparently, my C– average at East Los Angeles College did not impress. On the other hand, Wayne State University's Monteith College welcomed me with open arms. For the next weeks, the old student center there was my home away from home where I hung out and kibitzed with my fellow classmates, among them Dave Marsh, who was one of *Creem* magazine's original editors and later a rock critic for *Rolling Stone*, the author of twenty-five books, and a host on SiriusXM.

As much as I enjoyed the idea of attending Monteith, known for its small interdisciplinary program offering refuge for restless, free-range students like myself, the reality was that burning both ends of the candle was taking its toll. Within two months of starting the paper, I was exhausted from the day-to-day grind of editing and publishing while also trying to be a full-time student. Finally, I had enough. The *Fifth Estate* needed a full-time staff, I announced at a meeting of the Detroit Committee to End the War in Vietnam, and without one, the paper's days were numbered.

Nobody raised their hands.

Except Peter Werbe, who, after leaving Michigan State University, became a Detroit-based political activist and, fortunately for me, also an avid reader of the *Fifth Estate*. I may have created the paper, but once they joined the staff, Peter and his wife, Marilyn, saved it.

It wasn't a hard sale. "Considering the state of journalism at the time," Peter later recalled, "and especially the fragmented universe of the local peace, civil rights, youth, and women's rights movements, I realized the *Fifth Estate* had a role to play."

Read all about it! With Marilyn and Peter Werbe.
(Courtesy of Peter and Marilyn Werbe.)

An Artsy-Craftsy, Shoestring Paper Popping Up Like a Weed

Once Peter was on board, I didn't do as much writing and reporting as I would have liked. As editor and publisher, my job was to get the ball rolling, and then, with Peter's and the Sinclairs' help and a growing staff of volunteer writers and photographers, make sure it didn't stop.

And it didn't. "Shoestring papers of the strident left are popping up like weeds across the US," wrote *Time* magazine about what was fast becoming known as the underground press. "Their editors, writers and subscribers represent a curious coalition of hipsters, beatniks, college students and teachers and the just plain artsy-craftsy."

"Ovshinsky," continued *Time*, "is planning a long career in journalism." "I intend to be publishing this paper when I'm 35," I was quoted as saying. At the time, that was an unimaginable point in the future.

As it turned out, it was Peter who stayed with the paper until he was thirty-five and more than thirty-five years beyond that. He was always an excellent writer and copy editor, but in truth, his greatest contribution to the paper was to provide the strident left to my just plain artsy-craftsy.

Bringing the news home now.
(Photo by Leni Sinclair. Courtesy of Leni Sinclair, Harvey Ovshinsky, and
Bentley Historical Library.)

We started out, according to the paper's first editorial, being "Detroit's New Progressive Bi-Weekly Newspaper," but Peter was the driver who helped turn the *Fifth Estate* into something more forceful and persuasive and, eventually, more vociferous and radical than I ever could have imagined. Or even, at times, preferred. "The differing perspectives," wrote the authors of *Detroit: I Do Mind Dying*, "reflected a real division between advocates of an alternative lifestyle and hardcore political revolutionaries."

Or, as I told Peter, "We were like the Beatles, only I was Paul and you were John."

The more issues we published, the more our circulation grew, as did our staff of volunteer contributors. "Almost overnight," Peter recalled, "the paper's office became a bustling center of writers, photographers, and artists, all anxious to contribute their efforts in writing about psychedelic drugs, the antiwar movement, rock and roll, the alternative culture, and anything that was anti-authoritarian."

In time, Frank Joyce, a local civil rights activist who later became communications director for the United Auto Workers union, became an essential staff member. Frank was an excellent news editor who was also a gifted investigative reporter. It turned out, though, I had met Frank years before he joined the paper. During my parents' Seven-Year War, on one of my weekday nights alone with him, Dad said we had to make a stop to bail out young Frank, who was being held for his participation in a civil rights protest.

Me, Fifth Estate *news editor Frank Joyce, and co-editor Peter Werbe planning the next issue.*
(Photo by Tony Spina. Courtesy of Tony Spina Collection, Walter P. Reuther Library, Wayne State University.)

Tommye Wiese was our circulation manager, and she certainly increased mine. She was a blond, long-haired beauty (when you could get away with saying such things) from a working-class suburb who became an early and essential part of our growing full-time staff, at first doing the thankless job of typesetting our articles. "She's a Trotskyist, you *do* know that, don't you?" Peter would remind me every time he caught me staring, reminding me that, even then, sexism didn't play well with feminists and women revolutionaries.

Which brings me to Cathy West, our devoted editorial assistant. Cathy was a precocious fifteen- or sixteen-year-old runaway from Paw Paw, Michigan, who stopped by our offices one day to offer her services. Until she died many years later, she never left the paper. I still think of Cathy; she was devoted not only to the paper but also, in those early days, I suspect, to me. If that was true, I regret I could not offer her more than my gratitude and my appreciation. She was the kindest, most accessible, and openhearted person I knew, and I wish I could have given her more of what she offered me.

We Wanted to Show Everything

In a 2009 interview, I told *Detroit Free Press* columnist Desiree Cooper that I believed the mainstream media was like a hand mirror that only showed part of the body, whereas alternative papers like the *Fifth Estate* insisted, " 'No, there's more!' We were like this full-length mirror that wanted to see and show *everything*."

For me and Peter, Frank, and the rest of our army of guerilla journalists, "everything" included reporting on the existence of the so-called red squads organized by the Detroit Police Department, Michigan State Police, and the FBI. Their goal? To surveil and infiltrate "subversive" groups like the Sinclairs' Artists Workshop as well as area civil rights and antiwar organizations and even, as we later found out, the *Fifth Estate*, which the police identified in their files as "the Detroit hippie colony's underground newspaper . . . catering to beatnik and left-wing elements."

It's a story I love telling, most recently to participants in a workshop at Wayne State University's school of business where I taught members of the Detroit Police Department Leadership Academy how storytelling could help strengthen their leadership and management skills.

Of course, in 1966, teaching cops how to become leaders and effective managers was the last thing on my mind. It was bad enough how the police distorted our work in their reports, but discovering our trusted accountant was a police informer was a real kick in the head. Who knew, in addition to being a jolly good fellow and a brilliant bookkeeper, he was also a spy? "I didn't want to do it," he told Peter years later in a tearful apology. "They made me do it," he said, claiming the police blackmailed him into informing on us by threatening to prosecute him for what was then called a "morals" crime.

Reading my red squad files years later was a revelation, especially when I discovered that so many of the entries were "read and approved" by the City of Detroit's Criminal Intelligence Bureau. Sounded like an oxymoron to me, but who knew such a thing existed?

As misinformed as many of these files were, the detailed reports of Peter's and my activities were enormously helpful in recalling the details of my *Fifth Estate* days, reminding me of long-forgotten dates, times, and locations. I especially appreciated rereading an early article from the long-defunct *Detroit Scope* magazine about my father and me. "Although some of Harvey's hippie friends," read the article, "might consider his father's alternative energy work [*with the auto industry*] a sell-out to the system, Harvey says 'I support my father in everything he does . . . He's doing what he has to do and I'm doing what I have to do.'"

What the reams of red squad surveillance trivia and minutiae failed to disclose was how, from its very first edition, the *Fifth Estate* was vigilant in its coverage of local civil rights and social justice events and activities. Except for the city's Black newspaper, *The Michigan Chronicle*, the *Fifth Estate* was the only local newspaper to routinely cover and take seriously the years of discrimination against and harassment of African Americans by the police and others that led to what I came to call Detroit's 1967 "ri-bellion," splitting the difference as to whether the July 1967 uprising (another label we used) was a full-fledged **ri**ot or, as the *Fifth Estate* also called it, a people's re**bellion**.

A City on Fire

The summer of 1967 tested our skills as journalists. Our mandate to ourselves was that we not only cover the so-called riot but also, and more importantly, *un*cover it. Officially, it began when the Detroit police raided an unlicensed, after-hours bar on the west side of the city, but that was just the spark. The subsequent beating deaths of three African American teenagers during what infamously became known as the Algiers Motel incident, fueled by decades of abuse by Detroit's

THE FIFTH ESTATE

Vol. 2, No. 9 (35)
Aug. 1-15, 1967

10¢

15¢ OUTSIDE DETROIT

city ablaze

by Harvey Ovshinsky

On Sunday, July 23, at 3 o'clock in the morning, the DOORS 'Baby Light My Fire' was the number one song in Detroit.

It couldn't have been more appropriate.

At 3:30 a.m. a large crowd of black people watched as their brothers and sisters were arrested for drinking in a blind pig.

At 4:00 a.m. they stopped watching and began throwing things. The rest is history.

As of this writing, 40 people are dead, 2,000 are wounded and 3,500 people are in jail.

It started with mass looting in the inner city, but soon spread quickly into other areas. It was black and white together as looters gave way to arsonists and arsonists gave way to snipers. Young children watched as their parents broke into hardware and grocery stores. When the paratroopers came in with machine guns and tanks the looting stopped. Not so much because the people were afraid but because there wasn't anything left to loot.

When the fires started on Sunday afternoon, Mayor Cavanagh asked that suburban fire departments come in and help out. Several times the fire fighters were forced to leave the area because of heavy sniper fire. At first the fires were limited to clothing, furniture and grocery stores, but on Monday the shit hit the fan.

Bands of arsonists left the ghetto and by late Monday many homes and businesses in Northwest Detroit were gutted by fire, as were many on the East and West side.

As this paper goes to press, over 1,300 fires have been set, 30 firemen wounded by sniper fire and everybody wants to know why.

Cries of 'outside agitators fall on deaf ears for this reporter.

The looting was interracial and unusually cordial and friendly until the paratroopers began firing. Teenagers joined with black militants in arson and sniping. Six whites were arrested for firing on troops and while many deaths were blamed on snipers, the black and white residents of the ghetto say that the troopers were responsible for most of the killing.

In a discussion with FIFTH ESTATE co-editor Peter Werbe, one black militant acknowledged that residents were arming themselves and in his words "getting themselves together."

Fighting between snipers and troops reached fantastic proportions as armed assaults were made on police precincts, command posts and even the downtown headquarters housing presidential assistant Cyrus Vance.

Bands of Negroes, armed with army machine guns kept two police precincts from functioning for almost an hour as they lay siege to them. Also on several occasions guardsmen and police were forced to abandon entire sections of the ghetto due to sniper fire.

Not outside agitators. Just plain folk. Plain folk, some white, most black, who were angry at America. Plain folk who set Detroit on fire and made Watts look like a Love - In.

picket at lbj speech

Lyndon Baines Johnson, 36th President of the United States of America, the man who sends troops to Vietnam, Santo Domingo, the Congo, and now our own home town is scheduled to speak in Detroit on August 2nd.

Peace activists across the country have promised that Johnson will be met with demonstrations wherever he goes as long as he continues the war in Vietnam. And if Johnson is not frightened away by a little rioting the major peace and civil rights group plan a large reception for him in the form of a giant picket line.

He is scheduled to speak to the Association of County Employees at Cobo Hall in downtown Detroit, 7:30 p.m. on the 2nd. In the event LBJ doesn't appear an Administration representative will speak in his place and the demonstration will still be held. Be there and tell Johnson to get out of Vietnam now!

"get the big stuff"

by Peter Werbe

"The chickens are coming home to roost" Malcolm X, Nov. 22, 1963

Malcolm was right, of course, and the chickens have come home so many ways since that grim day four years ago. Vietnam, Malcolm's own death, riots across the country and now the biggest chicken of them all -- the Detroit riot.

Detroit always does things up in a big way. The destruction, looting, killing, and violence have been chronicled to such an extent that no repetition is necessary here.

This newspaper has concentrated its observations on the hippie, new left, and avant garde community it serves.

The geographical center of that community -- the Warren Forest area near Wayne University -- was relatively untouched by the holocaust.

The FIFTH ESTATE office at Warren and John Lodge was unharmed as were the adjacent offices of the Artists' Workshop, Trans - Love Energies, and the Detroit Committee to End the War in Vietnam. Our newspaper office sported a "soul brother" sign and two large banners were hung from Trans-Love reading "Peace on Earth" and "Burn, Baby, Burn."

Hippie and political residents of the Warren Forest area reacted to the situation just like their poorer neighbors -- they took whatever wasn't nailed down.

They joined the Negros and Southern whites in cleaning out the stores on Trumbull and Forest, which now lie in ashes, the Krogers on Second and Prentis and other stores. Looters came back laden with goodies, swapping stories of harrowing experiences with the guardsmen and bartering goods that they had in excess. The mayor was certainly right about the "carnival atmosphere." Everything was FREE.

Kae Halonen, a resident of W. Hancock, described the scene as that of integrated looting. "There was complete cooperation between the races in their common endeavor," she said. "There were children carrying toys they never would have been able to afford."

Detroit's Communications Company, which distributes leaflets in the area

(continued on p. 8)

Front page news: Covering Detroit's "ri-bellion," July 1967.
(Courtesy of Harvey Ovshinsky, the Fifth Estate, *and Bentley Historical Library.)*

police as well as the city's malignant history of neglect toward and discrimination of its Black citizens, led to the ri-bellion's five nights of looting, arson, and bloody confrontations between the police, civilians, and National Guard troops. Before President Johnson's "peacekeeping" was over, 43 people were dead, many from rifle fire and other wounds, 1,189 were injured, over 7,200 had been arrested, and more than 2,000 buildings were destroyed.

At first, everyone assumed the rioters were responsible for the sniping. But it didn't take long for us to discover the guilty parties were mainly the National Guardsmen, many of whom were from as far away as Muskegon and who had never set foot in a big city like Detroit.

When Peter and I left the office to see for ourselves what was going on, we couldn't believe what we were seeing. The looting in our neighborhood was biracial. "We were out in the streets and found no hostility toward us whatsoever," Peter later recalled for the *Detroit Metro Times*. "We were around Trumbull and Forest, which was an integrated neighborhood, so there was integrated looting. And I remember Mayor Jerry Cavanagh took a tour while the riot was going on and said he was horrified there was a 'carnival-like atmosphere.' "

The riot was a first for us mainly because it was the only time Peter and I ever actually covered a story together. We drove to Central High School, where we were told the Guard was bivouacked. Peter recalled what happened next better than me, but I do remember our welcome was not a friendly one. "An armed soldier met us at the gate and demanded to know our business," Peter said of the incident. "We said we were from the media and showed him our new press cards issued by the Detroit Police. The soldier looked at the cards, pointed his rifle at me, and said, 'I know who you are; get the fuck out of here.' "

It was surreal. One day, you're watching the president on television saying he was calling in the troops, and then you're looking out your window, and there they were, their tanks rolling through your neighborhood. *Welcome to the sixties,* I remember thinking to myself. *The war is home now. It's there and it's here. It's everywhere.*

You Scared the Shit Out of Me, Harvey

One of my most powerful memories of the riot had nothing to do with our journalism. Once shots were fired and the flames began spreading, I promised my father I wouldn't leave my campus apartment until things calmed down. I lied.

Peter and I were determined to discover the truth of what was happening, especially in the area near our Warren-Forest office.

We were successful in our reporting, but later in the day, when Dad couldn't
reach me by phone, he got worried and drove in from his home in Bloomfield
Hills, first to my apartment and then to our office. He had a good reason to be concerned. The one casualty we suffered during the riot was a tear gas grenade that was
gratuitously shot through the window of our office by the National Guard. As we
wrote in our August 15, 1967, issue, "the *Fifth Estate* really went underground for
about a week as we set up our operations in the basement of the building."

When Dad saw no one at either my apartment or my office, he got worried,
especially when, after peering through our office window, all he could see was
my favorite sweater, the one he and Iris gave me on my eighteenth birthday,
strewn on the floor.

Looking back, in his shoes, I would have been worried, too. Our building
at West Warren and the John C. Lodge Freeway service drive was home to not
only the *Fifth Estate* but the Detroit Committee to End the War in Vietnam, the
Artists Workshop, and, on the second floor, the Sinclairs and the White Panther
Party. During the ri-bellion, John and his people couldn't resist hoisting a large
sign on top of our complex urging, "Burn, baby, burn!" which, not surprisingly,
led to a raid by police, during which the cops threatened to burn him.

Eventually, my father forgave my broken promise, especially after he read
our "riot" issues and saw the results of our reporting efforts, including a series of
articles by Frank Joyce investigating the death of John Leroy, an unarmed Black
man killed at a National Guard checkpoint. But even then, Dad's praise was
qualified: "You scared the shit out of me, Harvey. Don't do it again."

It didn't take long before the straight (aka corporate) media like the *Detroit
Free Press* and even the more conservative *Detroit News* joined the *Fifth Estate*
and the *Michigan Chronicle* in our attempts at "full-length" mirror reporting
what happened during the ri-bellion, but I consider our own coverage among my
and the paper's proudest moments.

A Revolution in Content and Design

Inevitably, the paper often found itself under attack from what Peter liked to call
the "Four Ps"—parents, police, principals, and priests—who were often horrified
by the paper's irreverent content and radical politics. "It's so foul. I can't hold it

Fifth Estate *co-editor Peter Werbe exiting the* Fifth Estate *office following a National Guard tear gas attack.*
(Courtesy of Peter Werbe and the Fifth Estate.*)*

up for display," Royal Oak city commissioner Wallace Gabler said of the paper when he tried to close a local head shop for selling the *Fifth Estate*. "I don't want my kids reading stuff like this," Gabler told the *Detroit News*. "Today's youth should grow up to be All-American boys, not hippies."

Eventually, the paper drew the attention of the FBI, which, according to the red files, reported that "the *Fifth Estate* supports the cause of revolution everywhere," a charge we did not deny.

And the revolution was spreading.

Michael Kindman's *The Paper* had already begun publishing in East Lansing, and Barry Kramer created his national rock 'n' roll magazine, *Creem*, from an office in the city's Cass Corridor (now rebranded Midtown). Before producing his award-winning documentaries, Michael Moore published the *Flint Voice* (later renamed the *Michigan Voice*). Wayne State's staid student newspaper, *The Dailey Collegian*, reinvented itself under the leadership of Art Johnston as the radical and controversial *The South End*. Ken Kelly started the *Ann Arbor Argus*. John Sinclair and his White Panther Party began the *Ann Arbor Sun*, and the *Inner-City Voice*, a Black radical paper from Detroit's west side, published by John Watson and others, soon joined Michigan's burgeoning "anti-establishment" press movement.

Inspired by the *Fifth Estate*, young Detroiters began publishing their own underground papers by the dozens. When I started the paper in 1965, there were only five of us: the *Los Angeles Free Press*, the *Berkeley Barb*, the *East Village Other*, the *Fifth Estate*, and Kindman's *The Paper*. By 1970, according to the Underground Press Syndicate, there were five hundred regularly appearing publications with a total circulation of four million a week, all with the same message of peace, equality, and social justice. It didn't take long before antiwar GIs stationed in Vietnam and elsewhere joined an army of Detroit-area high school students in publishing their own newspapers.

But there was more to the underground press than our political reporting. The paper's emphasis on Detroit's alternative arts and cultural scene was for many of our readers like discovering there was light on the dark side of the moon.

Among the up-and-coming musicians and artists who benefited from our coverage were local bands like the Spikedrivers, Southbound Freeway, the MC5, and Iggy and the Stooges, plus popular Cass Corridor artists such as Gilda Snowden, Brenda Goodman, Bradley Jones, Ann Mikolowski, and Nancy Mitchnick.

Eventually, we were told, the *Fifth Estate*'s reporting on every aspect of our community's rising counterculture soon became required reading for reporters at both the *Detroit News* and the *Detroit Free Press*. At the *Freep*, a nickname the *Free Press* gave itself hoping to shed its conservative image, the editors took a cue from the *Fifth Estate* and hired rock writer Mike Gormley to add to the excellent work of its teen and music reporter, Loraine Alterman.

But for me, one of the most ironic, if not satisfying, signals of our impact on the local media was when the *News* began publishing its own underground section targeting young, hip readers, specializing in, as I used to call it, "news with a beat."

Under the art direction of local artists like Gary Grimshaw, Carl Lundgren, and Ed Bania, with additional contributions from area commercial illustrators and artists, underground newspapers like the *Fifth Estate* began to impact the design and layout of the city's two dailies. Eventually, both papers emulated

Designing *the news* and *covering it.*
(Courtesy of Harvey Ovshinsky, the Fifth Estate, *and Bentley Historical Library.)*

our use of varied type styles and text we often laid out in uneven, unjusti-fied columns. Even their photographs started to appear cropped in a variety of shapes (not just square or rectangular) and, when we were feeling especially artsy-craftsy, were laid out in collages.

"Never again will we see anything like the underground press," wrote John McMillian in his book *Smoking Typewriters*. "Underground papers captured the zeitgeist of the '60s, speaking directly to the readers and reflecting the spirit of cultural and political protest." Long before the internet revolutionized how the media reported and distributed the news, underground newspapers like the *Fifth Estate* were the original media disrupters.

In time, our impact attracted the attention of the national television networks—all three of them. In 1967, I was invited by David Susskind, the late-night television talk show host, to appear on his syndicated program. Sinclair and I were already frequent guests on local programs like *The Lou Gordon Program*, famous for the local curmudgeon's insistence on, "no teleprompters, no cue cards, no idiot boards, no reruns—just plain, ad-lib conversation."

Trying to explain the "hippie revolution" to the local mainstream media was fun, but it was more than a little surreal to be flown to New York to appear on Susskind's program with radical lawyer and peace and civil rights activist William Kunstler, *East Village Other* founder and editor Walter Bowart, and fashion critic Richard Black-well, who was famous for his annual "Ten Worst Dressed Women List."

And of course, it was a proud moment years later to discover in *Freaky Deaky*, Elmore Leonard's twisty, turny crime thriller, a one-time radical Detroit cop, who, while investigating a gang of over-the-hill, bomb-making revolutionar-ies, rediscovers a suspect's stash of old issues of the *Fifth Estate* and other under-ground newspapers.

Still, as successful as we appeared to be, our newfound fame and prowess as paper revolutionaries didn't prevent us from nearly crashing and burning. In the summer of 1966, the reality was grim: the *Fifth Estate* was broke, and we were com-ing frighteningly close to shutting down our fledgling publishing venture.

And truthfully, I wasn't feeling too well myself.

I was fine as long as I submerged myself in the daily churn of putting out the paper. "Ovshinsky is devoted to the *Fifth Estate*," wrote *Playboy* in its review of the underground press, "his own organ for hippies, liberals and anarchists." True, but what was missing in my life was my devotion to anyone else.

And vice versa.

THE FIFTH ESTATE LOVE-IN

Vol. II, No. 4 (30)
May 15-31, 1967

10¢
15¢ OUTSIDE DETROIT

C. T. Kelley

by Sheil Salasnek

Two thousand people had a love-in on Belle Isle. Unfortunately 8,000 people were present. Whatever happened on the island that night, it shouldn't be allowed to overshadow the 6 or 7 hours of dancing, singing and sharing that preceded it.

The hippies came out in force to celebrate their love. They wore their most colorful clothing and brought things to give away to their brothers.

Describing the event becomes absurd. It is impossible to do justice to it because so many things were going on at once. If you approached the bridge anytime after 11 o'clock you would have noticed that most of the cars were filled with bearded long-haired young people who, for this one special day had left their everyday costumes at home and came dressed as they felt. Everyone was smiling and waving at the other cars around them. After 1 o'clock traffic was backed up for miles and it took an hour to drive across the bridge.

The first impression as you got out of the car is that there is a large crowd over by the bandstand. Families on picnics are spread out all over the grounds and they look up curiously as you walk by in your long robes. Where are the hippies?

You kept walking toward the bandstand and from a distance you hear someone pounding a rhythm on a drum. Looking around you spot a few other figures dressed incolors and carrying balloons heading toward the bandstand.

Most of the people look very straight and you have to look very hard to find somebody smiling. What's going on here? Where are all the smiles and the lovers? You reach the outskirts of the few thousand people and start looking for a crowd you can feel comfortable with.

Walking through the staring crew-cuts and tribes of motorcyclists you begin to feel a little awkward. The robe hangs a little heavy now and the "LOVE" balloon looks kind of absurd. You push your way on through the beer drinkers toward the bandstand hoping to find some smiling faces.

Then you notice some sticks with colored ribbons flowing in the breeze and you head in that direction. As you move into the center the whole atmosphere changes. Smiling strangers are now offering to share with you whatever they have.

People are hanging brightly colored beads on sticks and Psychedelic Rangers are vibrating with widely dilated pupils. Here, inside the shifting masses of curiosity seekers, sit 2,000 hippies at one huge picnic.

Outside there are thousands of people in flowing groups moving constantly from one place to another trying to find out where something is happening. Inside 2,000 people are feeding one another.

The feeling is now one of joy. It is a love-in! It worked! I never thought there were this many hippies around. Where did they all come from?

People you haven't seen in years come to break bread with you. Two young people who came all the way from Toronto for this smile in ecstatic disbelief.

A stranger hands you a painted Easter egg and waits to share it with you. Someone else sets up cases of oranges and tomatoes and offers them to everyone passing by.

A woman in a pure white nun's habit with a diffraction grid on her forehead is handing out slices of kosher salami and a grey-haired old man is passing out balloons. Their eyes meet and they stop to smile at one another.

A stranger walks by and looks in your eyes telling you you're beautiful. Something hits you from behind and you turn around annoyed only to find that someone had thrown a carnation at you.

One long-haired man sits and chants the Hare Krishna mantra with such intensity that he ends up with 200 people chanting with him. The juiceheads stare with disbelief at the maniacal zealots rocking in time to the sacred words.

Two young girls are picking dandelions and placing them under the windshield wiper of the WXYZ station wagon while the occupants of the car are out asking the hippies what their movement is all about and whether there is any social significance to love-ins.

The newsmen are out in force. Love-ins are hot copy now and their readers are anxious to find out what's going on. Most of them are smiling condescendingly and asking the same silly questions they have asked a hundred times before.

A few of the younger newsmen are smiling because they like what they see and feel. They understand when we decline to give our names and seem to appreciate that rather than a day for individuals

continued on page 5

HAVE HATE-IN

Cops Riot at Belle Isle

by Frank H. Joyce

"When you have $50 billion invested in defense what you need most isn't allies but an enemy," Nelson Algren said in Ramparts, May, 1967.

When you have policemen on horses and Tactical Mobile Units with little baseball bats and "riot-trained" commandoes, what you need most is not a Love-In but a riot.

And when the Detroit Police Department wants a riot bad enough, they get one; manufactured it right out of plain ordinary friendliness, like the one they invented on Kercheval last summer.

This one they pinned on the Outlaws instead of the Negroes. But then the Outlaws are almost as good an excuse. Besides, once it's started, you can crack heads without regard to race, creed, color or national origin.

To a policeman that is apparently what a head is for.

One of the heads belonged to the son of a Dearborn doctor named Clem Kocinski. The police claim he was hit by someone other than a policeman. Dr. Kocinski, whose son was not even on Belle Isle and hadn't been all afternoon, said his son was struck as he emerged from the Howard Johnson's Restaurant at the foot of the Belle Isle bridge.

The doctor added that a Detroit area schoolteacher had called to inform him that he too had been attacked by the police when he sought assistance in getting from the restaurant to his car.

continued on page 5

Looking for love at Detroit's first Love-In on Belle Isle.
(Courtesy of Harvey Ovshinsky, the Fifth Estate, *and Bentley Historical Library.)*

Although I enjoyed watching Tim Buckley, the Jefferson Airplane, and other bands perform at Russ Gibb's Grande Ballroom, for me, the main attraction was the same thing that motivated me to attend Detroit's 1967 Belle Isle Love-In. I didn't go Belle Isle to cover it; I desperately wanted to pick up or, even better, get *picked up* by girls.

Despite my public persona as a crusading editor, below the surface, I was extremely lonely. And horny. At the Love-In, organized by Sinclair's "cooperative community," Trans-Love Energies, the *Fifth Estate* reported eight thousand straight and colorfully dressed hippies, who "came out in force to celebrate their love."

And I wanted some.

I tried to sweeten the pot by bringing along Dad and Iris's giant of a dog, a Great Pyrenees I affectionately called Buffy Saint Bernard, but sadly even my canine companion failed to help me attract the attention I was looking for.

Plum Street and the Rise of the Over-the-Counterculture

Detroit is famous for its abundance of funny-sounding street names. Growing up, I always thought Gratiot (or "Grass-shit" as Siri calls it) was a hoot, but I must confess, in its ordinariness and lack of imagination, the downtown neighborhood called Plum Street was never on my radar.

In 1966, Robert Cobb, yet another Mumford grad, was a twenty-four-year-old Detroit schoolteacher and budding real estate entrepreneur who teamed up with a local developer to purchase most of the buildings on Plum Street between Fourth and Fifth Streets.

Like "Uncle" Russ Gibb, who sought my help in identifying local bands to perform the San Francisco Sound at his Grande Ballroom and, like me, sought out John and Leni Sinclair to help me re-create my *L.A. Free Press* experience here, Cobb wanted to do the same in Detroit with his version of San Francisco's popular Haight-Ashbury district.

"Just what we need," Peter told me, appearing not at all eager to accept Cobb's invitation to visit the mainly empty, but newly renovated row of Victorian houses and storefronts bordered by what is now the Lodge and Fisher Freeways and Michigan Avenue. "Another place for acid heads to hang out and do *nothing*."

"Not nothing and not just hippies," I argued. "Cobb wants to make Plum Street an art community with coffeehouses, shops, art galleries, theaters, and restaurants."

Me and Buffy Saint Bernard.
(Photo by Leni Sinclair. Courtesy of Leni Sinclair, Harvey Ovshinsky, and Bentley Historical Library.)

And that's supposed to make me feel better, I heard the balloon above Peter's head say. *Grassroots capitalism at its finest.*

Considering the difference in our ages (he was seven years older than me), I was always impressed that Peter and I got along as well we did. We were both fire-brands in our own way, but while I was the quixotic fire starter, the ringleader in charge of the future, Peter was the paper's resident provocateur, the pragmatist in charge of fanning the flames of revolution and making sure there was someone left to take out the garbage.

"So, tell me again," Peter insisted as we passed the vacant buildings that would soon be home to Plum Street's planned head and bead shops and incense and candle stores, "why are we here?"

"To save the paper," I said, as we entered the seventy-five-year-old wooden building that was 923 Plum Street and the future home of the *Fifth Estate*.

Save Water, Shower with a Friend

Growing up in the 1950s, I was used to seeing political buttons like Dad's "Ban the Bomb" and my mother's "Madly for Adlai" pins. By the midsixties, these were

Members of the Siegel–Schwall Band on Plum Street.
(Photo by Wilson Lindsey. Courtesy of Wilson Lindsey and the Fifth Estate.*)*

replaced by more radical but equally dull statements like "War on Poverty—Not People," "Free Angela," and "Imperialist Racists Get out of Vietnam." They may have been accurate pronouncements, but they were not very inspiring. Or entertaining.

"Draft Beer Not Students," "Save Water, Shower with a Friend," and "Want Color TV? Try LSD" became new battle cries for a new generation and a new style of protesters. And, I argued to Peter, provided the opportunity for the *Fifth Estate* to supplement its meager newsstand and subscription sales with fresh new dollars.

"Fine," Peter relented. "As long as I don't have to work the counter."

"Ovshinsky sells more slogan buttons and bumper stickers than he sells newspapers," reported the *Detroit Free Press* in 1967, impressed with both the irony and the success of our budding new capitalist enterprise. "Sample bumper stickers: 'Nationalize AT&T,' 'Kill for Peace' and 'Pray for Sex.'"

To Peter and Sinclair's delight, our inventory also included radical and underground books, newspapers, and magazines from around the country and the latest

Plum Street visitors are invited to "Save Water, Shower with a Friend" at the Fifth Estate's *second-floor store.*
(Photo courtesy of the Detroit News *and Walter P. Reuther Library, Wayne State University.)*

alternative record albums from ESP label recording artists like the Fugs, Sun Ra, and one of my favorite bands, Pearls Before Swine.

It turned out the added value of our move to Plum Street wasn't only the revenue we generated from the sale of albums, buttons, and bumper stickers; I also saw it as an opportunity to expand the paper's circulation. The hundreds of nightly visitors (mainly from the suburbs) to "Detroit's New Bohemia" may have come to stare at the hippies and visit the various head shops, art galleries, and craft-oriented retail stores, but more often than not, they also left Plum Street with the latest copy of the *Fifth Estate*.

And just in time. "Dear Subscriber," I wrote in an urgent letter to readers earlier that summer, "Wayne State University is nearly deserted, advertising is down and many of our regular distributors are out of the city until the fall. This means that until the schools reopen . . . the *Fifth Estate* needs money for rent, bills and $325 per issue to pay the printer . . . You can help by renewing your $2.50 yearly subscription and extending it before its expiration date."

I closed my plea by offering readers lifetime subscriptions for any donation over twenty-five dollars. Now that the paper is in its sixth decade, I wonder how many of our early readers are still enjoying the benefits of that offer.

The *Fifth Estate*'s move to Plum Street also provided us with a flood of much-needed new advertising dollars from many of the 42 Plum Street head shops, art galleries, and craft-oriented retail stores. Soon, major record labels followed suit, purchasing ad space in the paper to promote their rock 'n' roll artists to the alternative press's growing (and targeted) readership.

Eventually, Plum Street collapsed under its own weight as an artificial, manufactured "alternative lifestyle" community. And when bikers and vagrants began to replace the teenyboppers and their suburban parents who were our paying customers, once again I saw the writing on the wall, and reluctantly agreed with Peter that it was time for the *Fifth Estate* to relocate back to the Warren-Forest area of the Wayne campus.

I'm a Little Jealous

Jefferson Airplane's Paul Kantner once famously said, "If you can remember anything about the sixties, you weren't really there." Not true. Some underground papers lasted only a few months, others a few years. More than a half century after it was introduced as "Detroit's New Progressive Bi-Weekly Newspaper," the fearless *Fifth Estate*, as it did in the 1960s, continues to engage and provoke, only now, in its current reincarnation, it's a quarterly magazine providing a new generation of readers a radical and anarchist perspective on such challenging topics as the environment, technology, civilization, and industrialism.

Who knew that, in addition to helping change history, we were also making it? In 2015, to help celebrate the paper's fifty years of radical publishing, the Detroit Historical Museum opened an exhibition, *Start the Presses: 50 Years of the Fifth Estate*, celebrating the half-century anniversary of the paper. Shortly after, the Museum of Contemporary Art Detroit (MOCAD) opened its own exhibition, *You Can't Print That! 50 Years of the Fifth Estate*.

"I thought we'd just have a potluck dinner," Peter said only half kidding when we met months earlier over bibimbap to discuss all the ways we could celebrate our anniversary. "Marilyn and I could bring the salad."

"I'm a little jealous," I told Ron Williams and Laura Markham thirty years earlier, when we met to discuss their plans to start their own weekly alternative paper. The two friends and business partners wanted my advice on how to survive in the 1980s, in an era when underground papers were increasingly *becoming* history instead of making it.

"Hold on to your politics," I told the future publishers of Detroit's *Metro Times*, once one of the largest circulating weekly newspapers in the country, "but not at the expense of your journalism. And you'll be fine."

8

I Get Drafted and Meet the Man with Three Hearts

In screenwriting, this is the part in the movie when everything changes. Script consultant Michael Hague calls these major plot points "spins," when something happens so suddenly and unexpectedly the event turns everything around and nothing in the story is ever the same.

A spin is when in *Star Wars: Episode IV—A New Hope,* Darth Vader's Storm-troopers kill Luke's aunt and uncle. Or in *The Godfather,* when Marlon Brando's character is gunned down in the streets and threatened yet again in the hospital unless his son Michael rises to the occasion and *does* something. And in *Frozen 2,* when the sisters discover what they believed to be the legendary benevolence of their grandfather was actually a devastating betrayal that led the indigenous Northuldra tribe to exile themselves from the world.

Although I've experienced many, the most significant of all my life's spins happened in 1968 when I received my draft notice and was ordered to report for induction into the armed forces.

At first, it seemed like my choices to avoid the draft were grim. Do I exile myself in Canada, or do I resist like Joan Baez's husband, David Harris, and self-deport myself to federal prison? But neither seemed like a good solution. After all, it was the war in Vietnam I was opposed to, *not* the idea of serving my country.

That's when it occurred to me to apply for status as a conscientious objector. "Like Gary Cooper?" my mother asked, recalling the actor's role as a pacifist in the 1941 movie *Sergeant York.* "More like Richard Dreyfuss," I assured her, once I heard he, too, was a conscientious objector and fulfilled his two years of alternative service as an aide in a state mental hospital.

"Don't get your hopes up," my best friend and fellow *Fifth Estater* Mike Kerman cautioned me when I told him I was applying for CO status: "Better you should wear a dress and act crazy. You'll have a better chance." His suggestion was tempting, but it wasn't me.

I faced two challenges: First, I had to write a statement making the case to my local draft board that I was a pacifist. That wasn't hard. "The conscientious objector," I wrote in my application statement, quoting Albert Einstein, "is a revolutionary. In deciding to disobey the law he sacrifices his personal interests to the most important cause of working for the betterment of society."

My father appreciated the nod to a fellow scientist, even though like Mike, he later told me, he doubted the draft board would buy it. At the time, more than one-third of the country's fighting forces were drafted into military service, and as the war escalated, so did the number of draftees.

What I didn't know at the time was that, because my permanent residence was at Dad and Iris's home in Bloomfield Hills and my draft board was five miles away in Pontiac, most of the area's draftees were young, economically disadvantaged African Americans, who, even if they wanted to resist the war, most likely never would have known applying for CO status was an option.

The mythology is that I left the *Fifth Estate* because I was drafted, and in large part, that's true. But not entirely. The reality is that emotionally, I began to withdraw from the paper months before I left physically. There were several reasons for this, but the main one for me was the simmering but, in my view, fundamental shift in the paper's editorial direction.

Although we generally got along and respected each other's talents, Peter and I had our differences. They started small: I argued against reprinting Timothy Leary's Turn On, Tune In, Drop Out columns from the *L.A. Free Press*. At first, I didn't mind Leary's rants; psychedelics were certainly part of our beat, and after so many arrests for his use and distribution of LSD, Leary had become somewhat of a cultural icon.

I didn't disagree with his "think for yourself and question authority" attitude; it was the "dropping out" part that rubbed me the wrong way. "You are a God, live like one," Leary advised our readers. "If everyone in Manhattan were to 'turn on' and 'tune in,' grass would grow on First Avenue and tie-less, shoe-less divinities would dance down car-less streets."

That sounded like crazy talk to me, but Peter supported Leary's anarchistic, anti-authoritarian brand of anti-politics, so when he insisted, I relented and reluctantly agreed to keep Leary in our mix. "Acidheads, another way of saying people who take LSD," wrote the *Detroit Free Press,* "must account for a great chunk of the *Estate's* 6,000 regular buyers, how else would you explain the paper's obsession with the subject?"

But it wasn't just the drugs. It was when the paper increasingly started calling police "pigs" and urging peace and civil rights activists to express their revolutionary fervor by arming themselves that I started tuning out.

And considered dropping out myself.

It wasn't just Peter. I was tired of fighting other battles. Sinclair was insisting we add more sex, drugs, and rock 'n' roll in the paper. "You really need to get high," was John's message for me. "Let loose, kick out the jams, man!" Even Barry Kramer, a fellow Mumford grad who started the Mixed Media head shop on Cass Avenue, resisted the paper's relentless political bent. Not long after we rejected one of his music reviews and he lambasted me for our ignoring his version of Detroit's music scene, Barry, with the help of my old Monteith College classmate Dave Marsh, decided to publish his own music publication, *Creem* magazine.

Get the Fuck Out of My Face

Once I achieved CO status, the question remained: Where was I going to be sent to fulfill my two years of alternative service? I was not optimistic. In those days, if they couldn't draft you, the board reasoned the least they could do was to make you suffer by insisting your next two years would be as inconvenient and disruptive as possible.

To my surprise and great relief, I was assigned to my first choice. Not only was Detroit's Lafayette Clinic one of the best mental hospitals in the state, it was only thirty miles away from the draft board in Pontiac, Michigan. And less than five miles away from my apartment off the Wayne campus. In retrospect, I was lucky to get a job at any state hospital, considering the state police were still monitoring my "left-wing and subversive" activities. I know this because years later, I discovered a marked-up copy of my resume and clinic job application in my red files.

"This is the seclusion room," Travic, the clinic's veteran nursing attendant (I never knew his first name), told me in one of my introductory tours of 4-South's two unpadded "padded" cells. "It's where 'our people' go when they need to be quiet. And we don't want them to hurt themselves."

Later, when I started to know what I was doing, I found myself spending a lot of time in the seclusion room, either as a patient escort or as someone who just wanted to lend some comfort to a tortured soul. I still have a pencil-sketched portrait of me drawn by one of my bipolar patients during one of his more hyper manic stages. It's a treasure, especially considering I watched him finish it in what felt like less than ten seconds. Which was about how long it took for me to realize not all of the ward's residents were going to be as friendly or receptive to my participation in their care.

Portrait of a nursing attendant as a young man.
(Courtesy of Harvey Ovshinsky.)

"Get the fuck out of my face," screamed one of my favorite patients, a young woman hospitalized for her volatile and unpredictable mood swings. One day, early on, Travic had to rescue me when she threw her lunch tray at me, almost hitting me in the face. "Acting out," my mentor explained. "You have to watch out for that. It's why I always leave the tray on the floor," he added. "I never hand it to them."

As much as I appreciated the guidance and camaraderie of Travic and my fellow attendants, I especially enjoyed the company of the ward's psychiatric nurses, who took me under their wing and patiently tolerated my questions about the patients.

And I had hundreds. *Who are these people? Where do they come from? What makes them sick? What's the difference between manic depression and schizophrenia?* Oh, and recalling my own experiences growing up with my younger brother, *What do you know about aphasia?*

How Many Fingers Do You See?

Victor Bloom was one of several staff psychiatrists at the clinic who dropped by regularly to see patients and supervise the residents. "He's *amazing* with patients," one of the nurses, Nancy Gonnsen, told me, "but he's a bit of a rebel."

I liked him already.

The first time we met, Dr. Bloom was in the nursing station reviewing a chart and, unbeknownst to me, watching the day area where I was becoming increasingly frustrated in my attempt to interact with a new patient, a transfer from the chronic schizophrenic unit. Afterward, he called me aside, introduced himself, and gave me this advice: "You know, Mr. Ovshinsky, you can't talk a patient out of his delusion."

```
            DR. BLOOM (cont'd)
    So, the next time you're speaking to a
    paranoid schizophrenic who insists on having
    three hearts, you may want to reconsider
    talking him out of it.
        (beat)
    Unless you're prepared to replace the other
    two hearts.
```

Check.

One weekend I escorted a teenager into our seclusion room who was hallucinating and extremely agitated. The boy had no history of mental illness, and the young resident doctor was stumped. What was the problem here? Where was this behavior coming from?

This was all so new to me; after all, where I came from, in *Fifth Estate* world, when people hallucinated it was because they wanted to, they couldn't wait. Or get enough.

"How many fingers do you see?" the resident asked the youth, holding up one hand.

"Beautiful!" the patient replied, staring wide-eyed at the hand.

"Work with me, son," the resident insisted. "Count the fingers and tell me what you see."

"Amazing," was all the kid muttered. "Fucking amazing."

"What is? What's fucking amazing?" The resident turned and asked one of the nurses, "Do you know what he's talking about?"

They didn't.

I raised my hand. "It's your ring," I said, disregarding protocol regarding lowly attendants offering their opinions on such matters. "He's tripping on your ring."

"How do you know?" the doc asked me incredulously.

                              HARVEY
        He's high.
             (beat)
        I've seen it before.

Fortunately for me, Dr. Bloom was in the room.

Not long after the ring incident, he asked Nancy Gonnsen and me if we would help facilitate a new series of group therapy sessions he and his associate (and later his wife), Dr. Shirley Dobie, were planning for adolescent drug users. I agreed, eager for the chance to bring my experience and my street cred to the table.

The patients dug it. And although Drs. Bloom and Dobie appreciated both my input and the direction I provided to the group, I later learned their enthusiasm for my participation was not shared by Travic and my other fellow attendants, who were largely African American and, because of their tenure, experience, and history at the clinic, felt they at least merited consideration for my position in the group. Looking back, I can appreciate their resentment; despite their fondness for me personally, I suspect they might have felt Bloom's "flavor of the month" was no more than a tourist, counting down the days until he was a free man and released from his two years of mandatory servitude.

Open City Isn't the Name of a Rock Group

Travic wasn't entirely wrong in his analysis of my situation. As much as I appreciated the learning and exposure to new experiences the clinic provided, there were times I longed to return to my life underground, at least for a visit.

I had no interest in getting soaked at Woodstock or beaten by police at the 1968 Democratic convention in Chicago. Instead, I threw myself into writing a three-page war dance imagining how else I could express my politics during my hiatus. Ours will be "an ambush of creative energies," I wrote about a multi-phase passion project I called Open City, "a full-scale attack on Detroit's cultural front" aimed at "organizing and developing a free lifestyle in a city where we can spend ourselves instead of money, where we can exhaust ourselves in struggle and dance."

But first things first.

The longer I was away from Detroit's underground scene, the more I felt a gnawing sense of responsibility, an obligation even, to do what I could to help heal the ravages of what felt like an out-of-control drug culture permeating our community.

Or what was left of it.

"We pushed drugs on kids who had no social consciousness or context with which to handle it," I told the *Detroit News*. "We didn't create the epidemic of drug abuse, but we sure justified it, pushed it along, gave it our blessings, and made it seem like a good idea, didn't we?"

The 70s are coming and we're not ready, I wrote in one of my war dances, imagining how I could help attack this problem. *We got the ball rolling but now it's rolling over us. Where's the help? Where's the hope?*

My first order of business was to call a meeting at Alvin's Finer Delicatessen on the Wayne campus, where I knew I could count on help from local underground disc jockeys Jerry Lubin and Larry Miller, and my friends Mike Kerman, Fred Frank, Karen Davies, Bob Kovac, Sharon Burke, and a dozen other

Open City's first meeting, held at Alvin's Finer Delicatessen.
(Courtesy of Harvey Ovshinsky and the Bentley Historical Library.)

representatives from the "hip" community. "It feels like we're at a meeting of the fucking United Nations," Miller observed, not incorrectly.

With the help of several of the 4-South nursing staff and their friends, it didn't take long for us to get help from area medical students and doctors, who offered to help us start a free medical clinic. Not long after, lawyers and law students also came forward, eager to provide free legal assistance. To accommodate the demand for our services, we rented a second-floor office off the Wayne campus and installed several extra phone lines to handle the calls from what the *Detroit Free Press* later sarcastically called "suburban pseudo-hippies [who] run away from home, come to the big city and blow their minds on all manner of bad dope."

"Open City isn't a rock group," the *Free Press*'s Mike Gormley announced after our first meeting, "a coffeehouse or another underground newspaper. Open City is a hip community service. It tries to help people who need help. It's a friend to those who happen to need one."

But not everyone was impressed. Once again, I attracted the attention of the Michigan State and Detroit police departments, who, unbeknownst to us, sent undercover agents to spy on our meetings. In rereading their reports from my red files, I was depressed with the cops' attention to detail but also amused by the number of times they insisted my name was Harvey Openshinsky.

Still, we persisted. And the need couldn't have been greater. In 1971, following Open City's lead, a coalition of young people, parents, and community leaders based in the northern suburb of Birmingham founded their own version of Open City, a self-help organization they called Common Ground, in response to their concern "about an increase in substance abuse and suicide among young people."

I Get to Know My Feelings

In the movies, spins generally come one at a time, but my being drafted, then becoming a conscientious objector, and then being sent to work at Lafayette Clinic set off a tsunami of major, life-changing plot points.

Among them was when I decided to ask the rebel psychiatrist Victor Bloom to take this rebel on as a patient.

My request surprised even me. Years later, when I worked as a producer and a director at WXYZ-TV, I hung out on the set of the station's locally produced, nationally syndicated *Hot Fudge* children's series. Although, truthfully, as much as I enjoyed watching the actors and the puppets perform their catchy musical numbers, I didn't get the series' emphasis on children's emotions. During the Seven-Year War, the themes of songs like Professor Emotion's "Get to Know Your Feelings" and "Sharing Shows You're Caring" were unfamiliar and alien concepts to me.

And yet, in therapy, Dr. Bloom and I hit it off right away. I liked the way my very own Professor Emotion just sat there, stroking his goatee, often sitting on one of his hands and just *listening*, hanging on to my every word. At least that's what it felt like to me.

"That explains your favorite movies," Bloom observed early on.

"Which ones?" I asked, certain he was referring to one of my monster movies. "The other ones, the ones you watched on TV," he said. "*The Man in the Iron Mask* and *The Prisoner of Zenda*."

"Oh," I said only half kidding. "You mean the documentaries."

He smiled. I liked when my shrink laughed at my jokes.

But in 1969 there was nothing funny about what caused me to seek his help. Although Dr. Bloom was interested in my family history and certainly curious about the *Fifth Estate* years and what brought me to the clinic, that was all ancient history compared to the sudden and unexpected crisis I now found myself facing.

An acute, existential crisis of the heart.

"You need to figure this out," Catherine Kurek, one of our 4-South and Open City nurses, told me after the glow of our first dates got even more intense and we started to imagine a more permanent future together. "Either you see someone and go into therapy," she told me after the second or third time we broke up. "Or I'm moving to Alaska."

And she meant it.

Miss Kurek was a twenty-three-year-old psychiatric nurse, a graduate student who was working afternoons to help pay her expenses and, on her days off, helping me staff the Open City free clinic. From the get-go, she was the warmest, most attractive, and *cheerful* woman I had ever seen. She couldn't stop smiling! I worked days, so I rarely saw Catherine, but whenever I did during our change-over reports, her beaming face never failed to convince me to want to work a double shift.

"Is she dating anyone?" I asked Nancy Gonnsen, about her roommate. "Don't even think about it," she insisted. "She has a boyfriend, and they've been together for years. And he's a lieutenant in the army!"

That didn't bode well until I learned that Miss Kurek and her high school sweetheart had recently broken up. Still, in the beginning, our budding romance was only in my head. "Sorry, I thought you were a patient," she eventually explained when I properly introduced myself.

"That's OK," I told her, finding that I had absolutely no control over the words that were spilling out of my mouth. "I thought you were a nun."

We were both right.

Fresh off the boat from her Catholic, working-class Wisconsin life, Catherine was the daughter of a Milwaukee policeman and a graduate of Alverno College, an all-women's Catholic college whose motto was *In Sanctitate et Doctrina* (in holiness and learning). That may have worked for her on the southside of Milwaukee, but newly landed in Detroit just after the 1967 riot, her education in the ways of the city was sorely lacking. Catherine never heard of the *Fifth Estate*, Plum Street, the Grande Ballroom, ABX, Sinclair, or, worse, me.

Catherine Kurek, RN, 1967.
(Courtesy of Catherine Kurek-Ovshinsky.)

Fortunately, and in time, our love for each other and our mutual senses of humor helped us get through. A good thing, too, because my new girlfriend needed all the help she could muster as I attempted to educate her on the finer points of Detroit's counterculture. In time, Catherine came to love Joe Cocker and Jackson Browne as much as I did, but sadly, no amount of instruction on my part could help her tell the difference between Leon Russell and Dr. John.

We're still working on that.

Dad and Iris were instant fans. In addition to her beauty and her intelligence, it didn't hurt that she was from Wisconsin; my father took every opportunity to remind his future daughter-in-law that among his favorite politicians (in addition to onetime Socialist Party presidential candidates Eugene Victor Debs and Norman Thomas) was Frank Zeidler, who in the 1950s was the enormously popular socialist mayor of Milwaukee.

My mother didn't get it. She liked Catherine well enough, but she couldn't hide her disapproval, not only because my true love wasn't Jewish, but also she was a Virgo "and you're an Aries, Harvey. I care for you both," Mom said, "but it'll never work."

So, Harvey, When Did You Start Dating Tricia Nixon?

I needed a reality check, which is why the first non-family members I introduced Catherine to were Mike Kerman and his girlfriend at the time, Sandy Feldheim. "What do these people wear?" Catherine joked as she debated how she would dress on the day of what she referred to as her "audition."

She passed with flying colors. "She's perfect for you, Harvey," Sandy said as she hugged me on our way out. "And we were starting to worry!"

Still, the auditions continued. Once, our Sunday brunch at Alvin's was interrupted by my fellow Monteith classmate and *Fifth Estate* colleague Bob Fleck. "So, Harvey," he asked me as if Catherine wasn't in the room, "when did you start dating Tricia Nixon?"

In the end, none of that mattered. Catherine and I shared the same core values and even the same politics when it came to the issues that mattered to us. Our surfaces may not have appeared to have much in common, but once scratched, our combined Good Stuffs were in perfect sync.

Which, for me, was the problem. And what compelled me to go into therapy.

Harvey and Catherine Kurek-Ovshinsky's wedding announcement, November 24, 1970.
(Photo by Saul Ash. Courtesy of Harvey and Catherine Kurek-Ovshinsky and the Bentley Historical Library.)

What was the point, I asked Bloom, during one of our early sessions, of committing yourself to someone you absolutely adore, knowing that it's only temporary, and that even though you might *think* you're in love now and you might think you're happily married now, it's only a matter of time before lightning strikes, the heavens open, and you meet someone new and exciting and fall hopelessly and passionately head over heels in love with your one *true* soul mate?

Like my father did when, in 1955, at a Workmen's Circle New Year's Eve party attended by both my parents, he met the woman he fell in love with and left my mother for.

While Bloom and I tackled the old stuff, Catherine pitched in on the here and now. It was her idea that I read *The Mirages of Marriage*, which according to its jacket was "a profoundly original look at the marital relationship with no-nonsense procedures to help solve its problems." Finally, I thought, an instruction manual, a *guidebook* that would answer all my questions and teach me how to be in love. And stay that way.

It wasn't easy.

Once, I recalled for Bloom how, in the middle of the Seven-Year War, Dad and Iris took my brothers and me on a road trip to visit the co-founder of Alcoholics Anonymous, Bill Wilson, and his charming wife, Helen. It was a lovely time until, on the drive back, Dad confided to "the boys" that Helen and Bill weren't really married; she was his mistress. *What? What's going on?* I remember thinking. *Doesn't anyone get married anymore?*

"Give it time," Catherine said, during my darkest days on the couch. All this talking and listening. And remembering! Why was it so hard? Why did it take so long? Why couldn't I just wave a wand?

And say the magic words?

"Because it doesn't work that way," my true love tried to tell me. "It takes a long time to be real," she reminded me, quoting from her own guidebook, *The Velveteen Rabbit*. "That's why it doesn't happen often to people who break easily, or have sharp edges, or who have to be carefully kept."

"Sounds like Detroit," I told Bloom shortly after Catherine and I were married in 1970. "No," said my shrink, "sounds like you. It's Bloom's law, Harvey. First you have to heal your own wounds before you can heal others."

9

FM: I Didn't Know Radio Could Do That!

Months before I met Catherine, Travic showed me how to survive working midnight shifts, instructing me on how to make coffee without spilling the grinds all over the floor and reminding me that whenever I felt the need to doze off in the "day" area, it was better to do it with my back to the door. That way, the docs or the nursing manager wouldn't catch me snoozing.

Because the patients were asleep, I had plenty of time on my hands. Fortunately, I also had my trusty Motorola transistor radio.

Growing up in the late fifties and early sixties, I enjoyed listening to the area's Top 40 stations, but it didn't take long before boomers like me got bored listening to the same songs over and over again. In those days, some stations played rock, others played soul. Or country. But the genres never mixed. And worse, the corporate-mandated playlists consisted only of best-selling singles. No albums, no EPs. No downloading or streaming.

Enter WABX-FM. "We were a different animal," Dan Carlisle, the station's evening jock, recalled. "Our rock was more than progressive. It was free-form. It was kick-ass!"

I know it kicked mine. ABX played what the *Detroit Free Press* called the "New Sounds of Hip Radio in Detroit." Technically, the station had a program director, but really, in the decade between the midsixties and the late seventies, each one of the jocks acted as their own, free to choose and program their own music regardless of the type of music or the length of the cut.

During the day I listened to Larry Miller, one of the first progressive rock jocks in the country, who famously introduced the format on KMPX-FM in San Francisco. "There were no singles cuts from the *Sgt. Pepper* album," Larry recalled. "So, if you wanted to hear the Beatles' latest album on the radio, you were out of luck."

I enjoyed listening to Larry because I was familiar with so much of his softer blend of folk music and rock 'n' roll, but Dave Dixon's all-night *Night Tripper* show was an altogether different animal.

A graduate of Birmingham's Seaholm High School and a classmate of Noel "Paul" Stookey, with whom he co-wrote Peter, Paul and Mary's hit single, "I Dig Rock and Roll Music," Dave had an instinct for playing just the right mix of musical genres that was pitch perfect. He was also fearless, thinking nothing of segueing from a Phil Spector tune to the Moody Blues, to the classical music that inspired "Nights in White Satin," then on to Gershwin and Bix Beiderbecke, and finishing with Orson Welles's spoken-word recording of *Desiderata*. Why? So he could follow the line "you are a child of the universe" with Buffalo Springfield singing "I Am a Child."

In 1968, I didn't know radio could do that!

Sadly, like most geniuses, Dave could also be what even his friends affectionately described as "difficult." He was a curmudgeon of the first order, "rude and abrupt," said Don Hicks, who created the facetiously named "I Hate Dave Dixon" fan club. "He was not known for his warm personality. He always managed to piss me off somehow."

Ah, Dave. As exhilarating as it was to listen to him on the radio, he could be equally cantankerous off-mic. "I don't take requests, asshole," I heard him yell at a caller when I sat in on one of his late-night shifts. "I take *suggestions*."

I once asked Dave about the source of his talent. "Free association?" I offered, hoping he'd be impressed with the latest new expression I'd picked up from my work on 4-South. He held up a stack of more than twenty albums he had pulled from his own and the station's record library and slammed them on the console.

```
                         DIXON
              (snorting)
      I don't know, Harvey.
              (beat)
      Does this look like free association to you?
```

What Kind of Operation Are You Running?

Of course, it was only a matter of time before it wasn't enough for me to just *listen* to the radio. When my friend and fellow *Fifth Estater* Mike Kerman gave up his

Sunday night *Hound Dog* music show on ABX, I happily agreed to take over his time slot, playing the music we both loved (Fairport Convention, the Incredible String Band, Tim Buckley, the Flying Burrito Brothers, etc.). But instead of only playing music, I changed the format to a hybrid music/talk show I renamed, in the spirit of the times, *Up Against the Wall.*

It wasn't long before I found myself hosting a Sunday morning talk show on ABX's rival station, WXYZ-FM, later rebranded as WRIF. Unlike so many of my passion projects, *Spare Change* was a surprise, an unforeseen and unanticipated event in my life, worth noting mainly because I only got the job as a result of losing my temper.

Long before he became vice president of industry relations at the Specs Howard School of Media Arts, Dick Kernen was WXYZ-FM's program manager. He's a lifelong friend now, but in 1969 our future together didn't look so bright. "Dear Mr. Kernen," I wrote to him on Open City stationery, "I am sickened by the hypocrisy of a slick, corporate radio station like yours and your lame attempt to pass itself off as a hip alternative to plastic, commercial radio."

The source of my outrage was the decision by ABC, the station's parent company, to launch what it called its "Love" format consisting of syndicated, pre-taped, automated rock music "interspersed with poetry and spiritual readings" hosted by someone called "Brother John," who claimed he was an ordained minister.

"What kind of operation are you running?" I ranted in my letter. "Brother John's so-called 'Love' format is a joke. He's not even from Detroit! Your station can talk about love and peace and community all it wants, but where's the live news and public affairs programming that even begins to cover our scene? Where's the *authenticity?*"

Poor Dick, he didn't know what to make of my outrage. *Who is this raving madman?* he wondered. *And why is he so pissed?*

Fortunately, he wanted to find out. "Look Harvey, I don't know you, but if this is something you feel so strongly about," he wrote back, "let's meet and you can tell me what *you* would do to try and fix my slick, corporate radio station."

Less than a month later, I found myself co-hosting *Spare Change* on Dick's station with *Fifth Estate* food columnist Judy Davis. Ours was a show where listeners could expect to hear, according to the station's newspaper's advertising, "music and people in Detroit's revolutionary community." One of our most memorable guests was Diana Oughton, from the University of Michigan chapter of Students for a Democratic Society (SDS) and later an active member of the much more radical Weather Underground. I remember my interview with Diana well, not only because she was as intensely articulate as her politics were radical, but also and especially, it wasn't long after our discussion when I read that she accidently blew herself up in a Greenwich Village townhouse explosion that also killed two of her comrades.

Flying High with the ABX Air Aces

After my two years of alternative service ended in 1970, I was eager to return to full-time work in alternative media. Although Kernen offered me more money to work full-time at his station, John Detz, ABX's general manager, made me a better offer to become the station's news director and to help provide the station's musically diverse audience with some much-needed context and, I argued, connective tissue.

I wish.

At the time, I'm not sure what Detz was looking for, other than trying to find a way to satisfy the Federal Communications Commission's news and public affairs requirements. Still, I was a true believer and, just as the *Fifth Estate* spoke to and gave voice to a new generation of Detroiters in print, so I pitched Detz, telling him I could help do the same for his listening audience.

He agreed, and within months, I stopped hosting *Spare Change* and began working full-time at ABX, proudly accepting the mantle of, as the local media described me, "the voice of Detroit's underground."

When asked about my work schedule, Detz was evasive. "In typical ABX fashion," he wrote in a press release announcing my hiring, "we cannot predict when Mr. Ovshinsky will be heard. Suffice it to say that he will be heard whenever he has something of value to say."

Which, as it turned out, was often.

In those days, young people had few outlets from which to listen to news they cared about and that mattered to them. I never considered myself a pioneer, but where else could you get in-depth coverage of the Goose Lake International Music Festival, the Balduck and Memorial Park riots between young people and police, and, of course, the John Sinclair Freedom Rally and concert protesting John's ten-year prison sentence for marijuana possession. While performers like Phil Ochs, Yoko Ono and John Lennon, and local artists Bob Seger and Stevie

Wonder took the stage, ABX jock Dennis Frawley and I were in our downtown studios delivering color(ful) commentary on the event, which was necessary for our listeners, who were less familiar with the rally's speakers, among them Leni Sinclair, Black Panther Bobby Seale, poet Allen Ginsberg, Yippie prankster Jerry Rubin, and civil rights activist Fr. James Groppi.

I was especially proud of our coverage of the Vietnam veterans Winter Soldier investigation held in Detroit in 1971. The three-day event, moderated by former senator and secretary of state John Kerry, then a decorated navy lieutenant, featured testimonies about war crimes and atrocities allegedly performed by American GI's during their tours of duty. One of the perks of covering that event was having the actress Jane Fonda visit our home. The notorious antiwar activist was in town with her *Klute* co-star, Donald Sutherland, to show their support for the testifying soldiers, but she pulled a muscle in her back and needed a place to get a massage. Catherine and I were happy to offer our bedroom. "I hope I changed the towels," she quipped afterward.

Have microphone, will travel.
(From Peace, Love and the Motor City. Courtesy of WDIV-Local 4/Graham Media Group.)

No Revolution before Breakfast. Please.

The old writer's maxim "content dictates style" was never truer than when I decided to play music behind some of my newscasts. And not just any tunes, but songs that spoke to the subject matter of each story. For example, if I was covering an antiwar march, I'd play Phil Ochs singing "I Ain't Marching Anymore," or, behind a story about abortion, the Beatles' "Your Mother Should Know."

That way, even if our listeners weren't particularly interested in the news, they could at least look forward to hearing the tunes. The jocks were happy to provide me with recommendations. It certainly never would have been my idea to put Ike and Tina Turner's "Contact High" behind a story about Common Ground's new drug rehab program.

Still, not everyone was impressed. "Listening to WABX in the morning," wrote the *Free Press*'s Charlie Hanna, "is like being served a fried jellybean sandwich for breakfast. I mean, no revolution before breakfast. Please."

One of my proudest collaborations with the jocks was the on-air news thesaurus I created for them. It was necessary because whenever I was in the field and they had to "rip and read" Associated Press (AP) wire copy, our newscasts ran the risk of sounding like every other station's.

"AP is always padding their stories with stuff that is useless for us," I wrote at the bottom of the one-page glossary I taped beneath the studio clock. "For example, when they describe someone as being a Black militant, either disregard both adjectives or consider using the position of the person in his community. Instead of using 'Black Panther militant Huey Newton,' consider using 'Black Panther Party Minister of Defense Huey Newton.' And on our air," I continued, "who AP calls 'the enemy,' we'll refer to as the Viet Cong, South Vietnamese rebels, the National Liberation Front, the North Vietnamese; My Lai was a massacre, *not* an incident."

And of course, on ABX, his name was always Muhammad Ali, *never* Cassius Clay.

The irony is that, before working at ABX, I had absolutely no experience writing or delivering the news on the radio. Someone once asked me if I was ever nervous or concerned about my lack of experience at the beginning of each of my varied careers. The short answer is no, because on ABX, as with my work on the *Fifth Estate*, I never knew what I didn't know.

Sitting down on the job.
(Courtesy of WABX, Harvey Ovshinsky, and Bentley Historical Library.)

"Rapping" about Open City with our free medical clinic doctor and the ABX Air
Aces, Jerry Lubin, Dave Dixon, Dan Carlisle, and Larry Miller.
(Photo by Leni Sinclair. Courtesy of Harvey Ovshinsky, WABX, and Bentley
Historical Library.)

"That seems to run in your family," Mrs. Martin, my junior high school journalism teacher, once wrote to me. "It's so much easier for Ovshinskys to break the
rules if they don't know what they are."

That certainly was true in my case, although my father would have disagreed. He always insisted he knew what the rules were, he just disagreed with
them. As for me, the downside of my passion for learning and mastering new
skills from scratch has always been that the work came with steep learning curves,
some steeper and sharper than others. Which explains why in junior high, while
I often received excellent grades for the content of my writing, I was frequently
called out by my teachers for not following instructions in my assignments and
handing in improperly structured reports. "You have much to say, Harvey," one
teacher wrote on one of my cover sheets. "In the future, please be more careful
in your formatting."

Different Hats

One of the rewards of working at ABX was my expanding role as Detz's confidant and content adviser. When one of our jocks left for greener (aka more lucrative) pastures, I urged John to replace him with a female Air Ace. "We need to stay innovative," I counseled him, "and diversify our bench." With John's blessing, I recruited, and Catherine helped me move, our new Ace, Ann Christ, from WTOS-FM in Milwaukee.

As receptive as Detz was to my input, our relationship was tested on more than one occasion, especially when my lefty politics butted heads with the economic realities of running a radio station. When our sales guy, Richard Golden (years before he took over his father's D.O.C. eyeglasses business and later created the successful SEE designer optical franchise), signed a contract with the US Army to run ads on the station, several others on the staff and I revolted. Eventually Detz relented, but only, as I recall, after I left the station.

We pushed the station's non-musical programming in a variety of directions. Our fifteen-minute reports, "Rock & Roll News," started the ball rolling, but soon after, I invited local film aficionado Elliot Wilhelm, who hadn't yet created the Detroit Institute of Arts' popular Detroit Film Theatre, and a brilliant young writer, Bill McGraw, to tell their stories on the radio. Although I thought Elliot's movie reviews of the latest, edgiest independent films would make a fine fit for our audience, I did have to caution him more than once not to use the word *cinema* quite so often. *I don't suppose you could call them "flicks?"* I wanted to ask but dared not broach the subject.

Bill's features were a risk, too, especially for our Birkenstock-, tie-dye-, poncho-wearing listeners, but how could I resist airing his hip, new outdoor and travel series he insisted we call *Trips?* Forty years later, Bill returned the favor when, during his induction ceremony into the Michigan Journalism Hall of Fame, the award-winning *Detroit Free Press* reporter and best-selling author gave me a shout-out from the dais for giving him his first paid job as a journalist.

In addition to being news director, I was also in charge of ABX's public affairs department, responsible for coordinating many of our off-air, non-musical programs and events. "Radio is a fine media tool," I wrote in a letter to the editors of all the area high school newspapers, "but it's also a passive and generally non-participatory experience." Our goal was to "stretch our community involvement to the farthest possible point, and in almost every case that meant breaking out from the confines of radio." I was especially proud of the voter registration drives. The station's free concerts at Wayne State's Tartar Field and Kite-Ins at Belle Isle, the city's island park, were fun, but for my part, the idea of attempting to register ten thousand seventeen-to-twenty-year-olds to vote in the 1972 presidential election was thrilling.

Another effort to stretch our community engagement was the WABX Conference on Youth and Community produced by my friend, antiwar activist and part-time ABX reporter Bill Pace. Bill recruited the recently freed John Sinclair to speak, along with Fr. James Groppi, a Catholic priest and civil rights activist from Milwaukee, Congresswoman Bella Abzug of New York, John Shuttleworth of *Mother Earth News*, radical attorney and Kennedy assassination scholar Mark Lane, and many others. John Denver concluded the event with a rousing concert that urged the young audience to register and vote. His "Ballad of Spiro Agnew" was a crowd pleaser, but Denver had me in tears when the audience joined him in singing "I Wish I Knew How It Would Feel to Be Free."

Terry King Signs Off

Although it wasn't in my job description, one of my more interesting contributions to the station was, until this writing, unattributed.

On a summer's night while I was still working at Lafayette Clinic, the *Fifth Estate*'s Cathy West and I were hanging out at my father and Iris's home in Bloomfield Hills. I don't recall what brought us there, but I do remember typing away in Dad's basement office while we listened to ABX. Terry King was on the air, pontificating, as I recall, about honesty and truthfulness and how authenticity played such an important role in the music he played.

"What a crock," I yelled at the radio. "Let's call him out." And Cathy did; she picked up the phone, dialed the station's request line, and asked Terry, why, if he was so keen on being honest and truthful, was he was still using his old Top 40 on-air name? Cathy hung up without waiting for an answer, but several minutes later, Terry, one of the station's most popular jocks, announced this was his last broadcast as Terry King, and from now on, he, as Dan Carlisle, would be taking over his shift.

Years later, when I asked Dan if he remembered the incident, he said he couldn't recall the details, but in David Carson's otherwise excellent *Grit, Noise and Revolution: The Birth of Detroit Rock 'N' Roll*, "it was, according to Dixon, he who convinced Lubin and Carlisle to drop their on-air personas in favor of their real names."

Once, when I spoke at a high school career day about ABX and the origins of Detroit's underground radio scene, a student asked me if I was ever tempted to change my own on-air name to something less ethnic-sounding, considering that before ABX the trend in radio was jocks choosing Top 40, Irish-sounding surnames like O'Neill, Kelly, Regan, and Ryan.

"Never," I responded, although I did confess on St. Patrick's Day I was once tempted to deliver the news as Harvey O'Shinsky.

Where's Harvey?

Between what I was learning in therapy and what was rubbing off on me from my relationship with Catherine, I could feel my radio voice changing and the content of my on-air work deepening. Instead of only reporting the news, increasingly, I heard myself telling *stories*. And not only about what was happening in the community, but with greater frequency, about what I was thinking and feeling about the people and events on my beat.

Years later, I created a line of imaginary vitamins for my younger creative writing students. Write-A-Mins weren't stringent rules or commands, but simply friendly observations and playful suggestions in the form of acronyms, each one intended to help boost the power and impact of their writing.

For example, Write-A-Min **D.S.G.F.** encouraged students to, in their work, **Don't Stop, Go Further**. Write-A-Min **W.A.** was especially potent, as in "I appreciate the information and facts in your essay," I would tell Ashley, "but where are *you* in your report?" More Write-A-Min **W.A.**, please: "Where's Ashley?"

Looking back, it's a question I first started to ask myself at ABX. Where's Harvey?

"Lyndon Johnson was a man who had a tremendous impact on people my age and a remarkable effect on my own political maturation," I wrote about the sudden death of Lyndon Johnson in 1973. "He wasn't just our president, LBJ was also our target. We flaunted our hostility and wore our contempt like a badge. We giggled when we saw the bumper stickers that read, 'Lee Harvey Oswald—where are you now that we need you?'"

Little did I know that in writing President Johnson's obituary, less than six months later I would be drafting one of my own when I made the decision to leave my radio days behind for new adventures in film and video production, yet another profession I knew nothing about and had absolutely no training, education, or experience in.

10

Exit Wounds

"I think I like you, Harvey Ovshinsky," wrote *Free Press* columnist Charlie Hanna in early 1973. "My wife and I met you at the WABX-FM fifth-anniversary party at the Roostertail, remember? We were standing around, looking straight, and you came up in your beard and your roundish glasses and your curly hair and said you were Harvey Ovshinsky."

I remember the event well and Charlie's recollection of it. His column was flattering in its remembrance of me and Catherine, but unfortunately, he had less positive things to say about the station.

"Harvey, I always figured ABX was a revolutionary force for free-minded young people dedicated to shaping a new kind of order just as soon as Mom had the maid sew some new patches on that great new pair of Levi's."

And then apparently, Detz must have said something that let the air out of the columnist's balloon. In response to Charlie remarking to him that the station seemed to be becoming calmer and less radical, John insisted we were simply "moving more away from hard acid rock to suit the need of what Detz called the station's changing demographics."

That's when we *really* lost Charlie.

"Detz talked as though ABX was just another station," wrote Hanna, "willing to do anything to hold its categorized audience (18–34) and thereby turn a buck . . . I came away from the WABX fifth anniversary party thinking the station is more of a business and less of a cause than I thought. Sort of a sheep in wolf's clothing."

The station could have let it go, but since we hit it off so well, the staff elected me to draft a response to what they felt was an attack on their authenticity. I wanted to show solidarity with my fellow Air Aces, but my heart wasn't in it, and I was not at all eager to yet again reinforce my reputation in the "straight" community as counterculture's resident "good hippie," the responsible flamethrower.

It was an old problem. As deeply involved in and committed to the underground media movement as I was, first with the *Fifth Estate* and then with ABX, the fit didn't always fit. I wasn't a flaming revolutionary like Peter nor a pot-smoking poet like Sinclair and his fellow hipsters at the Artists Workshop. And although I prided myself on being an Air Ace, I certainly wasn't a jock like Jerry Lubin, Dave Dixon, Dennis Frawley, or Dan Carlisle. We weren't friends, we didn't hang out together, I didn't get high with them. I wasn't aloof, exactly, but in those days, although I was perfectly comfortable working among my coworkers and teammates, I knew and they knew I was never *of* them.

Which is why Ann Delisi is probably still wondering why, when we were both working at Detroit's public radio station, long after I left ABX, during a fundraiser at the old State Theatre, I ran off the stage in a panic when the delightful host of WDET's *Essential Music* program asked me to dance with her.

I'm still kicking myself for that.

Still, in 1973, I was a loyal soldier, so I did my duty.

"I think I like you, too, Charlie Hanna," I wrote in the *Free Press* the next week. "But there are some things about your article we have to talk about. Forget everything you've heard about the 'establishment' or the 'revolution.' It has nothing to do with the kind of radio we are talking about. For five years ABX has been broadcasting unformatted rock and roll, community news and public interest programing. Off the air we've sponsored free concerts, voter registration drives, youth conferences, kite-ins, cycle-ins, etc."

As pleased as Detz and the Aces were at my response, I regretted writing the letter as soon as I sent it. Not because Charlie was wrong in his assessment, but because he was right. Only it wasn't the station that was masquerading as a sheep in wolf's clothing.

In 1973, I started to feel like I was, too.

For as long as I can remember, my father chafed at the press's persistent use of the word *maverick* to describe his work. ("The Self-styled Maverick Science Is Trying to Figure Out," "A Maverick Inventor Who Fought and Won," etc.) I tried to console him once by appealing to his socialist and radical roots, reminding Dad that being a maverick also meant he was a "dissident" and a "rebel." It didn't help.

"Look it up," he told me. "It *also* means you're an eccentric and an idealist. That's not who I am. I'll always be a footnote," he insisted, "the 'maverick inventor' who *almost* won the Nobel Prize."

Although winning a Nobel Prize was never on my bucket list, as I approached the beginning of my fourth year working at ABX, I was beginning to understand how my father felt about being tagged with a label that no longer applied.

As satisfying as it once was to be known as the "voice of Detroit's underground" and the "Prince of the Hippies" (to Sinclair's "king"?), I was starting to get weary of wearing the mantles. Before therapy, before Catherine, I'd always resisted the idea of working for the establishment, like my father, feeling much more at home swimming *against* the mainstream instead of simply going along for the ride.

But the closer I got to my twenty-fifth birthday, the more I felt something else stirring, the beginning of yet another new creative surge of energy and excitement I hadn't felt since I left Los Angeles to start the *Fifth Estate*. Or Lafayette Clinic to work at ABX. But it was also a scary, achy feeling, reminding me of an article I once read about certain types of lobsters who, when they can't shed their skin fast enough and their insides grow faster than their shells, find themselves crushed by the weight of their own armor.

Which was exactly how I had been feeling when Catherine and I bumped into Charlie Hanna at the Roostertail.

"It seems to me," Bloom said, when I explained all this to him during one of our last therapy sessions, "you have a decision to make."

"You mean, do I want to stay in radio?"

"No, I think you've already made that decision."

```
            DR. BLOOM (cont'd)
    My question is, do you want to be Harvey
    Ovshinsky?
        (beat)
    Or Jerry Rubin?
```

Part 3

They Shoot Pictures, Don't They?

11

I Wanna Be a Producer

The Air Aces had already begun to dabble in video production even before I arrived at ABX, hosting *Live from Earth*, a local music show produced at studios at Wayne State University and broadcast on WTVS, Detroit's public television station. In my CO days, when I was a guest on one of the programs to talk about Open City, I remember thinking how much the makeshift, ramshackle set reminded me of the He-Man Woman Haters Clubhouse from the original *Our Gang/Little Rascals* TV series.

Except on *Live from Earth* we sat on the floor.

Later, ABX's *Detroit Tubeworks* series debuted on WXON-TV, first on weekends and then on occasional weekdays and holidays. Like its predecessor, it was a disordered, sloppy show produced, according to the *Free Press*, in "an easygoing and informative way by an ad-hoc assembly of local Detroit counterculture folk heroes and various FM disc jockeys."

As one of the designated "counterculture folk heroes," my job was to interview political guests like folk singer Phil Ochs, actress Jane Fonda, and Jim Garrison, the Louisiana district attorney who was conducting his own independent investigation of President Kennedy's assassination.

While I handled *Tubeworks'* news and public affairs segments, the jocks were responsible for the music interviews and introducing local groups like Bob Seger, the MC5, Iggy and the Stooges, Alice Cooper, and Commander Cody and His Lost Planet Airmen.

It didn't take long before national acts discovered the show. Among the performers who stopped by the studios to perform and be interviewed were Rod Stewart, Sly and the Family Stone, Joe Cocker, Patti Smith, Dr. John, Procol Harum, John Lee Hooker, Johnny Winter, Jimi Hendrix, Country Joe

McDonald, the Byrds, Captain Beefheart, and Frank Zappa and the Mothers of Invention.

"I suppose you could have stayed in radio," observed my friend Mike Kerman when I told him of my plans to switch careers, yet again. "But then when was the last time you ever did the same thing twice?"

He was right. Just as my being drafted gave me the excuse to leave the *Fifth Estate* and ABX helped smooth my transition back into the underground community after my CO service, so did my work on *Tubeworks* provide the impetus for me to jump ship from radio to stretch new creative muscles in the alien, alternative universe of film and video storytelling.

Not Bad for a Christmas Movie That Opened in January

In the fall of 1973, I left ABX to work for the Video Group, a small, upstart video production company created by the technical and financial team that helped produce *Tubeworks.*

At first, my Aunt Selma, who was always a fan of my work, was confused by my new job; she thought a television producer made televisions.

I tried to explain that, as vice president and creative director, I was responsible for producing the Video Group's television commercials and public service announcements. And once in a while, I seized the opportunity to produce a project of my own, starting with a 33mm stop-motion animated film short directed by my friend and local animator Larry Larson.

Like many listeners, I was a fan of ABX's morning man Jerry Goodwin and his annual Christmas reading of *Barrington Bunny*, Martin Bell's inspiring story about an orphaned forest bunny who goes from hovel to hovel in search of a family to spend the holiday with. All hope is lost for Barrington until he meets a large, mysterious silver wolf who tries to console the bunny by reminding him that no one is ever *really* alone on Christmas because, "all of the animals in the forest are your family."

In retrospect, it probably wasn't the smartest idea for me to insist on producing *Barrington* before we had all our funding or even a distributor in place, but my boss, Sydney Lutz, was an amenable and generous collaborator, a fellow magical-thinking, carrot-pulling entrepreneur who, like me, was eager for his company to impress and make an impact.

Which, it turned out, was exactly what happened when the marquee at the old Northland Theater announced *Barrington Bunny* was sharing the bill with

On the set of Barrington Bunny *with animator Larry Larson and associate producer Rebecca Smith.*
(Photo by Randy Edmonds. Courtesy of the Video Group, Harvey Ovshinsky, and Bentley Historical Library.)

Mike Nichols's and George C. Scott's *Day of the Dolphin*. "Extra World Premiere!" the theater's newspaper ads boldly exclaimed. "*Barrington Bunny*, the Detroit-made short *everyone* is talking about!"

"How the hell did you manage that?" one of the Video Group's executives, Jake Tauber, asked incredulously. "They must have really liked the film."

"Not that much," I admitted sheepishly. "What they liked was all the publicity I promised the film would get if they agreed to *show* the film."

Still, Jake was not impressed. "I admired your passion and your hubris in thinking you could pull it off," he told me years later. "But to be blunt, I also remember thinking what a complete waste of money that project was. I viewed it as a vanity project that ultimately did little for the company, which was already financially stressed."

Maybe. Probably, but still, I forgave myself when I saw how contagious the passion I felt for my passion project was. "A little Detroit-made film . . . about a Christmas bunny," wrote the *Free Press*, "is stealing part of the limelight from a big budget Hollywood movie about dolphins."

"An enthralling vision . . . *Barrington Bunny* will be the best Christmas gift you'll receive," *Freep* columnist Bob Talbert gushed in his column. "I've seen it and all I can say is it's a vision that sort of hangs with you for life."

"Not bad," my boss, Sydney Lutz, admitted, "for a seven-and-a-half-minute Christmas movie that opened in January."

An Uncertain and Risky Venture

As gratifying as it was to produce a longtime story crush like *Barrington*, after two years of creating commercials and public service announcements for the struggling Video Group, once again, I felt the ants in my pants urging me to leave the colony and strike out on a path of my own.

Even by my standards, starting my own company, Creative Media Inc. (CMI), was an uncertain, risky venture, especially considering we had no clients and no savings account, and Catherine, who was teaching full-time at Wayne State University, was seven months pregnant with our first child, Natasha (aka Sasha).

Working out of a spare room in our downtown home in Lafayette Park, I was determined CMI would be the base from which I could offer freelance writing, production, and creative services to area advertising agencies, production companies, and television stations—especially TV stations.

"I'm a fan of your work, so I don't want to insult you," Toby Cunningham, WKBD-TV's director of production, called to tell me, apologetically. "But while my guy recovers from surgery, I'm looking for a temporary continuity director. Can you direct continuity?"

"Of course, I can," I assured him, while my inside voice was completely baffled. *What the hell is continuity? And how on earth do you direct it?* Fortunately, I was a fast learner. When I wasn't filling in the blanks for announcer copy like, "Now playing at a theater near you" at the end of commercials for upcoming movies, I was reminding Channel 50 viewers this movie "starts Friday" or is "opening soon!"

Although I appreciated the income, the work was temporary, and anyway, continuity was not what I had in mind when I left the Video Group. Still, writing commercials for Creative Media's hometown mom-and-pop retail clients like Unity Auto Products, Clyde's Carpets, and Meadowbrook Village Mall did give me the opportunity to fulfill my lifelong dream of writing song lyrics. The jingles

I wrote for my clients weren't exactly chartbusters, but to my ears, they sounded like pure Sondheim.

Can You Feel the Spirit?

Creative Media may have been floundering, but in 1975, America was in the mood to celebrate; the country had just elected as president a refreshing new political face, Georgia governor Jimmy Carter, NASA's Viking 1 space probe was landing on Mars, and in a galaxy far, far away, the fourth draft of George Lucas's new film, then titled, *The Adventures of Luke Starkiller*, was about to go into production. Good times.

Unfortunately, not in Detroit. To borrow the title of a popular Neil Young song, "Helpless," the city was feeling "hopeless, hopeless, hopeless."

And with good reason.

According to the *Michigan Historical Review*, my hometown was fast becoming "one of the most racially divided cities in the country. Unemployment in the city had reached 13.1 percent compared to the 7.4 percent national average; more than 90 percent of those unemployed in Detroit were minorities. And between 1974 and 1976, at least twenty-three major employers had moved their manufacturing businesses south, taking 150,000 Michigan jobs with them."

The city was in crisis yet again, and to many, it seemed like a waste of time and money for Mayor Coleman Young, Detroit's first African American mayor, to try and paint a happy face on it by planning a year-long celebration of its 275th birthday.

It's an old argument that men like Mayor Young and his friend and fellow mountain mover Father Bill Cunningham had heard many times before. When he was first transferred to the Church of the Madonna on Oakman Boulevard near the Lodge Freeway, Father Cunningham, the charismatic priest and co-founder of Focus: HOPE, a local nonprofit civil rights and jobs training program, could see the impoverished parish was on its last legs. That wasn't just a dire prediction; before arriving, the archdiocese informed the priest of its intention to close his new ministry.

Not on my watch, Father Cunningham insisted, spending the last two hundred dollars in the church's bank account to lay sod in front of the rectory and school building. He couldn't afford plants, but even if he could, Cunningham was consistent in his vision for a church left by others for dead. "No funeral flowers," he told his mourning parishioners. "No lilies. We're not sitting shiva here."

While grateful for their new priest's energy and creativity, some in the church's neighborhood couldn't help but wonder, *What's wrong with this young fool? What the hell is he thinking?* After all, who in their right mind plants a new lawn for a dying church?

"Exactly," Father Bill retorted with a twinkle in his eye. "And *that's* the point!"

My hero.

Which is why, with the help of my friend and *Barrington Bunny* director Larry Larson, I looked forward to making my pitch to the committee responsible for celebrating the city's 275th birthday. Our idea was as simple as it was hard to imagine: to create a video public service announcement featuring the city's giant Marshall Fredericks statue of the *Spirit of Detroit* resting on its marble perch in front of the City County Building.

Only in our story, the city's spirit was going to wake up and come to life.

"And how do you propose to make *that* happen?" asked Joyce Garrett, the committee's executive director and Mayor Young's unofficial first lady.

"With magic," I told her and her assistant, Tina Bassett, who later went on to become the city's chief communication officer. "The statue is a metaphor, a symbol of the city's resolute and indomitable spirit, but these days," I continued, "when it feels like the Motor City is losing its wheels, we need to inspire people to revive and reawaken their own spirit."

Tina's blank expression plus the fact that Ms. Garrett seemed to be repeatedly checking her wristwatch suggested this patch of ice may have been too thin for skating.

"So, with the help of stop-motion animation," I charged ahead, pointing to the storyboard we brought for the occasion, "we're going to wake the statue up. After he yawns and wipes the sleep from his eyes, the giant green behemoth scans the bleak environment that surrounds his marble perch and, with a sweep of his enormous creaking green metal hand, summons an enchanted cascade of flowers to blossom all around him. 'Detroit!' a voice-over announcer asks, 'Can you feel the spirit?'"

"We weren't sure you could pull it off," Tina beamed after watching our final cut of the sixty-second spot, "but you did." The review in the *Detroit Free Press* added to her and Ms. Garrett's pleasure. "It's pure whimsy, even a little poetic,"

Larry Larson and I feel the spirit.
(Courtesy of Harvey Ovshinsky, Creative Media, and Bentley Historical Library.)

wrote the *Freep*. "I think it's fascinating," added a local TV executive. "Every time it comes on, my eyes are glued to the screen."

If only my whimsy and my supernatural magical powers extended to my ability to earn a living.

Creative Media was broke, and I was starting *not* to feel the spirit myself. "I don't suppose you have a Plan B?" Catherine asked, trying not to sound too discouraged when no one nibbled at my next pitch, a proposal for WTVS-TV, for a new weekly children's TV series I called *Your Body Knows Best*, featuring a diverse cast of singing and dancing preteens promoting drug-free and other healthy lifestyle choices.

It wasn't my first visit to Detroit's public television station. In 1962, my counselor at Coffey, Mr. Levitt, invited me and several members of the Purple Gang to appear with him on a televised panel to discuss how young people can prepare for their future careers while still in junior high and high school.

Nearly fifteen years later, Jerry Trainer, Detroit Public Television's programming director, shared my excitement for *Your Body Knows Best*, but like the poor carrot sprout in my brother's Styrofoam cup, it was too much, too soon. "Sorry, Harvey," Jerry said, when he returned the proposal to me a week later.

```
                    JERRY (cont'd)
        I like it. But it's too rich for our blood.
        Come back to us in a few years.
                (beat)
        When we're both ready.
```

12

I Get to Play in My Father's Sandbox

Four hundred years after the Pilgrims landed at Plymouth Rock, our country's indigenous people are often asked why they didn't simply attack the foreigners' ships and, with their numbers and their might, at least *try* to prevent that first invasion. Their answer was as simple as it was shocking: *Because we didn't see them. We never saw sails before; we thought they were clouds.*

And that's why, in November 1968, my father, the high-school-educated machinist and budding scientist and inventor, created such an uproar when a front-page article in the *New York Times* predicted his sea-changing discoveries in the obscure and often discarded field of glass-like, amorphous materials would one day pave the way for the creation of "small, desktop computers for use in homes, schools and offices, and a flat, tubeless television set that can be hung on the wall like a picture."

What profane heresy was this? Who was this brazen forty-six-year-old unknown, uncredentialed, self-taught charlatan who dared to call himself a scientist, let alone a *physicist?*

"That's very interesting, Mr. Ovshinsky," Dad was told by the scientific establishment. "But what you're proposing is impossible, [*your devices are*] digital, but what good is a digital device?"

And that was thirty years before my father announced his company, Energy Conversion Devices, had created a solar-cell-producing machine the size of a football field that could roll off sheets of thin-film solar cells by the mile. "Like a newspaper run on a giant printing press," he proudly boasted.

And *that* was after Dad convinced General Motors, Toyota, and Honda to put his revolutionary nickel-metal hydride batteries in their newfangled electric and hybrid cars, GM's EV1, the Toyota Prius, and the Honda Insight.

121

And before the *Wall Street Journal* predicted my father's mysterious "phase-change" computer memory and information technology would one day replace flash memory in all our computers, cameras, and cell phones.

"He was ahead of his time," *Smithsonian Magazine* later wrote about my father, his generation's Thomas Edison, "[*whose*] brilliance [*has been*] compared to . . . Albert Einstein."

Exciting stuff, but in his early days, Dad was also frequently misunderstood. And disbelieved. "Amorphous Semiconductor" blared the 1969 headline in the trade magazine *Information Retrieval*, "Zowie? Or Zilch?" *Forbes* magazine once wondered, is Stanford Ovshinsky a scientific visionary or, when it comes to peddling his goods, is he "a repeat pretender" and "a puppet master"?

Although he was certainly hurt and offended by the attacks, Dad could be considerably more forgiving than Iris. When Michael Shnayerson's book *The Car That Could* came out, recalling the dramatic creation of GM's EV1 electric car and the role my father's nickel-metal hydride battery played in its rollout, I told her how generous I thought the author was in his description of Dad's work.

My stepmother disagreed. Vehemently. "They said his white hair was wild and unruly," Iris complained indignantly. "They made him look like a billy goat. Your father is *no* billy goat!"

"It's not their fault," Dad said, trying to comfort her. And, I suspect, to remind himself, considering he was not at all satisfied with Shnayerson's description of the depth of his contribution to the EV1's development, "They can't see what they can't see."

It was an old story. Before he knocked it off its pedestal, the orthodoxy at the time was that only the traditional and more orderly ("like soldiers marching in formation," Dad would say), crystalline-structured materials could be used to receive and conduct energy and convey information. In the eyes of the scientific and electronics establishment, Dad's disordered, solid-state rejects were, as my observant Jewish grandmother used to say in Yiddish about non-kosher foods, *treif*.

I often refer to my father's struggles in my classes and workshops. At the College for Creative Studies, whenever they got frustrated over the latest rejection of their work, I reminded my young artists and animators of Keith Haring and the origins of his pop art and graffiti genius. While attending art school in Pittsburgh, Haring was fascinated by the twisty, convoluted shapes made by the break-dancers in his neighborhood. "While the music played loud, Keith started drawing wiggly lines," Kay A. Haring wrote in *Keith Haring: The Boy Who Just Kept Drawing*, her illustrated book about her brother for young readers. "His teachers didn't get it, asking him, 'WHY are you drawing pictures that look liked scrambled bodies? This is not what we told you to draw.'"

It's not their fault, I imagine Haring told himself as he continued to draw and paint exactly what he alone could see so clearly in his mind. *They can't see what they can't see.*

The Porcupine Effect

It was always good to hear from her, but this time, when I picked up the phone, I could sense some urgency in Iris's voice.

"Harvey, can you come in?" she said excitedly from her office at Energy Conversion Devices. "Your father needs to speak to you about work."

This was a surprise. His work? Or mine?

It turned out to be both.

Growing up, I was never quite certain exactly what it was my father did for a living. His Santa's workshop–like laboratory was an exciting place to visit for sure, but it must have been frustrating for Dad to see the blank stares in the eyes of my brothers and me whenever he tried to explain what it was he actually did when he went to "work."

Although he was an atheist, Dad's idea of heaven was taking the boys to the Cranbrook Institute of Science in Bloomfield Hills. "See that?" my father would say when he gathered us around to see the enormous, three-dimensional display of the solar system in the museum's main exhibition hall. "Isn't that something?" he would whisper reverently. "That's the sun, boys. That's *hydrogen!*"

I didn't know what he was talking about.

Flash-forward to the midseventies when Iris called to ask me to meet with Dad to discuss how I could help him tell his company's story. I jumped at the chance, not only because Creative Media was on the ropes but because this would give me a chance to share my father's enthusiasm for his work and, more importantly, to actually be of some use to him.

And for me, that felt like a first.

My father had no problem getting people excited about the *need* for his inventions. Arnold Spielberg, Steven's father, who was an electrical engineer and designer, was a fan. So was half of the Hollywood writing/producing team responsible for blockbuster movies like the two *Independence Day* movies and *Godzilla*, but I can't remember if it was Dean Devlin or Roland Emmerich who reached out to him.

So, when the call came for me to play in his sandbox, I seized the opportunity. Not only because my father asked, but also because I knew how much he needed what I could bring to his playground.

As alluring and charismatic as he could be, when it came to describing his devices and how and why they worked, Dad would often find himself at a loss for words, or at least coherence. In his own mind, he could "see" his thoughts and what he called his "connections" clearly, but in trying to *explain* his big ideas to others, my father's genius did not always apply.

Apparently, this is an occupational hazard. I learned this when, years later, the University of Michigan asked me to work with the National Science Foundation (NSF) to teach several groups of their highest-tech scientists how to use storytelling to help get their ideas out of their heads and into the marketplace. "Our participants are brilliant researchers and deserving of any success we can help them achieve," admitted Jonathan Fay, executive director of the university's Center for Entrepreneurship, "but many have no idea how to communicate their visions to anyone outside the lab."

This was an all-too-familiar problem for my father, who, when trying to explain the inner workings of his mysterious and unfamiliar materials, would frequently find his disbelieving audience scratching their heads in bewilderment. Literally. "When Iris and I [*first*] went to Japan," he told me, "they weren't that anxious to use our patents, and you could tell they were confused by our solution to their problems, and they would scratch their heads and would ask in a puzzled way, 'Oh, Mr. Ovshinsky, what do you mean by the porcupine effect?' Because we had elements like D and F orbitals or even B orbitals, going in all sorts of different directions and giving you interactions that you couldn't get any other way. To me, in my mind, that effect resembled a porcupine. I tried to explain it, but really . . . the porcupine was not part of their experience." It was hard enough explaining his work to fellow scientists; the challenge now was how to sell his deep thinking and advanced knowledge to ECD stakeholders, investors, bankers, and the media. In 1973, that's where I came in.

But first we had to clear the air.

"I need you to say what I see, not what you *think* I see," he told me at one of our early meetings, recalling the time when I once asked him if he thought his early research on the analogous connection between his disordered, amorphous materials and memory, brain, and nerve cell function might have been kindled by my younger brother's early childhood struggles. Dad was insulted by the very idea and quickly changed the subject. Still I persisted. Years later, when I was in deep in the throes of therapy and trying to make my own connections, I asked him if he ever considered that there might be a link between the scrap collecting he did as a child with his beloved father in Akron and his own fascination as an adult with materials just about everyone in the scientific establishment considered to be scrap.

My father was not at all impressed with my attempts to analyze the origins of his work. "Those are your stories, Harvey," he said.

```
                    STAN (cont'd)
       Not mine.
            (beat)
       Tell your therapist; sometimes a cigar is
       just a cigar.
```

Like Trying to Capture a Firefly with a Jar

In our work together, we started out small. I took over writing and producing ECD's annual reports and later the colorful, high-gloss brochures promoting the growing array of the company's energy and information products. These new visual aids proved essential in helping potential customers, ECD stakeholders, and others see in their own minds what Dad could only visualize in his.

As much as my father appreciated the brochures and annual reports, he often couldn't wait for them to help get the word out. Much of my early work for the company consisted of creating large poster boards mounted on Styrofoam that illustrated and helped explain the company's latest inventions. But just as often, the call was to ask me to create reprints or blowups from newspaper or magazine articles that compared ECD's work with other successful alternative energy or information companies.

Eventually, as more and more of his discoveries were recognized, we had no shortage of headlines to choose from: "Inventor Ovshinsky Says He's Near Goal on Solar Breakthrough," "Ovshinsky's Theories Finally Win Approval in the World of Science," "Ovshinsky: A Twentieth-Century Gutenberg?" and one of his favorites, "Pioneer in Solar Tech May Be Another Henry Ford."

Dad making his point with the help of my company's poster boards. (Courtesy of Creative Media, the Ovshinsky family, and Bentley Historical Library.)

But as much as my father was eager to seek out recognition for his own accomplishments, he was often quick to give credit to others. "My kind of science is very much like jazz," he once told me. "You do your solos, but you also interact with your fellow musicians. Everybody is a creator in a real jazz group. Everybody has within them something that is genius."

Although I was proud of the early print work I did for ECD, my later attempts at capturing my father's genius on camera proved to be more difficult, often reminding me of what it must feel like for a child to try and capture a firefly with a jar. Dad was a tough interview, and our work together was perhaps the hardest I have ever done, but in the end, with the right mix of questions, and some energetic editing, I was able to help my father find the words to describe for others the visions he could see so clearly in his mind.

"I recall the many times over the years you would interview him for one video or another," wrote my former producer, Alex Wright, soon after Dad died in 2012. "It was always a treat to watch you two interact, each in your own quirky ways, never quite seeing eye to eye, but always communicating with a sense of love and compassion."

And, during the worst of our interviews, a lot of nudging on my part.

"You're very fidgety," one of my interns, Wendy Reiss, once observed. "You talk to people like a conductor conducting an orchestra. Is that normal?" "It is for me," I told her as I tried to explain why, during my more difficult on-camera interviews, I tended to move around so much. "You have to help me out here," I would lie to my father at the end of a long day. "The camera sucks up 40 percent of your energy, so in your answers, if we could find some more energy of your own to convert, that would be great."

And when that didn't work, I frequently used my own energy and body language to model the lift I was looking for. Of course, the downside of channeling my inner Leonard Bernstein is that with all this moving around, my shoulders and hands would frequently make their way into the frame. "Voice-over!" Mike Shamus, one of my shooters, would announce whenever I would ruin an otherwise perfect take.

The Undisputed Leader in Range and Performance of Any Electric Vehicle

On January 4, 1998, I taped General Motors' rollout of its next-generation electric and hybrid vehicles at the North American International Auto Show. "No car company will be able to thrive in the twenty-first century if it relies solely on internal combustion engines," GM's CEO, Jack Smith, boasted to the press. "Issues such as global climate warming, clean air, and energy conservation demand fundamental change from all industries and all nations."

It was left to GM's vice president for research and development, Ken Baker, to wow the audience when he introduced the company's next line of vehicles powered by a radical new technology few in the audience ever expected to see in GM vehicles. "It's a nickel-metal hydride battery," Baker beamed, "that makes EV1 the undisputed leader in range and performance of any electric vehicle in the world. And Bob Stempel [*ECD chairman and former GM chairman and CEO*], Stan Ovshinsky, and Iris Ovshinsky certainly have been close partners in this process."

Eventually ECD attracted the attention of another admirer from the auto industry. In the late 1990s, Lee Iacocca appeared with Dad and Bob Stempel at a press conference to enthusiastically endorse ECD's battery technology for use in his new electric bicycle company.

"At some point," the former Chrysler chairman, president, and CEO told reporters, "we've got to realize that you're going to have to face up to a new millennium which for the young people is going to be an electric world."

But of all the accolades, I think, above all, Dad treasured this one from Harley Shaiken, a close family friend and a national authority on technology and its impact on labor. "Stan Ovshinsky is the last of his kind," Shaiken said in one of the last videos I produced for my father. "Henry Ford transformed the twentieth century with a moving assembly line and a car that was suited to mass production. Stan Ovshinsky did what Ford did, but he really went beyond him in that he also developed the science that allowed new materials and new approaches that laid the basis for a global transformation in energy and information."

As fruitful as our work together was on camera, off camera our collaborations could also be extremely frustrating. For both of us.

Once, after I finished interviewing several high-level employees for a new ECD video, I called Dad to report how well I thought the taping had gone. But rather than being impressed with the content of the conversations, he grilled me on how many times each person mentioned him compared to others in the company. And in which order.

This was not unusual. As extremely accessible, nurturing, and generous as my father could be, he was also prone to sudden and extreme bouts of irritation

*Proud father, proud son, with Catherine and Iris at Energy Conversion Devices.
(Photo by Dunns-B. Courtesy of Harvey Ovshinsky and Bentley Historical
Library.)*

and frustration whenever he felt threatened by a hostile board of ECD directors or when his leadership skills were being challenged by stockholders, the
media, or Wall Street bankers.

And, on more than one occasion, by me.

"You don't know what you're talking about" was one of Dad's favorite retorts
whenever he felt misunderstood or misrepresented. He could be especially hard
on ECD employees who were members of his own family. I remember his rages
against his brother, my Uncle Herb, for reasons I couldn't even begin to understand.
And he fired my brother Ben at least once or twice a year. Fortunately, I was an
independent contractor, so more often than not, I was spared that embarrassment.

One of the most frequent questions I have been asked about my work is,
considering my professional history with my father and all the material I had on
hand, why I never made a documentary about him. The answer is simple: in
order to tell his story and do justice to his amazing life, I would have to tell the
truth and scratch an especially hard and extremely complicated and complex
surface, one that my father spent his entire life protecting.

And I loved him too much to do that.

It's one of the reasons why it took so long for his biographers, Lillian Hoddeson and Peter Garrett, to complete their biography, *The Man Who Saw Tomorrow: The Life and Inventions of Stanford R. Ovshinsky.* "A big problem," Lillian recalled, "was Stan's opposition to our interviewing many former ECD consultants or staff members that he feared would make critical comments about him. We reluctantly respected his wishes, but after his death in 2012 we felt free to talk with everyone. Those who had been on his 'enemies' list did sometimes have critical, or even hostile, things to say about Stan, but in addition to giving us much useful information, they also enabled us to get a fuller sense of Stan's character, with its flaws as well as its many remarkable strengths."

My solution was to split the difference. In 1984, when I became director of production at Detroit's public television station, I pitched Paula Apsell on the idea of PBS producing its own documentary about Dad. The executive producer of the award-winning science series *NOVA* was intrigued, but I heard nothing back from her until two years later when *NOVA* produced its own version of Dad's story, Marian Marzynski's *Japan's American Genius.*

At ECD, President Bush Gets Excited about the Future

"Are you sure they're going to let you in?" my crew asked in 2006 when President George W. Bush visited ECD's United Solar plant in Auburn Hills. They were recalling my radical *Fifth Estate* days. "Do they know who you are?"

"Actually, the question is," I told them, recalling Dad's own radical politics, "do they know who *he* is?"

The actual taping of President Bush's speech at United Solar went surprisingly well. "I just had an interesting tour of United Solar here in the state of Michigan," the president told the assembled press. "I also had the honor of meeting the inventor of a lot of the technology and the machines here."

So far so good.

"I am very excited about what I've seen here," Bush continued. "I'm excited about the future, because we've got great inventors and great entrepreneurs here in our own country preparing for ways to enable the American people to get rid of our addiction to oil. And that will not only enhance our economic security but enhance our national security as well."

The problem was my father and Iris weren't in the room—they were nowhere in sight. Dad was recuperating from surgery, and although he and Iris had a chance to shake hands with the president in an earlier private meeting, unbeknownst to me and for reasons I never understood, while we were taping Bush's tour, Dad was confined to an office several hundred feet away from the president, which meant no shots of his reacting to Bush's remarks.

And I knew how my father would feel about *that*.

"What can you do, Harvey?" my shooter asked. "Your father's stuck in a conference room."

"So, let's unstick him," I said, and after caucusing with Bob Stempel, I concocted a solution to what I considered a gross injustice. Once the president's speech was over and everyone had left the podium area, I tracked Dad down, propped him up in a corner of the room next to Stempel, and, as I stood where Bush had made his remarks, asked the two of them to react as if I was the president gushing about ECD and United Solar.

I generally hate subterfuge like this. In my business we call this kind of after-the-fact footage a "pick-up shot," only in this case, considering Dad was never actually in the audience, and we missed taping his handshake with Bush before the press event, it was also a cheat. Still, I reasoned, this wasn't a news report or part of a broadcast documentary, and ECD and United Solar were my clients, and Dad was my father, so for me, it was a no-brainer to decide to put the man the President of the United States was talking about in the frame.

Where he belonged.

13

We Didn't Do That with Soupy

I love the works of George Bernard Shaw, but we parted company when it came to his version of how to live a creative life while trying to earn a living *and* raise a family. "The true artist," he insisted in his play, *Man and Superman*, "will let his wife starve, his children go barefoot, his mother drudge for his living at seventy, sooner than work at anything but his art."

As much as I welcomed the income ECD provided and the opportunity to help my father tell his story, the peaks and valleys (mainly valleys) of freelancing were beginning to wear thin. Our poor spouses! Artists and other creatives may get off on the heat that radiates from our hot flashes and wildfires, but it's our partners who get burned. "This is going to pinch," our pediatrician used to warn our children, Sasha and Noah, before plunging the needle. Which is exactly what Catherine must have said to herself each time I left the security of one job to take my chances with another.

"I'm not Iris," she wailed one morning in tears, "and you're not your father. I can't keep living hand to mouth like this."

Hippie Harvey Sells Out

In 1976, it was unanimous: I needed a real job.

I'd like to say I selected WXYZ-TV, the television station owned and operated by the American Broadcasting Company, because of its rich history of producing my favorite local kids shows (*Lunch with Soupy, Curtain Time Theater* with Johnny Ginger, and the teen dance program *Club 1270*). Or because the television station's roots grew from WXYZ radio, the original creators of such innovative local-for-national radio dramas like *The Lone Ranger, The Green Hornet,* and *Sergeant Preston of the Yukon*. Or even because of the station's commitment to producing dozens of hours a week of award-winning local news and public affairs programming.

But none of that had anything to do with why I applied to work at Channel 7.

The reality was WXYZ was the only television station hiring at the time, and even then, it was an entry-level position as a production assistant. Several of my friends were surprised I would even consider accepting a low-level, "establishment" job that, on the surface, seemed like a shocking betrayal of my radical principals. "The folks who knew Hippie Harvey," the *Detroit News* wrote, in an otherwise positive review of my multiple careers, "would probably say the man has 'sold out.'"

But that's not how I looked at it. "When your head's full of pictures," Bill Maynard wrote in his classic children's book, *Incredible Ned*, "they have to come out." And that's how I felt; I realized if my drawers full of dozens of unrealized and unfulfilled story crushes and passion projects had any hope of ever seeing the light of day, I'd have to swallow my pride and find work somewhere, anywhere, that at least was in the business of telling my kind of stories.

If only it was that easy. "Sorry, Harvey, I can't hire you," Jeanne Findlater, WXYZ's programing director, told me apologetically. "You're way overqualified. I wouldn't know what to do with you."

I was afraid of this. During my *Fifth Estate* days, I knew Jeanne when she worked at the *Free Press*. She later produced *The Lou Gordon Show*, where she booked me and Sinclair to represent the voice of Detroit's counterculture. Or "the turned-on, left outs," as Lou once called us.

But now, Jeanne was as eager not to offend an old friend as I was to find the words that would land me the job. "Please, Jeanne," I said, trying not to sound too desperate, "do not discriminate against me because of my skills. I promise I will do everything I can to make this work. All I ask is the chance *not* to impress."

Finally, she came up with a solution: Jeanne kicked the can down the hall. "You have my blessing," she cautioned me, "but if you really want the job, you'll have to talk to Dennis."

The Job of a Producer

Early on in our relationship, Catherine taught me how, before engaging in or confronting any difficult or challenging situation, it helps to perform an internal diagnostic, what she called a "setting of intentions."

In meeting Dennis Wholey for the first time, my intention was to, in Trekkie terms, set my creative phasers "on stun" and to try not to, as was my nature, over-sell or overwhelm.

Fortunately, Dennis went out of his way to make me feel comfortable. He began hosting his morning talk show, *AM Detroit*, in 1973 after stints as a tour guide for NBC in New York and hosting talk shows at television stations in New York and Cincinnati.

Our interview began with his asking me why someone with my background was interested in a straight job like this. Fair enough. He must have liked my answers, though, because I noticed he jotted down fragments of them on his copy of my resume, including the one to his last question, the one that to this day I share with any intern or student interested in pursuing a career in broadcasting.

So, Mister Underground Detroit, I imagined the balloon above his head thinking, "Why don't you tell me what you think the job of a television pro-ducer is?"

I know this! "The job of a producer," my outside voice announced proudly, trying not to sound *too* impressed with myself, "is to protect the show."

No, young Jedi, I heard Dennis's balloon say. *Listen and learn:* "The job of a television producer is to protect the *talent*."

Fortunately, Dennis forgave my lapse in judgment because I got the job. Working with him, producer Helen Love, and her dedicated team of talent pro-tectors was a delight. And when I was done making coffee for the green room, greeting guests, creating cue cards, and copying and distributing the segment breakdowns for the crew, I made sure I stopped long enough to feel grateful for the opportunity.

Eventually, of course, I fell off my intentions and couldn't resist offering to help the staff pre-interview and book guests and, eventually, produce promos and even segments for the show. After Georgia governor Jimmy Carter was elected pres-ident, I suggested we mark the occasion by playing the Eagles cut, "New Kid in Town," as an intro to a segment about his inauguration. But looking back, I think the song said as much about how I was feeling about those giddy first days on the new job as it did about the country's excitement about electing such a young, fresh face to run the country.

Unfortunately, there were times my unbridled enthusiasm and youthful eagerness to impress bit back. Once, while escorting Jerry Lewis to home base for his interview with Dennis, I urged the legendary comedian and film director to duck below the camera on his way to the set. That way, I said, he would avoid getting in the shot. In my naïveté, I thought I was being considerate, but Lewis turned, glared at me, and snorted something to the effect, "Thanks, asshole, for telling me something I didn't know."

Once I recovered from that teaching moment, it didn't take long for me to get back on the bicycle. When Norman Lear's groundbreaking late-night soap opera, *Mary Hartman, Mary Hartman*, became popular, I wrote and produced a series of mini–soap operas for *AM Detroit*. *Channel 7, Channel 7* featured the two-minute adventures of Ruby, Channel 7's fictional chatty phone operator and lobby receptionist, played to perfection by local character actress Judy Dery. I loved Ruby and identified with her spirited, Mighty Hubble–like, uber-positive worldview and how she faced life's struggles and seemingly impossible challenges head-on.

"When the world calls," Ruby reminded *AM Detroit* viewers, "you gotta answer!"

Growing Pains

Unfortunately, Ruby's eternal optimism couldn't get me out of a jam I found myself in not long after I arrived at the station. When one of the unions representing the producing staff voted to go on strike, because of my history as a rabble-rouser, Jeanne and others naturally assumed I was in on the conspiracy. It wasn't me, but because I refused to name my fellow producers as the ones responsible for instigating the strike, it took a while before Jeanne forgave me for what, at the time, I'm sure she perceived was a betrayal.

I was distraught, but my father, always the optimist, was impressed. "You should be proud," he said, reminding me of his days surviving the horrendous red-baiting McCarthy era of the 1950s. "You didn't name names."

Fortunately, Jeanne wasn't one to hold a grudge. And her new executive producer couldn't afford to.

Michael Krauss was a talented young producer who later went on to help create and produce *Good Morning America* and *The Mike Douglas Show*. But in the mid-1970s, Michael was my executive producer at WXYZ. Among his priorities was creating a special documentary unit that would tell Detroit stories that flew under the news department's radar. "It means you'll have to leave the morning show," he said. "I assume you won't mind."

He assumed correctly. Working with our three-person crew and an editor on loan from the news department, our first effort was *The Concrete Reservation*, a prime-time, 16mm film about the plight of Detroit-area Native Americans.

Detroit's indigenous peoples were descendants of Detroit's first residents, but despite their birthright, after the failed 1763 rebellion initiated by Chief Pontiac, Detroit's not-so "great white fathers" (British and, later, American) created and then broke dozens of treaties. The results doomed Detroit's invisible minority group to a life of isolation and segregation, impoverishment and despair.

My first decision was to change the rules, at least by local TV standards. Rather than producing a generic local news report on the problem, I decided to personalize the narrative by focusing on three generations of a local Native American family who were attempting to straddle the disparate worlds between Detroit's Cass Corridor (now Midtown) and life on the nearby reservation across the Detroit River in Ontario, Canada.

I had high hopes for my first prime-time doc, but unfortunately, I was not yet familiar with what the legendary documentary photographer Henri Cartier-Bresson had to say about his own early years as a visual storyteller: "Your first ten thousand photographs are your worst."

Before working on *The Concrete Reservation*, I had directed several commercials for the Video Group and supervised one doc directed by my friend and former ABX colleague Bill Pace. But other than that, I had no real, boots-on-the-ground field experience making documentaries.

And it showed. I foolishly edited the audio to my visual reels instead of the other way around. And my interview segments were way too long and stopped cold any sense of momentum that preceded them. Fortunately, my editor, Denny Rottell, stepped up and in the second pass helped me make the necessary fixes. (I later learned he was reluctant to correct my original errors in judgment because he mistakenly assumed I was Harvey Ovshinsky and therefore *must* know what I was doing.)

Fortunately, our rescue efforts worked. *Detroit News* radio and TV columnist Frank Judge observed that, rather than focusing on the depressing number of all-too-familiar challenges faced by Detroit's Native American population, *The Concrete Reservation* "is a rare look at . . . three generations of one family of Metro Detroit's 10,000 Native Americans." The *Free Press*'s Bettelou Peterson liked *The Concrete Reservation* enough to include it among "Your Best Bets" on her TV page.

If that kind of media coverage sounds unfamiliar, it's because once upon a time, the local papers dedicated entire pages to reviewing homegrown as well as

Filming a powwow for my first documentary, The Concrete Reservation, *with cinematographer Keith Clark and co-director Lyle Reese. (Courtesy of WXYZ-TV/Channel 7 and Bentley Historical Library.)*

nationally produced TV programs. I feel badly for today's up-and-coming film-makers and video storytellers who don't have the support, as I did, along with so many others, of local film and television enthusiasts Bettelou, Frank, and later, Mike Duffy, Tim Kiska, Marc Gunther, George Bullard, Ben Brown, Susan Stark, Catharine Rambeau, and so many others.

They are missed.

You Mean We Have to Move the Camera?

When Michael Krauss left for greener pastures in New York, it fell to his replacement, Bob Woodruff (no relation to the famed ABC newscaster), to help me take off my training wheels.

Although our relationship was often prickly, I will always be grateful to Bob for sharing his tricks of the trade, starting with introducing me to his idea of creating "dummy" treatments in pre-production to help clarify a story's content and structure before wasting valuable time in the field. He also encouraged me to

stick Post-its or 3x5 cards on the wall, each one containing a handwritten description of a scene we had shot or a "best bite" from our interview transcripts. That
trick was extremely helpful in postproduction, when it came time to prepare a
"paper-cut" instead of simply trying to wing it in the edit suite, as I was so fond of
doing for *The Concrete Reservation*.

Meanwhile, I was learning how to show my stories as well as tell them. Painfully. The lessons began on *The Concrete Reservation* when, after our shoot, I
kicked myself for not positioning my crew *inside* the ceremonial powwow dancing circle instead of passively recording the event outside of it, too far removed,
for my taste, from both the action and, most importantly, any sense of *feeling* for
the event.

It was a mistake I did not repeat when, years later, I executive produced *The
Whole Child*, a PBS series for caregivers and educators working with preschool
children. The first day of shooting B-roll was a disaster. The kids were great, but
our crew shot the entire action from their own perspective, as adult giants, rather
than getting down and dirty with the kids.

At WXYZ, I was learning all kinds of new tricks, such as how to edit in the
camera, making sure that, in addition to shooting the usual suspects (close-
ups and medium and wide shots), my videographers followed the action in a
single take. "Let's not draw attention to our process with unnecessary edits," I
told my crew. "And while we're at it, let's hide our microphones. Seeing them
only breaks the trance and reminds viewers that we're in charge of their story,
not them."

As helpful as these techniques were, there were days when executing some
of them proved to be a challenge. Most of the crew in WXYZ's programming
department were seasoned lifers who had cut their teeth on three-camera
studio shows like the station's local newscasts, morning talk shows, and, of course,
classic children's programs like *Lunch with Soupy* and Johnny Ginger's *Curtain
Time Theater*. "You mean we have to *move* the camera?" one of my cameramen,
Jerry Zuckerman, once protested when we were in the field, shooting on the
run. "You never heard of a tripod?"

To be clear, each one of these guys was a sweetheart and surprisingly tol-
erant of the new kid on the block. But once in a while, especially whenever
I suggested we try something one of the older directors considered "artsy-fartsy," I
could swear I heard the ghosts of WXYZ producers past reminding me in no
uncertain terms, *But we never did that with Soupy!*

Sharing a moment with Jerry Zuckerman.
(Photo by Les Raebel. Courtesy of WXYZ-TV/Channel 7 and Bentley Historical Library.)

And yet, we managed to play well together. In 1979, on one of our prime-time *Special Report* magazine programs, hosted by the station's popular local news anchor, Bill Bonds, my intern Chris Stepien and I produced an opening sequence for a segment exposing the sweetheart deal between the owners of the Detroit Red Wings hockey team and the City of Detroit that led to the construction of the controversial (and now demolished) Joe Louis Arena. And this was forty years before HBO Sports produced a segment reporting on a similar sweetheart deal between the Red Wings and the City of Detroit for the construction of what became the Wings' Little Caesars Arena.

In creating an "open" for our investigative piece, we purchased a large heart-shaped cake box, and when Chris opened it on camera, we chroma-keyed an image of the arena accompanied by Mario Lanza singing "Be My Love."

"This is great shit!" our director, one of *Soupy*'s old-timers, hooted from the control room. "What planet did you say you were from?"

A *Far Cry from Glittery Production Numbers*

When it came to choosing the subject matter for our projects, WXYZ field producers generally had carte blanche, a policy I took extreme advantage of. After congressional hearings revealed the FBI was aware in advance and did nothing to prevent the brutal attack by Ku Klux Klansmen on our old family friend Dr. Walter Bergman, his wife, Francis, and their fellow Freedom Riders, I talked Woodruff into letting me take a crew to Grand Rapids to do a story on their story. Neither he nor our talent local psychologist, Sonya Freidman, was particularly enthusiastic about my passion project, but I insisted. "This is not my idea of a good idea," Woodruff said as we packed our gear. "You owe me one."

It didn't take very long for me to pay him back.

In 1979, independent filmmaker Arnold Shapiro shook up the broadcast television industry with his Emmy- and Oscar-winning documentary *Scared Straight*.

It was a shocker, guaranteed to scare the hell out of audiences with its depiction of hardened inmates at New Jersey's Rahway State Prison (now East Jersey State Prison) attempting to terrify juvenile offenders into going straight. *Scared Straight* was controversial because the inmates would sometimes threaten their young visitors with physical abuse and ridicule them with in-their-face shouts of every one of George Carlin's "seven dirty words you can never say on television."

I was not impressed. For me, *Scared Straight*'s scare tactics were cheap and easy thrills, and the program was self-serving, exploitive, and overly sensational. In other words, everything I didn't want to watch or make on television.

Bob Woodruff disagreed. This was his kind of TV, titillating, arousing, and *dramatic*, a far cry from what was being shown on the networks at the time. In many of the markets where *Scared Straight* was broadcast, ABC preceded the doc with *John Denver and the Ladies*, featuring, according to the *New York Times*, "the eternally boyish singer with an ensemble of assorted woman types . . . performing glittery production numbers."

The fact that *Scared Straight*'s ratings were through the roof only added fuel to Bob's enthusiasm for WXYZ to create a local version of the documentary featuring inmates from a similar program at Jackson State Prison, Juvenile Offenders Learn Truth (J.O.L.T.).

And his desire for me to produce and direct it.

"Do you know what it's like to lose your manhood, boy?" J.O.L.T.'s Jimmy the Pimp screamed at one of the youths during our taping of the climactic confrontation scene between the juvenile offenders and their J.O.L.T. hosts. "You'd fight for your manhood? Really, you'd fight for your *manhood?*"

```
        JIMMY THE PIMP (cont'd)
   Well, if you'd fight for your manhood, you'd
   fight me right now for putting my stinky
   finger in your face. Do you know why? Because
   I just pulled it out of my sissy's ass!
```

The problem with our doc, which we called *The Boys Next Door*, was less the intensity of the material or even the quality of the storytelling as it was the controversy that surfaced because of a study released months earlier. *Scared Straight* efforts like the one at Rahway, according to the report, simply didn't work. "Long term behavior patterns are not changed by brief exposures," concluded another study, "no matter how threatening and vivid the consequences of a life of crime. In fact, some kids may even be attracted to the roughneck romance of the convicts."

Still, the *Detroit News* applauded our film's "technical expertise" and the prevalence of deeply personal testimonials expressed by the inmates and the juveniles in their charge, which "filled in the gaps to show the human beings behind the terrorists."

Lights Out

Like patients in the beginning stages of therapy, prison inmates are generally masters of "fronting." Until they get to know you and trust you, they will generally resist confiding in you or sharing their innermost feelings. And they will not—*cannot*—under any circumstances reveal any part of their true selves to strangers.

At least on camera. To do so might be interpreted as a sign of weakness and vulnerability. And in prison, given the wrong set of circumstances, that could prove dangerous, if not fatal.

One J.O.L.T. inmate was the exception, giving truth to documentarian Cartier-Bresson's description of what he called a film's clarifying and "decisive moments."

Every doc has one. And in *The Boys Next Door*, Lawrence delivered mine.

At first, the interview did not go well. They rarely do in the beginning because that's when the subject needs time to get used to the camera and the lights. But twenty minutes into the interview, Lawrence still could not relax, speaking only in vague generalities about his life behind bars. The razor-bald, broad-shouldered African American with an imposing Arnold Schwarzenegger physique and bulging Oakland Raiders T-shirt was reluctant to discuss the crime that brought him here.

"Just J.O.L.T.," he grumbled at me. "That was the deal."

What to do? In drips and drabs, it seemed Lawrence was genuinely attempting to offer me his best dots, but despite my best efforts, I couldn't find a way to connect them. I was just about to give up and scrap the interview when Lawrence surprised me with his answer to an otherwise clichéd question about what he thought was the hardest part of being imprisoned at Jackson. Armed with my intern's research, I expected to hear all about "bumpin' titties" (fighting among prisoners), or the "bushes" (ambushes) he might have witnessed, or if he personally knew anyone who "caught cold" (was killed) while in prison.

Talking "lights out" with Lawrence, one of The Boys Next Door.
(Photo courtesy of WXYZ-TV/Channel 7 and Bentley Historical Library.)

Instead, Lawrence's answer was as brief as it was unexpected.

"Lights out."

I didn't get it. "What does that mean?" In the back of my mind I searched my glossary of prison slang. "I don't understand, Lawrence. What happens at lights out that makes it so hard to be here?"

Silence.

> HARVEY (cont'd)
> C'mon, Lawrence. We've gone this far. Why are
> we here? What do you want the kids who are
> watching this program to know about what
> happens in prison when the lights go out?

I held my breath. And then the convicted thief and rapist took off his wire-frame glasses, wiped his eyes, and putting them back on, stared at me for what felt like minutes.

> LAWRENCE
> When I'm laying up and in my cell at
> twelve o'clock at night . . . it's quiet,
> it's about the only time it gets quiet,
> when the electricity goes off, TVs are off,
> tape players are off, radios are off. It's
> quiet in the block . . . and I think about
> what has happened that day . . . I think
> about the things I may have seen, like for
> instance, someone chasing someone around
> with a shank . . . And I'm thinking about
> the different reasons people have for wanting
> to hurt one another in the penitentiary. I
> sit back and wonder if I'll ever get out,
> so I can start a new life. I think about my
> feelings; I think about crying. Sometimes I
> hear other people crying. I think about how
> much I hate being here. I think about how
> badly I wish I could go back to that moment

before I committed any crime. I think
about the times my parents would tell me,
"Lawrence, you're doing wrong." I think
about my daughter, eleven and a half years
old. I think about how much I love her. And
how much I wouldn't want her to go to any
prison. I think about my brothers; I think
about my parents and how I may never see
them again.
        (struggling to wipe the
        tears from his eyes)
I think about how much I'd like to be home.
        (beat)
And I think of how much of a fool I've been.

14

Channel Who?

"But where will you *eat?*" Woodruff asked me in 1980 when I announced my plan to leave WXYZ for a move to the not-so-greener pastures at another local station, WDIV-TV. I laughed because one of the many perks of working for a network-owned station like Channel 7 was that employees were invited to purchase their meals (including deeply discounted hot breakfasts) in the old farmhouse that shared the station's grounds.

But none of that mattered when I met for dinner with Alan Frank and Channel 4's executive producer. Alan was program director at WDIV, recently renamed from WWJ after the *Detroit News* traded its station for the Washington Post Company's flagship DC station, WTOP-TV (now WUSA).

"Your mission, should you choose to accept it," the executive producer told me, "is to help us create a new prime-time public affairs talk show and a series of locally produced documentaries."

"We're committed to doing this," Alan added. "It's been two years since the ownership transfer. We love this city, but we seem to be having a hard time communicating that to our viewers."

Alan was not wrong in his analysis. Many viewers, as well as those of us in the broadcast community, were convinced that Channel 4's new owners, Post-Newsweek Stations (as in the *Washington Post* and *Newsweek* magazine, now renamed the Graham Media Group), were carpetbagging outsiders, what the radical right would have once called "East Coast cosmopolitans" and "elites," who believed their job was to teach the yokel locals in this Podunk, backwater town how to report *real* news. And make *real* television.

They weren't too far off. In her otherwise magnificent autobiography, *Personal History*, Post-Newsweek's owner, Katharine Graham, described Detroit as "a strange town, unlike any I had known" saddled with a "mediocre station in a market mired in a recession."

"We need your talent," the executive producer told me. "But honestly right now, we could also use your reputation."

I had three reasons for saying yes.

First, it was refreshing just to be asked, to feel like I was *needed* at a station and not still learning the ropes. Second, I believed Post-Newsweek could be my ticket for greater exposure and distribution of what I came to call my Detroit-centric, "local for national" documentaries like *The Concrete Reservation* and *The Boys Next Door*.

But what *really* sealed the deal was that the station's executive producer was my best friend and former WABX and WXYZ producing partner, Bill Pace.

Of course, those were Bill's early producing days, years before he moved to Los Angeles and became a successful Hollywood producer of award-winning movies like Penny Marshall's *A League of Their Own*. Even then, my friend was determined, like me, to tell stories and make movies that mattered. "There are two kinds of light," was our credo, quoting author, journalist, and playwright James Thurber, "the glow that illumines, and the glare that obscures."

And Bill and I knew which side of the light we were on.

It'll Be a Great Adventure

My first job at the new station was to create a vehicle to promote the skills of the station's hotshot new news anchor. But as it turned out, Mort Crim heard about me before we ever met, and it wasn't from watching my docs or reading about me or my work. At the time, he didn't even know my name. All Mort knew was what a psychic and intuitive medium had prophesized for his future after he decided to leave Chicago to become WDIV's new lead news anchor. "It will be a great adventure," the psychic told him. "You'll work with a young, dark, curly-haired, bearded man who will help you create a future in Detroit."

```
              PSYCHIC (cont'd)
    I can't tell you who he is.
         (beat)
    But I can tell you his first name starts with
    the letter H.
```

From the beginning, ours was an unlikely pairing.

"Who do you have to screw around here to get some respect?" was the mantra heard around WDIV when I arrived. It was true; despite new investments in staffing, equipment, and on-air talent, the station's newscasts were being stomped in the ratings by the likes of the flamboyant and popular Bill Bonds and even WJBK-TV's news reader, Joe Glover.

"Channel who?" WXYZ's star news anchor, Bill Bonds, teased me when I told him of my decision to cross enemy lines.

WDIV's new guy was supposed to change all that. After all, we were told, Mort Crim was the "real" thing, having worked alongside national newscasters like Ted Koppel and Peter Jennings at the ABC Radio network before anchoring local newscasts in Philadelphia with a rising news anchor, Jessica Savitch.

Unfortunately, Mort's entry into Detroit's atmosphere was not a smooth one. I wasn't surprised; the Motor City has always been a hard ride. "When I came to Detroit, I was just a mild-mannered Sunday school boy," Ty Cobb famously said, referring to the early 1900s, before he became one of the angriest, most foul-mouthed, mean-spirited, *frustrated* baseball players who ever played for the Detroit Tigers.

Fortunately, none of that was Mort's problem.

"I was considered by some critics to be stiff, and maybe too somber," Mort wrote in his autobiography, *Anchored.* "*Detroit Free Press* columnist Bob Talbert enjoyed tagging me with the handle, 'Mort Grim.'"

Which, perhaps, explains why Will Ferrell credited Mort for inspiring his Ron Burgundy character in the *Anchorman* movies.

"He's very vanilla," Bill Pace cautioned me. "He could use some of your Neapolitan."

Poor Mort. His sterling reputation as a "thinking man's journalist" in larger markets like New York, Philadelphia, and Chicago did him little good in Motown. Despite WDIV's best marketing and promoting efforts to convince viewers that its new anchor was the real thing, nothing seemed to click. Where was the "grab and stick" needed to hold the audience's attention and elevate their heart and EKG levels?

Bonds had it; he was full of it. He could be glum and even sullen, but he could get away with it because he also knew how to read the news with wild abandon and unbridled enthusiasm. In other words, Bill Bonds had *feelings* and he wasn't afraid to show them.

Unfortunately, Mort's were nowhere in sight, at least not on the air.

WDIV's new star was also missing something else. Above all, Bonds had *history* in this town. Local television viewers are nothing if not loyal to their own, and it didn't at all hurt that WXYZ's viewers were already big fans, having practically grown up listening to the spirited radio newscasts of Detroit's leading television news anchor.

"How do we compete with that?" was the challenge Bill Pace laid out for me. The answer was for me to produce a weekly prime-time public affairs talk show starring Mort that would reintroduce, reinterpret, and reimagine Channel 4's new lead anchor, who, despite his and the station's best efforts, was clinging to last place in the news ratings.

But if that was the problem, we were determined our new show, *Mort Crim's Free4All*, would be the answer. At least, one of them.

Inspired by a public affairs show Alan Frank helped create when he was an executive at WBZ-TV in Boston, we imagined *Free4All* to be what might happen if, as the *Detroit Free Press* described it, "*What's My Line* panel met *Meet the Press* in front of a *Donahue* audience."

But we had a problem. Separate from his sterling out-of-town credentials and his reputation for being a "newsman's newsman," really, who was Mort Crim? The audience didn't know—they didn't have a clue. And worse, they didn't seem to care. Viewers had absolutely no sense or *feel* for who the man was. What did Mort look like in *front* of the news set? Did he have legs? Could he take a joke? Did he even *know* any jokes?

In other words, who *was* this guy?

To find out, Bill Pace, my associate producers Esther Frank and Ann Oswald, and I surrounded Mort with a carefully selected cast of three-dimensional, fully developed characters, each one with a mission, not just to hear themselves talk but also and mainly to help entertain, provoke, and, if necessary, poke, if that's what it was going to take to bring out the best of Mort.

Our dirty half dozen included Mike Sessa, an Archie Bunker type (but articulate) who was active in the local tax-cut movement; Larry Simmons, a civil rights activist and Urban League staffer; Diane Trombley, a registered nurse, suburban homemaker, and passionate anti-abortionist and pro-lifer; Joan Israel, a firebrand, *Maude*-type social worker and active member of the National Organization for Women; and finally, Janice Burnett, a mental health worker who was dedicated to helping disadvantaged unwed mothers make the best of their

On the set of Mort Crim's Free4All *with Mike Sessa, Janice Burnett, me, Mort, associate producer Ann Oswald, executive producer Bill Pace, Joan Israel, Larry Simmons, and Diane Trombley.*
(Photo by Ameen Howrani. Courtesy of WDIV-Local 4/Graham Media Group, and Bentley Historical Library.)

lives. We also auditioned a local attorney, Dennis Archer, who, years later, went on to become mayor of Detroit. Dennis was a nice enough fellow and eventually a decent mayor, but at the time I felt he didn't have the chops to join the *Free4All* panel. "Too dry," I remember writing on his audition sheet. "Where's the *juice?*"

When we showed Mort the panelists' final audition tapes, he was grateful for our effort and impressed with the results. But he also expressed concern.

"I see what you're aiming for, really I do," he said, choosing his words very carefully. "And I appreciate the work that went into finding me these excellent co-stars. But the show is called *Mort Crim's Free4All*, isn't it? And I'm worried I might get lost in all the excitement."

"Three things," I told Mort, recalling Dennis Wholey's advice to me about how, above all, it's the producer's job to protect the talent. "First, on this program, I promise you will always be the picture and the panel will be the frame. And not the other way around. Second, you're the one holding the mic, while the panel is stuck on the set at home base; you get to get up, walk around, and join the studio audience, asking them questions, inviting them to join the conversation.

"Third, I don't expect you to provide the thrills, that's not who you are. Your job is to conduct this train, to lead this orchestra. Plus, bring something of your own to the table."

"And what's that?" he asked, not at all rhetorically.

"Mort Crim," I said. "Join the fray. Tell us *your* stories. Talk about your mother, your father. Your own experiences as a husband and a father. Whatever the subject or issue on the table, seek out—even better, *create*—opportunities to add your own personal experience and connection to it.

"In other words, Mort, less facts, please. Save them for the six o'clock news."

He winced but he got it. Mort understood that, unlike his newscasts, *Mort Crim's Free4All* would follow Don Hewitt's lead. Inform viewers of the facts, the creator of CBS's *60 Minutes* instructed his staff, but follow the story. "Noah will always be a more interesting subject than the flood."

The formula worked. The show was made all the more interesting by the brilliant wrangling of our studio director, Bob Brooks.

"*Free4All* is fizzy—and fun," Mike Duffy wrote in the *Free Press*. "A rare programming feat indeed: a local public affairs show that doesn't hit you like a glass of warm milk and an afternoon nap. *Free4All* offsets the dreary mumbo of most 'experts only' public affairs shows with some refreshingly emotional and articulate yakety-yak."

I Think We'll Have a Good Shot at Mrs. Sadat

Like any writer, I pride myself on my ability to use the best words in their best order, but I also have a reputation for being amazingly clumsy and sometimes even inappropriate when it comes to saying aloud the first things that come to mind.

Once, while deep in preparation for a *Free4All* taping, a news bulletin on the television monitor in our basement office reported an assassination attempt on President Reagan's life. One of our new interns burst into tears at the news. When she saw I wasn't paying any attention to the TV and instead continued to write that night's teleprompter copy, she turned and screamed at me in tears, "How can you just *sit* there like nothing happened? It's terrible! Can't you see the president has been shot?"

I stopped typing Mort's intro, looked up, and apologized. "I'm sorry, I forgot," I said, trying to sound sympathetic, before delivering the punch line. "This is your *first*."

Insensitive? Yes. Tactless? Of course. But at least my maladroitness never proved to be dangerous or life threatening. At least not until six months later when Mort and I traveled with our WDIV crew to the Middle East to shoot a documentary and series of news reports we called *Christmas in Crisis: The Search for Peace in the Middle East.*

Egypt was the first of several stops in our ten-day journey, part of a collaborative effort between the station's news and programming departments. Our goal? To seek out and document the work of everyday citizens, several of them former Detroiters, who were struggling to find (or create) peace in the troubled region. It wasn't easy, but with research and pre-production support provided by our associate producer, the talented Lisa Goldin Rabinowicz (who spoke fluent Hebrew and a little Arabic), Mort and I and our crew, Matt Combs and Jim Stanhope, ventured forth.

Our timing was lousy. We arrived in Egypt shortly after President Anwar Sadat was assassinated by members of the Egyptian Islamic Jihad. As a result,

Mort Crim and I on the run in Egypt.
(Photo by Mack Combs III.)

Cairo was on high alert, government buildings were fortified with sandbags and other barricades, and heavily armed police and machine-gun-packing soldiers patrolled the streets in preparation for the other shoe to drop.

My job was to spec out a suitable location so Mort could do his on-camera reporting. But before he had a chance to say anything, four armed (and armored) policemen approached us and took us into custody. "The arrest didn't last long," Mort recalled in *Anchored*. "Our interpreter discovered that he had been a classmate of the police chief, so we were released after a short interrogation."

But we weren't out of the woods yet. "That evening," Mort wrote, "Harvey placed a phone call to our news assignment desk back in Detroit. He wanted to let them know that we had failed to get an interview with the new president, Hosni Mubarak, but Harvey was optimistic that we could interview the widow of the late President Sadat the next day.

"'Well, guys,' Harvey said, 'we missed Mubarak today, but I think we'll have a good shot at Mrs. Sadat tomorrow.'"

And suddenly, after a loud click, the phone went dead.

It wasn't the only time my habit of using shorthand, cut-to-the-chase expressions raised eyebrows. Years later, when I taught screenwriting and video storytelling at Madonna University, I was always careful to shut the door. Madonna was a Franciscan university after all, and I was concerned one of the elderly nuns would walk by my classroom and overhear me teaching William Faulkner's advice to writers about how, in the best interest of our readers, we sometimes have to ditch the favorite parts of our stories and "kill our darlings."

Only instead of darlings, I urged my Catholic students to kill their babies. Later, after being admonished by a particularly religious student, I acquiesced, and in her next draft, I urged her to kill her puppies.

Or, in her case, her kittens.

Forget the Goddamn Cornfields

Although producing *Free4All* was a pleasure, once we launched the series and it was up and running, the work no longer felt particularly stimulating. I recognized the symptoms immediately from my success with past projects like the *Fifth Estate* and my work at ABX. Once the race was won, the challenge faced and obstacles overcome, what was left for this protagonist? I missed the trial, the test, the sense of excitment and adventure that came from creating something new and being in over my head.

And then came Poletown. I was familiar with Hamtramck, the mainly Polish enclave on Detroit's east side, where Catherine and I and the kids would often spend our Saturday mornings at the farmer's market, shopping for fruits and vegetables and binging on the Polish pastries.

But nearby Poletown was a different story.

In a desperate effort to prevent General Motors from building a new plant in the cornfields of non-union states like Alabama and Mississippi, Mayor Young made the company a counteroffer. "Forget the goddamn cornfields," the mayor insisted. "What would it take for GM to consider building its shiny new factory in Detroit?"

"Land," answered what was then the world's largest corporation, knowing full well there wasn't anywhere near enough vacant property in Detroit large enough to suit their needs.

Until Mayor Young made sure there was, which we illustrated in our doc's opening sequence when our narrator, WDIV's ace investigative reporter Mike Wendland, introduced the problem in a cornfield and then stepped out of that scene into a tree-lined Poletown neighborhood, complete with an elderly *babcia* leaving her home and, in the background, a young child cycling his big wheel away from the camera. But I wasn't done; Mike was eager to make the point by subtly waving a dried piece of cornstalk he brought with him from the morning's shoot.

But there was nothing cute or clever about the fact that, in order to close the deal with GM, the city had to call on its powers of eminent domain to purchase and then take over a swath of 465 acres of largely privately owned land south of Hamtramck in Detroit—and then turn around and sell it to a private company. The process dislocated thirty-five hundred people and closed a hundred neighborhood businesses, sixteen churches, two schools, and, before the land grab was completed, a hospital.

Detroit's first Black mayor was no stranger to eminent domain. "In the early 1950s," reported the *Detroit Free Press*, "in one of the most controversial episodes of mass gentrification in Detroit history, the virtually all-white city government bulldozed Black Bottom in the name of 'slum clearance,' eventually to replace it with the Chrysler Freeway and Lafayette Park."

And I don't think Mayor Young, like so many of his constituents, ever forgave the city for destroying his neighborhood.

With Bill Robbins and Mike Wendland in a Jewish cemetery for Land Grab: The
Taking of Poletown.
(Courtesy of WDIV-Local 4/Graham Media Group and Bentley Historical Library.)

I thought I knew what I was doing when I began work on the doc that
became *Land Grab: The Taking of Poletown*, but I soon learned I had no clue.
Which for a documentary director at the beginning of a project is not necessarily
a bad thing. "No surprise in the producer," I used to remind my interns, tweak-
ing an old writer's maxim "no surprise in the viewer."

Or, years later, as I tried to explain to my fourth- and fifth-grade creative writing
students, you don't have to know what you're talking about *before* you start writing.

That's what the writing is for.

To help soften the blows, I asked my interns, Carole Gibson and Diane Cross,
and my associate producer, Ann Oswald, to find a variety of experts to help point us
in the right directions. Among my favorite guides was Father Malcolm Maloney,
although, in the beginning of our work together, he was a reluctant chaperone.

Newly arrived at his Poletown parish, Father Maloney offered comfort to
his parishioners and helped ease their transition to their new neighborhoods. A

task, he insisted, that disqualified him from being able to offer an opinion about how he personally felt about the project. And besides, he added, what was the point of editorializing? Considering the planned GM plant was a done deal, why pick at a closed wound? But not everyone agreed with Father Maloney's analogy. Many Poletown residents, especially African Americans, welcomed the new factory to the neighborhood with open arms even if they knew it was at the expense of their own homes and community. "I love the neighborhood," community activist Bernice Winfrey told me.

> BERNICE WINFREY (cont'd)
> I like the area, but I also love the city
> of Detroit. I don't want to see GM leave
> Detroit. I feel like the Lord is using
> General Motors to help the city and to help
> stabilize the employment here.

And for those viewers who were sitting on the fence, I threw in a surprisingly emotional statement from Maryann Mahaffey, a vocal member of the Detroit City Council who, even though she supported the project, was not without her doubts.

"I *hate* gambling!" she insisted. "I'm absolutely opposed to casino gambling, to Bingo, you name it."

> MARYANN MAHAFFEY (cont'd)
> I don't like it, but in this instance we're
> talking about a minimum of six thousand
> jobs in the plant, *plus* the twenty-five
> thousand supplier jobs because that's the
> best estimate we have, [we're] talking about
> families! And that to me is a gamble I'm
> prepared to take as compared to gambling
> away my last five dollars on a Bingo card.

But as persuasive as these arguments were, opinions aren't *stories*, statistics aren't stories, and in the end, that's what made *Land Grab* such a compelling experience. For me and the viewing audience.

In Poletown, I pose with somebody's dziadia *and* babcia.
(Courtesy of WDIV-Local 4/Graham Media Group and Bentley Historical Library.)

No Offense, Father, but This Is Bullshit

As with Lawrence at Jackson State Prison, when I first sat down with Father Maloney, the interview did not go well. As I expected, the priest had the archdiocese's party line down pat, managing to successfully dodge each one of my questions, even my trusty, tried-and-true, scratch-the-surface ones. "How do you feel about what the church is asking you to do, are you cool with it? And forget about the residents—how are *you* holding up?"

"I can't help you there, Harvey," Father Maloney said wearily. "I try not to think about my own feelings. I tell my people God has a higher purpose even if we don't always know what it is."

Finally, I had enough. I can be attentive during my interviews, I can be patient, I can actively care about every word spoken, constructing a safe zone, what a trade industry magazine once described as "a cone of silence" around the people I talk to. But not today. I told my crew that if this kept up, we'd have to turn off the camera and pack up our gear. "No offense, Father," I told the priest. "But this is bullshit. Really, can you tell me *this* is why you went into the seminary?"

The priest was stunned.

Fortunately, my team was used to my last-resort, Hail Mary, take-no-prisoners tactics, and they knew where I was going with this.

And I think, deep down, in his heart of hearts, so did Father Maloney.

When he could tell we were still rolling, he shrugged and inhaled a long, deep breath. "You know what I think is going on in the community, *really*?"

I shook my head. "No, Father, I don't," I lied, hoping he'd finally say it out loud.

FATHER MALONEY

This project is going so *fast*, it's not even
human. I found out a week before I got here
what was going on. You know I got called
down to the chancery office, and they said,
"Guess what? You're losing it." And I made
up my mind I'm not going to fall in love
with these bricks, I'm going to try and
stay aloof from the people, because I don't
want to get emotionally involved because
this ain't going to be here. I'll deal
with it in an intellectual way, to protect
yourself, you know? Then you fall in love,
fall in love with the bricks, fall in love
with the people, their helplessness, you
hear them cry; they walk into the church,
they're crying. Why? "Father, are we going
to have mass here this Christmas? It'll
be the first Christmas in forty-four years
I won't be here for mass." And that makes
you angry because somebody wants it to
turn out *cars*? And I'm all for that, cars,
but now that it's touching people's lives,

```
grandmothers, grandfathers, people I'm close
to—if everybody had their grandma down here,
they'd feel the same way. They would.
```

It was an electric moment, what I have since come to call "the wallop," an unexpected reveal that shocks, surprises, and, on occasion, disturbs. And reminds documentary storytellers like me why we got into this business in the first place. At WXYZ, Woodruff used to call these "no shit!" moments, as in, *No shit*, the audience thinks, *I wasn't expecting this at all. I had no idea!*

As inspiring as Father Maloney's no-shit moment was, the first cut of *Land Grab* wasn't pretty. They rarely are. I can't speak for other documentary directors, but I generally want to throw up after watching my first attempts at finding the story.

Too much talking, my inner judge insists. *Not enough B-roll visuals. Too much B-roll. The structure is wrong, better to end with a return to the beginning. No, make that the other way around. Fuck me, who produced this piece of shit, anyway?*

And fuck Bill Pace for even thinking *I was up for this.*

There are two schools of thought about what to do with first passes. First of all, first drafts and rough cuts are *supposed* to suck; that's what they're there for. "Knock yourself out," I tell my students, "spill your guts, get it off your chest, but just know your first pass is for you, the second is for everyone else."

Not to be confused with filmmakers who are convinced there's nothing at all rough about their rough cut, who fall in love with their every word, sound bite, and frame of film or video. They hand it in as is. How could they not? After all, in their minds, it's a flawless masterwork, pristine and perfect in every way.

Unlike my first rough cut of my Poletown doc. After creating what I was certain was one of the world's worst rough cuts in the history of broadcast television, I returned to the edit suite to reimagine the next cut of what became *Land Grab: The Taking of Poletown.*

A good thing, too.

"Exceptional and eloquent," wrote the *Free Press*. "Harvey Ovshinsky delivered what is perhaps the finest hour of local television I have seen . . . [*he*] proved public affairs programming does not have to be boring and that it can be substantive, perspective, powerful and (surprise, surprise) entertaining."

And I still treasure Lou Heldman's card in which the *Freep*'s business editor wrote me to thank me and to say *Land Grab* "was the best television journalism I can recall in 10 years in Detroit. Far and away the best thing anyone in the media has done on Poletown."

But my success was bittersweet, and not only because of the sacrifices made by so many of the Poletown residents. As a result of the City of Detroit's "land grab" of Poletown, dozens of municipalities around the country were inspired to use the power of eminent domain to expedite their own urban renewal and economic revitalization efforts. More bittersweet still, in 2004, in an unprecedented move, the Michigan Supreme Court reversed its original 1981 decision that authorized the city's demolishment of Poletown.

And in 2018, sadly but not surprisingly, General Motors announced its intentions to close its Poletown facility, once a state-of-the-art factory originally touted as the plant that was going to save Detroit and pave the future of automotive manufacturing in the rest of the country.

Is There Going to Be a Problem Here?

At first I thought he was kidding when my boss and best friend, Bill Pace, called to tell me he had been fired.

And then I realized the rumors were true. Despite his helping to create and executive-produce *Land Grab*, *Free4All*, and the new morning talk show *Sonya*, hosted by local psychologist Sonya Friedman, there were whispers that changes were afoot at the station. We just didn't know what they were.

I felt terrible for my friend, but when Alan Frank informed me Bill's replacement (and my new boss) was Henry Maldonado, his friend and former collaborator at WBZ-TV in Boston, I started to feel not so good for myself. Alan came into my office to let me know Bill's abrupt departure was nothing personal, simply a result of his need to make some "necessary changes" at the station. And he wanted to assure me I was going to continue to play an important role in these changes.

I appreciated hearing that, but knowing how close Bill and I were, I think the true intention of that meeting, what Alan *really* wanted to know before Henry arrived was, *Are we OK? Is there going to be a problem here?*

Truthfully, I didn't know. I was going to miss working with Bill, and I also felt badly for what I considered his unfair treatment by the station. And I wasn't alone. Although his tenure at the station was brief, Bill's impact and his contributions were felt and missed by many on the production staff and crew.

I was not looking forward to meeting the new guy. I've always *wanted* to play well with executive producers, but, except for working with Bill, I never really seemed to get the hang of it.

One of my favorite scenes in Charles Dickens's A *Christmas Carol* is when Scrooge tries to explain his relationship with Mr. Fezziwig to the Spirit of Christmas Past. "He has the power to render us happy or unhappy," Scrooge mournfully observed, recalling how his beloved first employer had the power "to make our service light or burdensome, a pleasure or a toil."

That's how I have always felt about my executive producers. Woodruff was a genius, but an abrasive one. Henry Maldonado was no Fezziwig, but he wasn't a Scrooge, either. A producer's producer, Henry directed his share of award-winning docs before becoming an executive producer at WNBC and WCBS in New York and later a manager of cultural programming at WGBH.

But the surprise for me was that Henry's creativity was matched by his generosity in sharing his producer's playbook on how to produce television programs that were as compelling as they were entertaining.

A *Gift for Serena*

My mother was confused. "I thought you went into therapy to get *less* depressed." She was talking about my next doc for WDIV, the story of nine-year-old girl Serena Ecarius whose cerebral palsy, which she'd had since birth, prevented her from using her vocal cords, not to mention just about every other muscle in her body.

In other words, young Serena was totally mute. "She had so much to say," her mother told my interns, Laura Barroso and Marjorie Cato, in her pre-interviews. "You can see it in her eyes. But she couldn't utter a sound. And I'm sorry, but that's just not acceptable."

"This artificial language lab at Michigan State University may not look like Santa's workshop," observed our narrator, WDIV reporter and news anchor Jennifer Moore, in her voice-over introduction. "And the man with the beard may not be Kris Kringle, but to nine-year-old Serena Ecarius, it's Christmas."

JENNIFER (cont'd)

And in this unlikeliest of places, little
Serena, who has never spoken a word in her

```
life, will receive the greatest Christmas
present of them all—the gift of speech.
    (beat)
And everyone wonders what her first words
will be.
```

Including the several thousand prime-time viewers who embraced Serena's story. "Exciting" and "triumphant" wrote the *Free Press*. "*A Gift for Serena* was produced with obvious love and compassion . . . This deeply affecting 30 minutes is filled with Christmas season love and good cheer . . . a gift for TV viewers."

One of the reasons I believe viewers reacted so passionately to Serena's story, in addition to having the opportunity to witness her courage and vivacious personality firsthand, was that, unlike *Land Grab, The Boys Next Door,* or *The Concrete Reservation, A Gift for Serena* wasn't a strictly issue-oriented public affairs report. In fact, it wasn't a report at all, it was a *story*, void of any of the usual on-camera narration used to explain all and tie up loose ends. Except for the program's setup and tease, *Serena* was entirely unscripted and self-narrated with each of the characters showing and telling their own stories.

Although certainly not a first, that kind of intimate, almost cinema verité (cinema truth) style of storytelling was certainly unique and all too rare in local television. Without a news anchor or a reporter in charge of the story, who was going to feed viewers the facts? Where was the voice of God to tell us what was important in this story?

I took my cue from feature films. I liked Stanley Kubrick well enough, but he was too cool for my taste. The Austrian-born American director Billy Wilder was my role model. Give the audience something to do, he urged his fellow directors. It's fine to tell them two plus two, but for maximum impact, resist giving the audience the answer.

Let them do the math.

Power! Accuracy! All in One Pump!

"Why do you care?" Henry asked. "It's not exactly *A Gift for Serena*; there's nothing heavy or serious about deer hunting."

Good question. All I can say is that I was curious. I wanted to understand the appeal, the attraction, the allure of this ancient sport that during Michigan's deer-hunting season drives nearly seven hundred thousand hunters to contribute an estimated $8.9 billion to the state's economy.

I had no clue. Growing up, my brothers and I loved watching television shows like *Have Gun—Will Travel, Gunsmoke,* or Steve McQueen's *Wanted Dead or Alive,* but we had to wait until Dad was out of the house to get our firearms fix. Although he never mentioned it, I know my father the pacifist was not at all happy when Mom bought me a new Daisy Red Ryder carbine air gun ("Power! Accuracy! All in One Pump!").

To help me blow off steam, I'd like to think. "Why are you always angry at *me?*" my mother used to shout at me whenever I would resist taking sides during the Seven-Year War. "You have *two* parents. Why don't ever you get angry at *him?*"

The Deer Hunters followed the adventures of two different archetypes: traditional hunters who slept in tents and cabins, and the more urban recreational hunters who preferred the comfort of motor homes. We threw in a little suspense and drama by adding to the mix a profile of a Department of Natural Resources agent on the lookout for illegal "slob" hunters. All three stories were magnificently intertwined by my editor, WDIV's Sheldon Brown.

That part was easy. The hard part was securing the support and participation of local hunting and outdoors organizations, who were still wincing from the 1975 CBS documentary, *The Guns of Autumn,* narrated by Dan Rather. The *New York Times* loved the prime-time report, calling it "extremely powerful television . . . the combined impact of script, pictures and sound is extraordinary." But the *Washington Post* critic had other ideas, arguing that because of what it described as the doc's anti-hunting bias, *Guns* "should receive an award for the most biased TV reporting of the year, possibly the decade." Its focus solely on "fringe elements of a larger group . . . was an insult to all the hunters I know, to the ethics of fair and responsible hunting practices and even to the practice of fair TV journalism." My intern, Toby Tabaczynski, and I had our work cut out for us.

"Sorry, Harvey," the director of the Michigan United Conservation Clubs, the largest statewide conservation organization in the nation, informed me, "but we just can't take a chance on another *Guns of Autumn.*" Fortunately, he asked around and, after caucusing with area hunters familiar with my work, the MUCC decided to roll the dice and endorse the project.

But I still wasn't out of the woods. For the longest time, even while we were taping, the doc's theme, the story's spine, evaded me completely. We knew the story was about deer hunters, but for me that was only its plot. "We're not Bambi killers," one hunter insisted, trying to explain his passion for the sport. "We treat our dogs right. We treat our women right." OK, but I still had no idea what the point of my story was, what it was *really* about. Finally, during our last interview with the tent hunters sitting around the campfire, the young man tearfully explained why this year's hunt was particularly meaningful for him and his brothers.

> TENT HUNTER
> Hunting is our obligation to carry this on.
> As of Friday, we didn't even know if we were
> coming. About a month ago when we started
> thinking about going hunting and Dad's
> getting fired up, he's out helping us cut
> wood. He wanted to get up here with us, and
> he was planning to. And then about a week
> and a half ago and he had his little bout
> with the doctor, who told him his old cancer
> was flaring up again. And we were down there
> Thursday when he had his surgery. He just
> started coming out of his anesthesia, and he
> hardly said any words—I don't even think he
> said 'hi'—but he recognized we were there.
> And when we were saying goodbye and getting
> ready to go, he said, 'Shoot straight.' His
> eyes weren't even open.
>   (beat)
> Shoot straight.

The Hunt for Happy Accidents

Of all my WDIV documentaries, *City Nights* was the most controversial. Co-produced with a young protégé of Henry's, Mitch Jacobs, it was an hour-long special exploring the little-known and off-the-radar lives of working Detroiters who worked late night and midnight shifts—artists, musicians, emergency room docs and nurses, taxi dancers, and other night owls who embraced the calm and quiet of their nocturnal adventures.

Not to mention the adrenaline.

Although we agreed we didn't need a narrator to tell our story, I decided early on I wanted the popular, all-night FM disc jockey, the Electrifying Mojo, to provide the on-camera, free-associating connective tissue between each of the *City Nights* segments. That was the good news. But when we arrived in his studio with our crew, Mojo balked and insisted we use only his voice and under no circumstances show his face on camera.

"Don't want to mess with the magic," he told me, not at all embarrassed by the frantic position we were put in by his last-minute change of heart.

"We're screwed," Mitch said. "There goes our connective tissue!"

"Not necessarily," I said. "Let's find a way to make this work."

And we did. Using star filters and colored gels, my shooter, Kevin Ward, shot Mojo's sequences, revealing only indistinguishable parts of his face seen on the side and in silhouette, illuminated with a backlit aura while the back of his head bobbed in and out of the frame. "This works," Mitch later admitted, recalling our original intention to shoot Mojo in his entirety. "What do *we* know?"

For many viewers, *City Nights* was a Rorschach test. In profiling the last of Detroit's taxi dancers (and their paying dance partners) and by showing citizens being treated for gunshot wounds at a local ER, some critics argued we only reinforced clichéd negative stereotypes of the city, which only served to contribute to the media's all-too-frequent preoccupation with the darker and seamier side of life in the Motor City.

Or, did we, as was our intention with our emphasis on the below-the-surface, after-hours struggles of its residents—the *humanity* of the city—do exactly the opposite?

We got our chance with a late-night stake-out at Detroit's old Mount Carmel Hospital emergency room. Mitch had returned to the station distraught because he deliberately chose a weekend night to tape what he was certain was going to be a *M*A*S*H*-like atmosphere of heroic but frenzied lifesaving interventions by the ER staff. But instead, he came back empty-handed. Unfortunately, that night the docs and nursing staff saw few patients, and worse, the ones they worked on ended up dying. "What kind of story is *that*?" Mitch asked, already making plans to return to the ER for a reshoot.

Henry and I discussed it. We agreed Mitch should go back, but not for the reason he thought. "We're missing something," I told him. "We just don't know what it is yet."

To find out, Mitch returned to the hospital the next day for a pickup interview, among other things, to find out why, once her patient died, one of his ER nurses made a point of *not* covering the dead woman's face. What was that about?

"It's just how I feel," the night nurse explained the next night when Mitch returned to shine a new light on her story.

```
              NIGHT NURSE (cont'd)
When we lose a patient, it's like when
you cover their face up, you're denying
that they were a person, you're denying
they existed. And I don't like the act
of bringing their family in to see their
beloved and pulling a sheet over their
head. It's like we just covered them up,
like we're done with them. We're not done
with them, the family's not finished with
them. It just seems so final with the
sheet over their face. You don't have to
cover their face.
     (beat)
That's the movies, they cover faces.
```

These Planes Were Built for Flying

We never know where our projects will take us or what lessons we'll learn along the way.

In *Visions in Bubblegum, Canvas & Stone*, one of my last docs for WDIV, the station was eager to celebrate the exhibition *Black Folk Art in America (1930–1980)* on display at the Detroit Institute of Arts that was funded, in part, by our parent company, Post-Newsweek Stations.

When Henry pitched me on the assignment, I thought I was absolutely the wrong person for the job. "All the artists are dead!" I insisted. "Who am I going to *talk* to?" And besides, I protested, in order to tell this story, we'd have to hire a *narrator*!

But then something happened. The deeper my intern, Bob Kernen, and I delved into the story about these illiterate children of slaves and former slaves, the more I became fascinated, infatuated even, with how these unschooled, self-taught storytellers confronted the harsh reality of their seemingly impossible situations, a theme that has been, I have come to realize, regardless of the genre, medium, or platform, genetically encoded in every one of my stories.

For me, *Visions in Bubblegum, Canvas & Stone* was an important lesson on how to embrace a project even when it's not your baby and you're brought on as a "work for hire." My solution? When you think you have absolutely nothing in common with your subject and even less interest and/or experience in tackling the task at hand, the challenge is to find something, *anything* about the project that speaks to you. And once you make that connection, build from there.

Although not always easily.

Several years later, when I ran my own production company, a client insisted I insert an especially gratuitous and self-serving sound bite in his promotional video. I fought hard but lost the battle. "What are you going to do?" my interns Joyce Golden and Donna Maio, asked. "It'll ruin the scene."

"I'll try to talk him out of it, of course," I said, "but sometimes we just have to put the toilet on the stairs."

They didn't get it. "It's an old freelancer's joke," I explained, reminding ourselves that as independent contractors we're only the architects, we don't own our for-hire stories. It's their house, their rules, I explained. So, when a client insists we put the toilet on the stairs instead of in the bathroom where we know it belongs, we make our case, defend our argument as best we can, but in the end, we do what we're told.

And put the toilet on the stairs.

Fortunately, *Visions in Bubblegum, Canvas & Stone* was a toilet/stairs-free zone, and although this project wasn't my idea and I never would have chosen it in the first place, the artist who ended up speaking to me the loudest was the remarkable Leslie "Airplane" Payne.

Although he never actually learned how to fly, Leslie Payne (1907–1981) was an African American artist who created an alter ego for himself as a World War I aviator. Inspired by an air show he had seen as a child in the 1940s, Payne began to make what he proudly called his "imitations," full-size replicas of Lindbergh's *Spirit of St. Louis* and other planes of that era.

They were a wonder, each one created from scratch out of sheets of discarded planks of plywood, sheet metal, canvas, and anything else the artist could get his hands on. "Leslie used to joke about whether or not he actually flew his

Leslie "Airplane" Payne in one of his backyard "imitations" in Visions in Bubblegum, Canvas & Stone.
(Photo by Bob Jones Jr. Courtesy of WDIV-Local 4/Graham Media Group and Bentley Historical Library.)

imitations," my narration, read by *Roots* and pre–*Star Trek: The Next Generation* star LeVar Burton, informed the audience.

                    LEVAR (cont'd)
    But one look at the torn canvas and badly
    splintered wood and tiny gas-powered
    lawnmower engines attached to each plane,
    and you had to realize the answer was "no."
    But another look into the deep, dark eyes
    of Leslie Payne, the eyes that sparkled
    and came alive whenever he spoke about his
    imitations, one would have to say "yes,"
    these planes were built for flying. Leslie

```
Payne, artist and plane builder, did what
so many Black people wished they could do:
he took off. He was more than an artist,
Leslie Payne was also a pilot, in his mind,
traveling to distant lands and faraway
places in time . . .
```

And because we had superimposed an image of one of Leslie's imitations over a field, as LeVar spoke over a gentle George Winston piano track, we slowly cross-dissolved the plane out of the shot, leaving only the empty field.

```
                    LEVAR (cont'd)
    . . . and with his art, taking us with him.
```

15

Aren't You Going to Hit Me?
and Other Executive Decisions

In 1984 I felt I had put off becoming a production executive for as long as I could. "What is it with you and authority figures?" Woodruff once asked me. "You give us such a hard time, but you do everything in your power to avoid becoming one yourself."

He was right. When it came to work, my preferred gear was fifth, but when asked to hang out with my peers or make small talk with the station's higher-ups, I was, more often than not, tongue-tied, my social skills stuck in neutral.

I wasn't trying to be rude, it's just that I had little interest in spending any more time away from Catherine and the children than I had to. I love my work, but I have always tried, often with mixed results, not to take it out on my family. Besides, my wife and I were both cocoon-ists, so my having to arrive at work early and leave hours later than quitting time, as I had seen Woodruff and Henry Maldonado do so many times, was not my idea of a good time. Still, in 1984, when a managerial job as the director of production opened at Detroit's public television station, Catherine and I both agreed it was time for me to leave the nest.

It was good news all around. The *Detroit Free Press* gave DPTV "the Hire-of-the-Week Award" for having "the smarts to hire the Detroit-bred production ace" to "infuse (*its*) productions with the substance and touch of class that are all too rare in local commercial television."

It sounded good on paper. Now, all I had to do was deliver.

Fortunately, I had help. Robert Larson was the station's newly arrived general manager. "Doctor Bob" was a puzzle, an ordained Presbyterian minister and former president of WITF-TV in tiny Harrisburg, Pennsylvania, population

52,098. *What the hell is he doing here?* I remember thinking when I heard about his coming to WTVS.

"Because I was done in Harrisburg," he told me when I asked him what brought him here, to Detroit of all places. "Because this is where my work is. I knew I could make a difference here."

"Me too," I told him.

Still, making the leap from commercial to public television, going from being a line director and producer to a production executive was not an easy transition. It didn't help that I'd been warned by several friends about the myriad of problems confronting the station. "It's a real mess here," my friend Bill Pace said. He was now producing the station's nationally syndicated flagship program, *Late Night America.* "Are you sure you want to do this?"

Positive.

Because, like Bob Larson, I was ready. After my successful attempts at avoiding becoming a boss at WXYZ and WDIV, the closer I got to my fortieth birthday, the stronger was my desire to share with others what I'd learned about telling stories and making media that mattered.

We Can Only Do What We Can Do

It's not as if WTVS was a damsel in distress or a hick operation in need of a big city makeover. The station was already producing its share of successful locally produced programs, including nationally syndicated shows *Late Night America* (hosted by my first boss at WXYZ, Dennis Wholey), *Country Express,* and *The Beat,* and several public affairs programs including *Video Detroit* and *Detroit Black Journal,* later rebranded as *American Black Journal.*

Still, Detroit Public Television was no Post-Newsweek or ABC-owned station, where we had all the money and resources we needed to produce as many locally produced, network-quality programs as we wanted. But it didn't take long for me to discover the lack of funding and resources was going to be the least of my problems.

Apparently, my predecessor was notorious for having a volatile temper and a penchant for minimizing the contributions made by his staff. The result was what Bill and others described as a debilitating lack of morale and self-confidence that seemed to permeate just about every part of the production department.

At first, I thought my friend was exaggerating. After all, how bad could it be? I found out within a few months of my arrival, when one of my producers, Megan

Mainguth, came into my office to plead guilty to a breach of department protocol. Her crime, she confessed, was that she'd misplaced several of the expense receipts from her last trip to Nashville on behalf of her syndicated show, *Country Express*. I told her to try to trace her steps, find as many as she could, and then write me a note for the files that explained what had happened.

Megan looked at me in feigned shock. "That's it?" she asked incredulously. "That's all?"

I didn't get it. "Is there more?" I asked. "Well," she suggested coyly, "aren't you going to hit me?"

I assumed she was kidding, but I played along.

HARVEY

Sure, I can do that. Hold out your hands.

Megan did. And I tapped her on the back of her wrists.

HARVEY (cont'd)

Here. Consider them slapped.

If only all my problems were that easy to fix. Compared to WDIV and WXYZ, WTVS's crews had access to only the most basic and rudimentary production equipment. And even then, we couldn't always count on the cameras or even the mics to work properly. Although we had several studio cameras, I was shocked to discover that each one "registered" different versions of the same color. And it wasn't much better in the field, where our early generation wireless mics would often pick up as much static and radio transmissions as interview sound bites.

I realized lack of funding was an issue, but until I could fix that, I decided not to accept the station's poverty as an excuse for what I considered shoddy production values. "Sorry, Harvey," the chief engineer told me, as he tried to justify the frequent equipment failures. "We can only do what we can do."

"Then let's flip this," I insisted. "Until I can find the money for equipment that actually works, let's agree *not* to do what we *can't* do."

"What does that mean?" he demanded.

"It means that until at least the third camera can match the other two, we're going to shoot our studio shows with just the two cameras that are in sync."

Miraculously, within a few days, the three studio cameras began to register perfectly, and all our programs, including *Late Night America*, were back to looking shipshape.

Better Frames, Better Pictures

I decided early on I wasn't going to try to fix what wasn't broken.

When Ben Frazier, the host of *Detroit Black Journal*, didn't show up for a taping, I pulled the former intern and talented production assistant Ed Gordon off the bench and placed him in front of the camera as the new host of the program. Ed went on to host NPR's *News and Notes with Ed Gordon* and to work for the Black Entertainment Television network on such nationally syndicated programs as *BET News* and *Weekly with Ed Gordon*, and the nationally syndicated talk show *Our World with Black Enterprise*.

I was also happy to encourage Diane Atkinson Hudson to take a chance and leave her comfortable producing job at *Late Night* for the insecurity of working on a new nationally syndicated talk show hosted by a former Baltimore news anchor, Oprah Somebody.

But what to do with my reporters? Each of them—Trudy Gallant, Bob Rossbach, Darryl Wood, Shelley Czeizler, among others—was an excellent on-air talent, but I felt their producing work on the weekly magazine show *Video Detroit* was not as compelling as it could be. "Energy is power," I told them, "and the best way to determine the power of our energy is by its impact." I told my staff, including a talented up-and-coming producer, Jay Nelson, "So, let's go out there and make some impact!"

But where to start? During the Passover Seder, Jews ask themselves *di fir kashes,* "the four questions," to remind them why "this night is different than all other nights." With *Video Detroit*, I challenged my producers to answer at least five questions before going into the field: Why bother? Other than you, who will care? Who will give a shit about this story? Where's the fire? What's the urgency, the *need*, for telling this tale?

In other words, of all the tens of thousands of stories out there, why does it matter? Why this one, why *now*?

Next, once we had those answers, came the hard part. "We need a better frame for our picture," I suggested. *Video Detroit* was an OK title, but only OK. The problem was it didn't raise any EKG levels for our viewers. What did it *say*?

In content and tone, what did it communicate to viewers about what they could expect when they tuned in to the program?

"But it's about Detroit," one producer insisted. "And we feature video reports instead of talking heads. Isn't that enough?"

"It's a start," I replied. "But if the show is about Detroit, shouldn't the title at least reflect the tone and attitude of the city, its *juice?*" That sounded good on paper, but I shared my staff's pain; in my early days, I always found naming my stories, coming up with just the right title for each project, to be a difficult and frustrating process.

Unlike WDIV's Henry Maldonado, who was brilliant at it, a graduate of the Andrew M. Greeley school of title creation. "Give the thing a name," urged the leprechauns in his *Emerald Magic: Great Tales of Irish Fantasy*, "and it takes shape."

And invites others to want to watch.

Once, when I pitched Henry on a doc about the double life of Bernie Marquis, a local mannequin repair artist whose alter ego was performing as Santa Claus in what was then called the Hudson's Thanksgiving Day Parade, he got excited and instantly came up with the perfect title: "*Santa Claus is Alive and Well and Living in Detroit!* Who wouldn't want to watch *that?*"

Following Henry's lead, it didn't take long for *Video Detroit* to become reimagined as an award-winning, prime-time public affairs series, we called — riffing off Detroit's reputation at the time as a gun-toting crime capital — the *Friday Night Special*.

PBS Savors a Detroit Miracle

As soon as I read in the *Detroit Free Press* about the annual efforts by parishioners at Detroit's Fort Street Presbyterian Church to perform Handel's *Messiah*, I knew it was a project that had my name on it, one of many story crushes I brought with me in the hopes of finding a national outlet for the station's locally produced programs. And to answer the unasked question, no, it never occurred to me our Detroit stories wouldn't "play" outside the city. I come from the Jordan Peele school of storytelling: the more specific our stories are, the more universal. "When a story works," the award-winning director of *Get Out* and *Us* insisted, "you see yourself in it no matter who you are."

Or where.

Miracle on Fort Street, a city tale about an unlikely band of amateur singers and their brave attempts to find their voices through music and song, spoke to me in a way few other projects had. But despite my enthusiasm for the story, it took a while for me to get the project off the ground. For the longest time, we could neither afford to hire a director/producer nor rent the remote, multi-camera video truck necessary to shoot the chorale's performance.

Fortunately, Bob Larson wasn't discouraged. "It's so Detroit!" he gushed when I pitched him on my latest passion project. "Don't give up. We have to find a way to do this!"

And we did, thanks to a generous contribution from General Television Network, a local production house that loaned us a remote truck, and our station's newly revitalized production crew under the supervision of our director, the late, great Chris Felcyn. And, most importantly, the unbridled commitment and passion of a former seminarian named Carl Bidleman who confessed that, other than shooting a few short videos for Father Cunningham's Focus: HOPE's civil rights and jobs training program, he had never actually produced a documentary in his life.

But I wasn't worried; it wasn't Carl's inexperience that got him the job.

It was his empty refrigerator.

When I screened it, I thought his video about Focus: HOPE's meals for the elderly program was painfully OK, but there was nothing special or particularly compelling about it. But that was before Carl asked the frail, elderly man he was interviewing to show him what was inside his refrigerator. When the old man opened the door and Carl's camera pushed in, the audience joined me in seeing, that except for a half loaf of bread and a stick of celery, it was empty.

My heart stopped. It was a beautiful, sad, *perfect* moment, for its own sake but also, and mainly, because that was the moment I knew I'd found a natural storyteller who could help me bring my *Miracle* to life.

Still, producing *Miracle* was a challenge. My greatest concern was that, as compelling as I imagined the chorale's rehearsals would be, they would end up simply becoming a pacing device. "That's too easy," I cautioned Carl and his talented shooter, Jhimm Woods. "And obvious." The real drama, we both agreed, the real story, was not just in witnessing the arduous preparation chorale members endured for the concert but the dramatic, *personal* impact this journey was going to have on Carl's two main characters.

Milfordean Luster was a Detroit police officer who was worried her job was making her "too jaded" and cut off from her feelings. Pat DeLisle was a desperately lonely woman, who in her interview confessed to Carl that her despair was so deep "it was at the core of my being. I want someone's shoulder to cry on so bad I could cry."

Still, despite how exciting Jhimm and Carl's footage was, the first cut sheet/ edit script revealed an unexpected problem.

Miracle's first two acts were exactly right in terms of introducing Milfordean and Pat and documenting their painful learning curve in performing the difficult score in a way that would satisfy the choir director's relentless and demanding expectations. But the last act suffered from an occupational hazard experienced by many writers, directors, and other creatives: it simply did not live up to its premise, the *promise* of the story.

Carl was discouraged. "It sucks, I know," he said, "but I don't know how to fix it."

I didn't either. But I knew what the question was. There's always a question.

"Something's missing," I said after reading his cut sheet. "So far," I suggested, "you're showing us exactly what we expect to see. How can we surprise the audience and show them something they didn't know or expect to experience?"

"Or even better," I added, "something *you* didn't know."

Carl didn't get it, but I persisted.

> HARVEY (cont'd)
> Go back and talk to the chorale's conductor.
> Let's find out.

> CARL
> Find out what?

> HARVEY
> His secret. He seems so tense all the time.
> What's he hiding?
>   (beat)
> What *isn't* he telling you?

Carl found his answer the next day when, in a pickup interview with Ed Kingins, the chorale's co-founder and conductor, the maestro revealed that this year was a first for him, that in previous performances of *Messiah,* he had never conducted the musicians before. The chorale yes, but never with the orchestra. Not ever.

And it showed.

"The pressure mounts on all of us, people," Kingins barked at his war-weary pupils, angrily threatening to expel members, or at the least call out anyone who was mispronouncing the text or hitting a wrong note. "Don't let it collapse, people. If you *think* these words, you can't let that happen."

```
              KINGINS (cont'd)
      If you believe what you're singing, you
      cannot let that happen.
           (beat)
      You're singing this like it's a show tune or
      something!
```

Suddenly, Carl's baby was no longer ugly.

"A Detroit Chorale sings out," the *New York Times* proudly announced in its review published on Christmas day. "The film is about more than a production; it's about community and how one achieves it. In an unpretentious way, *Miracle on Fort Street* is about art and artistry as well. How are they achieved? Edward Kingins, the conductor, is demanding . . . [*but*] the effort . . . is justified."

And then some. By *Miracle*'s end, we see the sad, lonely Pat Delisle beam with unabashed pleasure and the smiling policewoman Milfordean Luster wipe away tears. "The members of the chorale . . . ," concluded the *Times*, "look transformed. *Miracle on Fort Street* . . . manages to be wonderfully warming without being the slightest sentimental. It is a lovely piece of work."

Closing the Circle

One of the rewards of being an executive at a PBS station was having the opportunity to participate in projects that involved other local stations and even the network itself. I looked forward to joining the consortium of founding PBS stations that consulted and advised the network's flagship documentary series, *Frontline*. Although, as much as I enjoyed being wined and dined on WGBH's dime (PBS feeds its consultants *very* well), my experience with *Frontline* was marred by the fact that, despite being invited to provide feedback and contribute story ideas, I couldn't help but notice David Fanning, the series' executive producer, never took notes.

(*Note to self: if you ever get a chance to run the show and one of the conditions for your funding is that you seek out feedback from an advisory council, pick up your pen, take notes, and at least* pretend *you give a shit.*)

Fortunately, I had a more direct and hands-on experience working with PBS on my next assignment for them.

"Welcome back," Josh Darsa greeted me at our first meeting to discuss our shared role as midwives to *Who Killed Vincent Chin?*, a new project being funded by the Corporation for Public Broadcasting (CPB). It was an exciting independently produced film about the brutal beating and subsequent death in 1982 of a Chinese American by two white Detroit auto workers who, according to witnesses, mistook him for being Japanese. "It's because of you motherfuckers that we're out of work" was among the taunts, according to witnesses, hurled at Chin and his friends when the fight began in a local strip club.

Josh was a real producer, a *macher* (Yiddish for someone who gets things done) who, before he helped create *Frontline*, was a CBS news correspondent and a key player in launching such groundbreaking PBS programs as *The MacNeil/Lehrer NewsHour* and Henry Hampton's epic civil rights documentary series, *Eyes on the Prize*. Josh was also one of the nicest, smartest, and most professional collaborators I ever had the pleasure of working with.

As a CPB senior program officer, he was one of the designated point persons for filmmakers and independent production companies hoping to get their foot in the door and then survive the required hoop-jumping necessary to qualify for CPB funding and, hopefully, PBS distribution.

That's where I came in.

As part of its efforts to diversify the producing pool, CPB was eager to fund projects like *Who Killed Vincent Chin?*, produced and directed by up-and-coming independent filmmakers Christine Choy and Renee Tajima. But as compelling as their proposal was, CPB required a presenting station be attached to the project to help provide the supervision it felt was necessary to ensure its investment would both adhere to the network's content and production standards and work within the confines of the approved budget.

I was looking forward to assisting on the Chin project; for one thing, by reputation, Christine's approach to video storytelling sounded not too unlike my own, when I wasn't wearing my hard hat. "Choy puts people at ease with the camera," wrote the *New York Times*, "encouraging them to pour out their most intimate dilemmas. She lets subjects tell their tales at leisure . . . and presents different points of view to flesh out the main story."

WTVS was a natural fit to help CPB shepherd the Chin project because, in addition to being Chin's hometown (and the city where he was killed), under Dr. Larson's leadership, the station was fast becoming nationally recognized for its production of award-winning, local-for-national, city-centric stories.

Editorial control wasn't as much a concern on the Chin project because the whole point of this new round of PBS and CPB support for independent production companies was that "works produced by filmmakers in association with a station or organization are acceptable if editorial control was entirely in the hands of the filmmaker." Or filmmakers. Christine's co-director and co-producer was Renee Tajima, a young Japanese American filmmaker who was committed to telling stories about race and gender, with an emphasis on the Asian American and immigrant experience.

Although neither Josh nor I had any argument with the terms and conditions for funding *Vincent Chin*, CPB did expect us to review the work in progress and provide our "third eye" input and feedback during certain critical stages of the project. Our job was not to interfere or intrude in the creative process, but to help make sure the producers' vision was completed to their satisfaction, on time, and within budget.

Josh warned me the relationship between a presenting station like ours and independent filmmakers was a delicate balance. "You're there to ensure their success," he said. "On the other hand, there's bound to be some resistance when you offer what they might consider 'too much' help."

He wasn't kidding. *Who Killed Vincent Chin?* was one of the most challenging and difficult projects I have ever been engaged in.

Not just for me, but also, I suspect, for the filmmakers.

For my part, I realized from the very beginning that for this relationship to work, I'd have to set my phasers on stun. "These are highly respected and accomplished professional filmmakers," Juanita Anderson, my executive producer of cultural affairs and special projects, cautioned me in advance of our first meeting. *In other words,* I imagined her saying, *Christine and Renee are not Carl Bidleman. They are nobody's protégés.*

Juanita is a force of nature, co-founder of the National Black Programming Consortium (now Black Public Media), a documentary producer and director in her own right, and later head of the Media Arts and Studies program in the Department of Communication at Wayne State University. We're friendly now, but thirty-five years ago, when I was Juanita's supervisor on the Chin project, to paraphrase a lyric from a popular Leonard Cohen song, our steps did *not* always rhyme. One of our core disagreements, pre-*Chin*, was that, because I came up in an era when local documentary producers were also their own directors, Juanita resented what she perceived as my intrusion into her own directors' creative process and decision-making.

Still, my plate was full with other projects, and, considering Juanita was the station's original point person for this project before my arrival, I was looking forward to her doing the heavy lifting on the station's behalf.

I did, however, have one request. At one of our first meetings, I asked for the team's latest creative treatment, so I could be brought up to speed on the status of the project. "I'm not going to micromanage you," I said, "but I don't like surprises, either. Just share your shooting schedules with me and keep me posted on any changes in your story that might affect the budget."

I thought the meeting went well, but for me, the team's reluctance to follow through on my request was a frustration.

Another problem, at least from my perspective, was that Christine and Renee appeared to be still researching and pre-interviewing while already in production. I expected some of that, of course—documentaries are not done deals, signed, sealed, and delivered in pre-production. During the reality of the shoots, we expect our stories to change and for the content to shift direction; the problem was that without an updated treatment, production schedule, or any tweaks to the line items in their budget, Josh and I felt like we were flying blind.

But that's not how Renee and Christine saw it. They seemed to view my requests as attempts to inhibit and control their creative process.

And then there was the issue of notes. When I was a line director and producer, I welcomed any feedback that I thought would make the work better, stronger, tighter, *deeper*. Seeing the trees and accepting feedback and notes from anyone "outside the forest" has always been an essential part of my work ethic. But for the relationship to work, it requires equal measures of good faith, receptivity, and trust.

Looking back, I think that may have been one of the problems that contributed to our rocky experience working together on the Chin project. "You can get really sucked into the idea of working for television," Christine Choy later told *Jump Cut* magazine, the bible for independent filmmakers "They don't care about quality, just a product. We artists have to find a way to combat our dependency, (*otherwise*) art becomes a commodity, and the artist does, too."

I don't know if Christine was referring to her work in public television, but it sure explains why she and Renee balked when, after looking at an early rough cut, I questioned why, out of the blue, they inserted a jazzy sequence of a Chinese youth dancing on top of cars in a junkyard. Other than confusing the audience, at the time I simply could not see how the sequence contributed to or advanced the story.

Since then, I've lightened up on that orthodoxy. A little. There's more than one way to tell a story, I now confess to my students, and sometimes, ours isn't the only one.

In the end, there was much in *Who Killed Vincent Chin?* that impressed. The *L.A. Times* described the film as "thought provoking" and "an absorbing piece of reporting." The *New York Times* agreed, saying it was a "complex, solidly constructed documentary." *Who Killed Vincent Chin?* went on to win a Peabody Award and was nominated for an Oscar. What struck me the most about Choy and Tajima's work were their spot-on interviews, especially with the film's main characters, Vincent Chin's mother, Lily Chin, the various eyewitnesses to his murder, journalist Helen Zia, and representatives from the American Citizens for Justice (ACJ). I also thought the footage of Detroit's Chinese community and the visual impact of imports on the ailing US automotive industry was terrific.

But all of that was in the final cut, long after I left the project and WTVS. Before leaving, though, I gave the filmmakers one last note, expressing my concern that, despite their best intentions, there was what I felt was a gaping hole in their narrative; something was missing.

Fortunately, and to their credit, the filmmakers knew exactly what I was talking about. All the major players connected to Vincent Chin's killing and its aftermath appeared well represented in the film, but, I asked, where were the two people who played the most important roles in Chin's murder, namely the two men who beat him to death, Ron Ebens and his stepson, Michael Nitz?

"We tried," Juanita explained. "But they wouldn't talk to us." On one level I wasn't surprised, considering what the film was about and who was making it. "They probably don't trust you," I said, stating a fact and not at all a value judgment. "What do you think you can do to change that?"

"Not very much," Juanita replied. "We tried everything, but they still won't budge."

"Try this," I replied, reaching into my pocket and handing over a piece of paper with the name and phone number of Ebens and Nitz's defense attorney, Frank Eamons. Juanita seemed genuinely surprised.

"Frank is a friend married to a friend," I explained. "He's agreed you can talk to his clients."

"On camera?" Juanita asked, sounding not at all certain she'd heard me correctly.

"That's for you and Frank to work out," I told her. "Good luck."

"Thanks," she said, getting up, in a tone I felt was considerably warmer and friendlier than we had ever exchanged before. "This will help."

"You're welcome," I told her. *That's what I'm here for*, I wanted to add, but I decided to leave well enough alone.

My premature departure from the Chin project was one of the reasons why, twenty-five years later, in 2011, I was happy to accept an invitation to address attendees at the 22nd Annual National Convention of the Asian American Journalists Association. The subject of my presentation was "How to Be a Great Backpack Video Journalist," and I looked forward to passing on what I had learned about telling stories on the run. And truthfully, my talk also gave me the chance to close a circle I felt was left open when I left the *Who Killed Vincent Chin?* project and Detroit Public Television to start my own production company.

And, like Christine Choy and Renee Tajima, become an independent filmmaker.

16

I've Got No Strings

One of the great pleasures of watching the original *Disneyland* television series so many years ago was having the opportunity to binge on classic Disney animated films from the 1940s. Although I felt sorry for Bambi and I certainly identified with Dumbo's hidden talent for flight, it was Pinocchio who struck a chord, especially when the boy marionette proclaimed in song how thrilled he was to finally be free with no strings attached.

In 1986, I had my Pinocchio moment when I left Detroit Public Television to start my own independent film and video production company, HKO Media.

"It's crucial to have a setup, a room to dream," filmmaker David Lynch wrote in his autobiography, *Catching the Big Fish*, "so that, at any given moment, when you get an idea, you have the place and the tools to make it happen." For more than twenty-five years, HKO Media was my room to dream, even though there were times in the early days of my company when I could swear I heard the Ghosts of Executive Producers Past ringing in my ears: *Who are you kidding, Harvey? You've always been an independent producer. Why do you think we fought so much?*

Although HKO Media (the K stands for Catherine's maiden name, Kurek) was my gift to myself, in my mind it was also a delicious, albeit belated, thirteenth-birthday present from my mother, who, at least in her death, found an opportunity to no longer feel the need to compete with my father.

Mom hated how sick the colon cancer made her feel and how it ravaged her body. During my last visit with her and Adolph in their Florida home, she surprised me by expressing regret at not being able to cry during her illness. "I want to feel sad," she told me. "Don't you think I *deserve* to feel sad?"

Always the producer, the problem solver, I came up with what I thought was an obliging, albeit risky solution. "I can make you sad, Mom. I know how to help make you cry."

She looked up with her hollowed eyes and, in a hoarse voice I barely recognized, whispered her approval. "I love you, Mom," I said softly, "but my plane leaves in two hours, and that means we're never going to see each other again. Not ever. This is our—"

"Stop, Harvey," she said, cutting me off. "That's *too* sad."

I stopped, kissed her goodbye, and never saw her alive again. Only there's a twist in this story, because unlike Charlie Brown's Lucy, my mother, upon her death several months later, found a way to return the football she had a habit of pulling away from me so many times in my youth. Dad and Iris have always gotten their share of well-deserved credit for supporting my life's work, but in the end, in *her* end, it was my mother who, with the help of a generous bequest in her will, gave me and Catherine the financial security that enabled me to leave Detroit Public Television so I could set up my own shop and create my own room to dream.

What World War II?

As with my first company, Creative Media, it was rough going at first. Producing testimonial-style and real people promotional and fundraising videos for local nonprofits was fun, but I was hoping my friends in the advertising business would also send work my way. It didn't happen. "I was tempted," one production executive told me, "but I didn't want to insult you by asking you to produce commercials."

Fortunately, Ross Roy Advertising had no such problem. In addition to directing commercials for clients like Blue Cross Blue Shield of Michigan and DTE Energy, Ross Roy brought me on board to create a series of promotional videos on the history of each of Chrysler Corporation's three brands: the Chrysler division, Jeep, and Dodge. I was happy for the business but not at all certain this was going to be a good fit. "I'm not much of a car guy," I warned my client. No problem, my team leaders, Roy Edmonds and Lance Aldrich, assured me. "It's one of the reasons we hired you." The only caveat? "Surprise us. Don't tell us what we already know."

My intern, Joe Phillips, and I started with the Jeep story. At the time, German company Daimler Mercedes was on the verge of purchasing Chrysler, and the then president of the company, Bob Lutz, and other Chrysler executives were eager to capture not only the history of these uniquely American brands but also and mainly, according to my executive producer, Roberta Beaudet, each brand's unique stories.

It was more difficult than I thought. I've walked on many a tightrope with clients, but none as delicately as when our team negotiated among ourselves how we were going to present for our German client the critical role Jeep played in defeating what the Allies called the Jerry "Huns" in World War II, or as my editor, the brilliant Christa Kindt Newhouse, and I used to call it, "What World War II?"

As much as I enjoyed solving that problem, as well as having the opportunity to hire my son, Noah, as a production assistant during our Camp Jeep shoot, it wasn't the Jeep brand that enthralled. In the end, it was the long-forgotten story of the Dodge brothers and their motor car and truck company that grabbed me by the throat.

And to this day, and for so many reasons, has never let go.

I Still Dream about the Dodge Brothers

Legend has it that one of the reasons Henry Ford's Model T was so successful was because over 90 percent of its parts were designed and manufactured by John and Horace Dodge. "Everything except the tires and the windshield wipers," a Chrysler engineer told me during our filming for the Ross Roy videos.

The Dodge brothers were consummate engineers and manufacturers, artisans even, who, like my father, were as principled as they were creative. Once, John tested tires by taking them to the top of a four-story building at the plant site, dropping them off the side of the building, and bouncing them on the pavement below. Later he drove two of his cars into a brick wall at 20 mph. When an employee asked why he did it, John said, "I might as well because someone else is going to do it when these cars get on the road."

But it wasn't only John and Horace's integrity or their manufacturing genius that captured my imagination. In my mind, theirs was also a love story. Whether it was drinking in their favorite bars (and paying for any damage when things got rowdy) or working in their creative "playpen" at their Dodge Main plant in Hamtramck, they adored each other and could not get enough of each other's company.

And I wanted to know, what must *that* feel like?

So, while working on the Dodge brothers' story, I decided to find out. Between shoots, I sat down and began doodling the book and lyrics to *The Brothers D*, an imagined musical about the brothers Dodge and the tremendous pull they felt for each other, especially considering their inability, I imagined, to feel and express the same kind of intimacy towards their wives, Matilda and Anna.

> ANNA
>
> The children missed you tonight. But they understood. I told them, "Your daddy is not like other people." Your father is an engineer, an inventor. An artist, I tell them.

> HORACE
> (lighting his cigar)
> I like the sound of that. Thank you.

> ANNA
>
> And Daddy can't help it if he prefers the company of his motors and his machines. And carousing at all hours. By the way, how is John?

> HORACE
> Fine. Splendid. He sends his regards.

> ANNA
> I'm sure he does.

"As Anna watches Horace reach in his vest pocket for his ever-present fountain pen and notepad," I wrote in the stage directions, "she watches helplessly as she sees his mind drift away from her so he can jot down his latest idea he wants to share with his brother. And in a tender, aching ballad, she asks her husband a question she already knows the answer to: 'Where Do You Go When I'm with You?'"

We Don't Do Teeth

Screenwriters talk about the value of "touches" to help characters express, in words or gestures, certain core aspects of their personalities. In Aaron Sorkin's hit TV series *The West Wing*, think President Bartlet's communications director Toby Ziegler, played by Richard Schiff, and his stress-relieving habit of bouncing a rubber ball against the wall. Or, in Clint Eastwood's harrowing 1993 film, *In the Line of Fire*, when Eastwood, as a veteran Secret Service agent, threatens to blow off the head of his longtime nemesis, John Malkovich, just as Malkovich is about to fall to his death. But instead of pleading for his life, Malkovich, who is clinging to the side of a building, defiantly raises his head to meet Eastwood's revolver and place the pistol firmly in his mouth. I *loved* that touch; it told me everything I needed to know about Malkovich's psychopathic character.

Although not nearly as dramatic, as far as our clients were concerned, HKO Media's touch was equally compelling. All two of them.

How the heck do we show cold? My intern asked when we were about to produce a fundraising video for the state's The Heat and Warmth Fund (THAW), known for its work informing low income residents how to receive help paying their heating bills during Michigan's harsh winter months. "Showing is important," I explained, "but the real question is, how can we make potential funders *feel* the cold and experience it for themselves?" My solution was to open the video with a completely white screen, and because we placed our camera in the driver's seat, viewers had a front-seat view of someone trying to scratch and scrape away the thick blanket of white snow and ice that enveloped the windshield. Brr!

HKO Media's second touch was not so much our ability to inform viewers about what our clients' products and services were *about* but also, and mainly, what they were *really* about.

For example, when the University of Michigan's School of Dentistry asked HKO Media to produce a marketing and fundraising video, I told the dean I wasn't sure if we could accept the assignment. "We don't do teeth," I told him with a less than straight face.

I wasn't playing hard to get, I just wanted him to know if we were going to help him sell his school's story, we'd have to do a little digging first to find out, on behalf of our target audience, more about the *experience* and *impact* of the school.

In other words, where was this story's hook, what was its *angle*?

This emphasis on theme over plot is one of the reasons why I believe HKO Media was so successful in competing with other production companies. In the end, our School of Dentistry video wasn't about teeth any more than *Miracle on Fort Street* was about singing or *The Deer Hunters* was about deer. Or *Michigan Football Memories*, our prime-time doc produced by my former interns Oliver Thornton and Alex Wright, which celebrated 125 years of University of Michigan football, was about football.

Eventually, my co-producer, Matt Prested, and I cracked the code and discovered the true value of U of M's School of Dentistry, what kept so many students, grads, and funders coming back for more. It turned out it wasn't just the school's worldwide reputation for restoring teeth; it had also received acclaim and recognition over the years for restoring so many of its client's *smiles*.

I wish I could take credit for such brilliance. I have always subscribed to E. L. Doctorow's thinking on storytelling. "Good writing," he cautioned us, "is supposed to invoke sensation in the reader—not the fact that it's raining, but the feeling of being rained upon."

I Could Stay at Home and Worry

I first met Detroit mayor Mike Duggan in 1990 when, as Wayne County's deputy executive under Ed McNamara, he invited me to present at a senior staff retreat to talk about how his administration could improve its communication and storytelling skills. "It's not hard," I told these movers and shakers, "all you have to do is find a way to make *your* story also feel like *theirs*."

Five years later Mike had a chance to test my theory when he asked HKO to produce a documentary-style television commercial that would encourage voters to support an upcoming millage that would help rescue the metro area's failing SMART trans-city/suburb bus system.

After pre-interviewing dozens of SMART riders, my intern, Alan Bernstein, and I spent a day riding one of the buses, taping what the SMART service meant to its passengers. "I go to the nursing home most every day to see my husband," an elderly woman who was visiting her ailing partner, told me on camera.

ELDERLY WOMAN (cont'd)

I could stay home and worry. When you call
them, they always tell you he's all right.

> But really, you don't know how he's doing
> until you go there and see him.

Needless to say, the millage passed with flying colors. *Nobody* wanted to be responsible for preventing the elderly bus lady from seeing her ailing husband.

The Perfect Balance of Urban Fashion

In pre-pandemic 2019, the national media couldn't write enough positive, even glowing, things about Detroit. Headlines reported the city was "in High Gear," "Detroit Revs Back to Life," "Is Detroit the Most Exciting City in America?" And one of the country's hottest new retail spots is called Détroit is the New Black, combining "minimalism and high street aesthetic to achieve the perfect balance of urban fashion."

It wasn't always so.

Riding a SMART bus, I get the message: "They can take away my keys, but they can't take away my bus."
(Photo by Ameen Howrani. Courtesy of Harvey Ovshinsky, HKO Media, and Bentley Historical Library.)

One of HKO Media's most successful promotional videos was *Heart of the City*, commissioned by Blue Cross Blue Shield of Michigan over twenty years ago to help support the efforts of the area's prominent civic organizations and corporations to reimagine and revitalize the city's East Riverfront and the downtown Campus Martius area.

In my *Fifth Estate* days, I covered my share of marches and protest demonstrations at the old Kennedy Square near Campus Martius. And later, when I reported the news for WABX, the jocks and I would often hang a microphone outside our studio on the thirty-third floor of the David Stott building so we could broadcast snippets of the speeches and passionate antiwar chants.

Today, Detroit's bustling Campus Martius area is the poster child for the city's latest attempts at revival. But back in the 1980s and 90s, it was a different story; in those days, downtown Detroit was essentially a ghost town, and except for the homeless and the few remaining downtown businessmen and women, Campus Martius was all but deserted.

Truthfully, I did not jump at the chance to tell this story.

Having lived through so many past failed attempts to revitalize Detroit's downtown, by this time I was more than a little doubtful about the chances for this project to succeed. How many times must we endure, I argued, year after year after year, the latest feel-good news reports touting the city's latest attempts at revival and then hear Detroit described by the national media as "a city on the verge" and "America's Comeback City."

"Don't get me wrong," I told Rick Cole, senior vice president in charge of communications at Blue Cross Blue Shield. "I'm still a fan; Catherine and I still have our autographed poster of the Noguchi Fountain at Hart Plaza framed and hanging in our living room. Call it buyers' remorse, Rick, but after all these years, I just don't believe it anymore."

And, I heard myself think, *I don't think anyone else does, either.*

Surprisingly, Rick wasn't at all offended by my reaction. "We need your skepticism on this project," he told me. "We need to convince lapsed Detroiters like you that *this* time we mean it, *this* time it's for real. Besides," he added, avoiding making eye contact, "I already told the folks at Detroit Renaissance you would do it."

And so, I did. But first I had to find a way to scratch this mother of all surfaces.

I had all the usual suspects: beauty shots of the city's Greektown, the riverfront fireworks, the People Mover downtown transportation system, the Motown Museum, Fox Theatre, and inspiring futuristic renderings of riverfront walking tours and bike paths. But it wasn't enough; there was an enormous hole in our story, and unless we could fill it, Rick and I agreed this campaign wouldn't be able to raise a dime.

Not this time, not if all Campus Martius was selling was bricks and mortar.

"Make me an offer," I challenged everyone I interviewed. "Forget the new bike paths and the ice-skating park; screw the sandcastles for the kiddies. Can you explain to me, from my own perspective, based my own needs and my own self-interest, why I should care, why *anyone* should care about what happens to Campus Martius?"

I was on a roll, but I had found no takers to pick up the baton, nobody who could find the magic words that would convince me to invest in the city's future. Yet again.

And then, on one of the last days of shooting, Matthew Cullen, then General Motors' general manager for economic development, delivered the goods. It took a while, and more than a little prodding on my part, but we finally found a perfect fit for Cinderella's missing shoe!

We're not writing this check for Detroit Renaissance or even the city, Cullen essentially said, all but reaching for his pen. "For me, this is personal."

```
              MATT (cont'd)
My kids are young right now. I've got three
young boys, but when they get older, I don't
want them to feel like, in order to be able
to experience an exciting urban area, that
they have to leave the city of Detroit. And
I think this [project] is a key enabler to
transforming the environment into one our
kids are going to be excited to stay in.
     (beat)
So I won't have to travel around the world
to find my kids.
```

If You Have an Apple and I Have an Apple

As much as I appreciated the creative challenges and the income generated by HKO's corporate and nonprofit work, the buzz on the street, and truthfully, in my own head, was who *is* this guy and what has he done with Harvey Ovshinsky? Has "the voice of Detroit's underground" lost his voice?

In other words, where were the docs? I found my answer when I decided to renew my relationships with my old friends and colleagues at the local television stations. It was a mutually beneficial collaboration between me and WDIV-TV, WXYZ-TV, WKBD-TV, and Detroit Public Television, and one that re-energized my career (and reputation) as a long-form documentary storyteller.

If you can call thirty minutes long-form. I would have preferred hour-long programs, but my broadcast partners could only afford to provide enough crews and airtime for half-hour shows.

My role in these co-productions was to come up with the idea and provide the support staff as well as my own services as writer, producer, and director. For its part, Detroit Public Television agreed to pay my salary while each of the commercial stations took turns providing the necessary production crews and editors, as well as agreeing to simulcast each of our programs on Detroit Public Television.

They also kept me supplied with videotape!

When I was at WXYZ, Woodruff enjoyed calling me out for shooting more footage than the station's other producers. At that time, my colleagues, especially in the newsroom, were shooting something like a five-to-one ratio, which meant they would end up using one minute of videotape for every five they shot. Not me. Despite my not-so-best best efforts to conserve, my ratio was, more often than not, notoriously ten or as much as fifteen to one. "If you keep this up," Woodruff would poke me, "we'll need more shelves."

"More like a new room," my editor, Tom Cleeves, chimed in, not at all exaggerating.

As much as I enjoyed the freedom and autonomy that came with having my own production company, the dirty little secret about independent filmmaking is that there is no such thing. It's why, as often as I have changed jobs, I always made a point of leaving without regrets or burned bridges, cognizant of George Bernard Shaw's theory about the collaborative nature of the creative process: "If you have an apple and I have an apple and we exchange these apples then you and I will still each have one apple. But if you have an idea and I have an idea and we exchange these ideas, then each of us will have two ideas."

That's how I have always felt about partnering with others, and not just with the TV stations, but also with area production and post-production houses and the dozens of freelance crew members who stepped up and contributed to the cause.

And not just mine, but theirs, too.

My need has always been to find the financing and crews that would enable me to produce my city tales, but the TV stations also had a need of their own. They were eager to, with very little investment on their part, co-produce highly visible, award-winning broadcast docs that would attract both viewers and the attention of the mainstream and trade media. Not to mention, in those days, they wanted to satisfy the Federal Communications Commission's mandate to generate a certain amount of locally produced programming that spoke to the needs of the greater community.

Everyone pitched in. Area videographers, audio and lighting people, and stagehands were especially appreciative of the freelance work. "It beats working on instructional videos about glove compartments," Mark Adler, who frequently provided video assist and playback on my shoots, remarked.

Which brings us to my First Most Important First Rule of Independent Filmmaking: funders and production partners will rarely participate in a project unless it satisfies their need, helps solve their problem.

Their problem, their need. Not ours.

That's how my doc *Close to Home: The Tammy Boccomino Story* got funded. Although Frank Newman, president of F&M Distributing, didn't know me from Adam, he was motivated to have his company invest in a doc that dealt with the AIDS crisis, a cause he and his family were deeply engaged in and committed to.

But here's the challenge: the "personal or professional interest" part only applies if the connection is a *direct* one. Secondhand relationships rarely count.

I learned that the hard way.

The Second Most Important First Rule

When I invited fellow Michigander Jeff Daniels to stretch his directing muscles and attach himself to my first screenplay, I thought I did everything right: I talked to his pal, *Free Press* columnist Bob Talbert, who not only told me what to say but gave me Jeff's best mailing address. "And make sure you tell him you and I are buds!"

It was all very exciting. In my care package, I told Jeff that I was a fan of his work (long before he starred in HBO's *The Newsroom*, Showtime's *The Comey*

Rule, and on Broadway in *To Kill a Mockingbird*), and I made sure I was not asking him to act but to direct my screenplay. As Talbert instructed, I also dropped his name and included a synopsis and a script and, most importantly, the standard industry release that assured Jeff he could read my masterpiece without fear of being sued.

The good news is that I heard from Jeff right away.

The bad news is my screenplay was returned to me unopened with a form letter that essentially told me I was an idiot for even trying to reach Daniels without going through his "people," either his agent or his manager, as I recall. Jeff may be a lovely fellow, and I look forward to one day working with his people at the Purple Rose Theatre in his hometown of nearby Chelsea, Michigan, but thirty years ago, "his people" blew me off.

So, learned the hard way, here's the Second Most Important First Rule of Independent Filmmaking: The next time you ask for help or a favor on a passion project, make sure the request is going to someone you have a personal or professional relationship with and, short of that, that they at least have a personal or professional interest or stake in the subject matter of your project.

That's the key. That's the rain, as my father used to say, that'll make the rhubarb grow.

Stayin' Alive

We can't all be Spike Lee, Aaron Sorkin, Ken Burns. Or Steven Spielberg. When, despite our best efforts, the pickings are slim and the work dries up, sometimes we mortals have to go whole hog. When butchers do it, they use every part of the pig, snout to tail, and, in some countries, some parts of the animal that aren't so readily available. It sounds gross, I know, but going whole hog is what we often have to do to stay sharp and stretch new creative muscles.

Not to mention keep the lights on.

It's not brain surgery; going whole hog simply means we identify each of our own unique and distinctive talents and skillset and then go out in the world to seek out anyone who might have a use or need for them.

But here's the trick: once again, the solution has to satisfy *their* need, not ours. In the land of whole hog, our success, more likely than not, will be the result of solving somebody else's problems.

And not only our own.

Sharing what playwright John Patrick Shanley calls "all these parts of yourself," is one of the main reasons I managed to endure and survive so many creative dry spells and painfully fallow periods. For example, to help augment my income from my work at the television stations, I began producing documentary- and testimonial-style commercials for corporate and nonprofit clients on the side. And after that, I put my interviewing skills to work on the radio, hosting *Harvey O on the Metro*, a Friday night talk show on Detroit's public radio station, WDET-FM. And in between, the Sunday night call-in program *Nightcall* (pre-Peter Werbe), and later, a new version of my old *Spare Change* program on WRIF-FM.

Radio came naturally to me, mainly because the work wasn't too much different than what I was attempting to do on television and, before that, in print with the *Fifth Estate*. "Who are you?" I would ask my guests. "How are we the same? How are we different? How can we better understand and communicate with each other?"

My radio conversation with Santa Claus is a good example. One Christmas, I booked Bernie (now Father Joseph) Marquis, Hudson's best-ever Thanksgiving Day Parade Father Christmas. Considering the trouble Michael Jackson was in that year as a result of newly surfaced accusations of child abuse (back when his people insisted Jackson was only *sleeping* with children), I asked Santa what he thought he should give the King of Pop this year. I was sure Bernie would have to think about that one, but I was wrong. "The benefit of the doubt," Santa said without missing a beat. "We could all use some this time of year, Harvey. Don'tcha think?"

Of course, that was then. Today, I'm certain both my question and Santa's answer would be entirely different. And, I suspect, at the risk of speaking for Santa Claus, less forgiving.

C'mon Fellas, I Don't Pay You to Stand Around All Day and Do Nothing

Going whole hog helps, but what do we do when our inspiration dries up and our muses go all AWOL on us?

That's when I call in the cavalry.

Charles Dickens had his stash of good-luck amulets consisting of "bronze toads, a green vase, and the statuette of an eccentric dog salesman surrounded by his pups." Children's author Andrea Beaty called her lucky charms her "desk

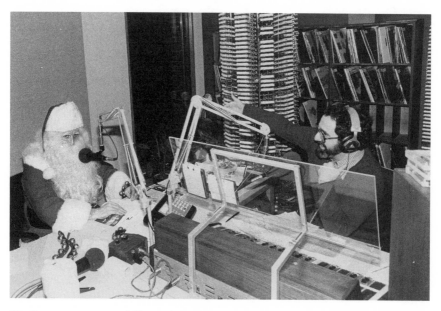

Honing my interview skills on the radio.
(Photo by Michael N. Marks. Courtesy of Harvey Ovshinsky, WRIF-FM, and
Bentley Historical Library.)

clan." My own power tchotchkes of choice are a miniature army of Lionel train construction workers I put to work digging, drilling, and pounding away at my blank computer screen. In one of my favorite scenes from my second screenplay, *The Keyman*, Sarah Doner, a once-successful screenwriter touted as "Detroit's answer to Nora Ephron," now a recovering alcoholic, lashes out at her own cast of toy miniature supporting characters for not helping her find the words.

                    SARAH
        C'mon fellas, give me a hint.
            (beat)
        I don't pay you to stand around all day and
        do nothing.

As comforting as my sacred objects are, I have found my most dependable collaborator and staunchest ally is my own unconscious mind. Whenever I find my gears stuck in Nowhere Fast, I convene a staff meeting of both my "un" and "overly" conscious minds to try and resolve the problem.

When we lived in downtown Detroit, I enjoyed jogging with my friend Ike McKinnon, a graduate of the FBI Academy who later became Detroit's chief of police and deputy mayor. But unfortunately, those jaunts were rarely productive because whenever my old friend spotted something suspicious going on in our neighborhood, he'd want to chase after bad guys. I never got a lot of work done during my staff meetings with Ike.

Eventually, I discovered the best opportunities for accessing my unconscious came while I was sleeping. By nature, I am a daytime person, happy to be in bed by 10:00 or 11:00 p.m. at the latest. But when I find myself hopelessly stumped or preoccupied, I often find myself bolting out of bed in the middle of the night. I used to try to shake it off and return to sleep, but not anymore. Instead, I head for my home office, seized with a new idea or a solution to a problem that I didn't even know I had. I transcribe the instructions in my head, and only after I've sapped myself of all creative thoughts do I return to bed, totally spent and exhausted.

The best part of these late-night and early morning brainstorms is that when I wake up the next morning and return to my desk, it's brimming with the results of all the heavy lifting my shoemaker's elves did for me while I was snoozing.

Catherine used to be alarmed by my nocturnal adventures, but now, whenever she expresses her concern about how many minutes these disruptions in my sleep cycle will take off my life, I remind her what Malcolm Forbes said: "People who never get carried away should be."

"Not funny," she says, waving me off before returning to her sleep.

That's Not an Artist. That's a Junkman

When she played Detroit in the early seventies, Bette Midler told her adoring audience how impressed she was with the city because she never met so many people who, in her words, "knew how to make the best of such an impossible situation." We laughed because it was true; in Detroit that's how we roll.

And to prove it, in 1990, HKO Media, along with our production partners WDIV and Detroit Public Television, produced *The Voodoo Man of Heidelberg Street*, a documentary about Tyree Guyton, a self-styled "proponent of graffiti art and urban environmental art." Tyree made headlines in the late 1980s when he tried to make the best out of his own impossible situation by waging a one-man war against the devastating blight that was destroying his east side Detroit neighborhood.

Tyree's solution? To hang old children's bicycles, broken dolls, and other found objects on the outside of Heidelberg's abandoned houses, and to paint polka dots and other wacky shapes and designs on what was left of the decaying sidewalks and streets. Even the mailboxes weren't safe from Tyree's brush.

"Hell," he told me, "I'd paint the damn trees if I could."

Other docs may have been produced about Tyree's work, but *Voodoo Man* was the first and, as far as I know, the only one that taped a rare interview with Tyree's mentor and biggest fan, his grandfather and fellow artist, Sam Mackey. "People wouldn't come through the street here, it was so bad," Grandpa told me. "But now it's clean, people coming through here who never been here before, who didn't know there was a short street named Heidelberg."

But not everyone agreed with Grandpa or Tyree's stone soup approach to beautifying their neighborhood. "I think Mr. Guyton is crazy," Conrad Herndon from the McDougall-Hunt District Council told me. "First of all, Mr. Guyton is not a self-appointed garbage collector. You have garbage cans, you have toilet stools, you have old douche bags, things of that nature. That's not art, that's not an artist. That's a junkman!"

The critics disagreed.

"Bold Art Is Riveting in Local Special" was the headline in the *Free Press* review of *The Voodoo Man of Heidelberg Street*. It's "a lively new film with not a dull moment." The Michigan chapter of the National Academy of Television Arts & Sciences agreed, awarding *Voodoo Man* a regional Emmy. In addition to being broadcast, special screenings of the film were held at venues like the Charles H. Wright Museum of African American History, the Detroit Institute of Arts, and the *Imaging Detroit* conference presented by the Metropolitan Observatory for Digital Culture and Representation (MODCaR). Working on *Voodoo Man* was a treat, not only because of how impressed I was with Tyree's commitment to making a difference in his community but because of how he managed to create his own solution to the myriad of seemingly hopeless problems confronting his neighborhood.

Tyree and Grandpa's creativity reminded me of the classic joke about two brothers who wake up one morning to find themselves stuck in a roomful of horse manure. All one child can do is wail and moan and pull his hair out.

Tyree Guyton, the Voodoo Man of Heidelberg Street, *with me, cinematographer Kevin Hewitt, audio engineer Jim Howard, and intern Diane Blasciuc. (Photo by Santa Fabio. Courtesy of HKO Media, WTVS Detroit Public Television, and WDIV-Local 4/Graham Media Group.)*

But the other brother, instead of whining and complaining and howling at the wind, immediately gets busy *doing* something about the impossibility of their situation. He claws, he digs, and with his bare hands he scratches and scrapes the shit away, determined to find the one thing he was certain was missing from this picture.

"What are you *doing?*" screams his brother. "Can't you see we're stuck in a room of horse manure?"

"Yes!" his brother squeals with delight. "And there must be a pony!"

For as long as I can remember, that's how I have felt about stories.

Pigeonholes Are for Pigeons

I once asked my father why he didn't pack up his alternative energy company and move to Silicon Valley. Dad had his reasons for staying, among them, what he called the "freedom, excitement, and dynamism" he found in his adopted city. Not one for false modesty, my father was also determined to see his sea-changing hydrogen storage and nickel-metal hydride battery technology "save the auto industry from itself."

My own reasons for staying were less altruistic.

Most artists are infatuated with their models, inspired by their charm, beauty, and splendor. Not me. Although I have always identified with my hometown's wounds, its "brokenness," in my mind that was always my city's sizzle.

Not its steak.

Nobel Prize–winning Yiddish author Isaac Bashevis Singer wrote that "every writer needs an address." For me, living and working in a city like Detroit, so famous for its genetically encoded, apocalypse-resistant survival gene, has been great practice for how to endure the tumultuous peaks and valleys and challenges that come from attempting to live a creative life.

Still, there was a time when I actively resisted being called a Detroit film-maker. "Pigeonholes are for pigeons," I told myself, concerned the label might mark me as being simply a one-trick pony, a musician who only knew how to play one note, tell only one kind of story.

It's not an unfamiliar issue for artists who stay true to their own passions and are guided by the glow of their own North Star. "I've been told that maybe I shouldn't focus so much on race," Brooklyn artist Alexandra Bell told the *New York Times* about her reputation for creating only mixed media works that went "against the dominant narrative put forth in the news. Art people try to get me to diversify my work . . . so I won't be seen as the 'race girl' in the art world."

Bell's success with what some critics called her "preoccupation" was heartening, but it was Detroit crime novelist Elmore Leonard who helped me snap out of it. For years, Hollywood producers teased Leonard about his insistence on not moving to L.A. "Eventually they stopped bothering me," he told me, "because they figured, 'Well, maybe he knows something we don't.'"

Years ago, I tried to explain this intense pull I have for the mother planet to Scott Simon, but the host of NPR's *Weekend Edition Saturday* was aghast. "Look around you, Harvey," he said. "I see a decimated, burned-out community. I see Beirut. I see a city in despair. What can you possibly see that I don't?"

"It's out there, Scott," I told him. "You just have to know where to look."

I'm not saying I've never succumbed to a bout of city envy or been tempted to heed the siren's call to become a bigger fish in a larger pond. Thirty-five years ago, when my friend Bill Pace left Detroit with his fellow producer Ronnie Clemmer to follow their dream of making movies in Hollywood with their new company, Longbow Productions, I was crushed. And for a while, I allowed myself to wallow in my regret that I wasn't willing to make the personal and professional sacrifices necessary to make the move.

Still, no regrets. I come from the Jeanette Pierce school of grow where you're planted. This town, said the executive director of the Detroit Experience Factory touring company, "is big enough to matter in the world and small enough for you to matter in it."

17

The Elephant in the Room

Although he was not superstitious, one of my father's favorite expressions was, "In the house of the hanged one does not speak of rope." That's how I have always felt about Detroit and the issue of race. Only in this town you can't be a filmmaker or a storyteller of any kind and *not* speak of it.

The First Hurrah, HKO Media's co-production with WDIV and Detroit Public Television, gave me a chance to attack the elephant in the room because in this film about two friends, one white and one Black, vying for the presidency of the University of Detroit Jesuit High School senate, race permeated almost every frame. It was both inspiring and painful to watch Sam and Laith compete for the office as they tried to hold on to their friendship and attempt to protect their "base." It wasn't easy, trying not to offend while questioning the merits of playing football versus "a white man's sport" like lacrosse and debating whose music should be played at school dances, rock 'n' roll or house music.

"I wouldn't say this race is about racism," Kendall Buhl, the editor of U of D's school paper, told me, "as much as race consciousness. For many students it will be very hard to look at the two candidates and not have that little voice in the back of their heads that says it's a Black candidate or this is a white. And the second they become conscious of that, it becomes impossible to not to have that become, for right or wrong, a part of the decision process."

In 1990, I got another chance to attack the elephant.

I was no stranger to Grosse Pointe's infamous "point system," the "systematic process of discrimination," according to the digital news magazine *Metromode*, "practiced by realtors between 1945 and 1960 which assigned a point value to prospective property owners based on appearance, race and ethnicity." In other words, if you had "swarthy skin," you were assigned a certain amount of points, ditto if you had an accent. And if you were Jewish, or worse, Black, and you were looking to buy in Grosse Pointe, your score was off the charts.

"These people are the worst kind of racists," my father would remind my brothers and me when we would conduct our meetings driving down Lakeshore Drive in the "exclusive" east side suburb. "They don't just discriminate against Negroes and Jews; they have to write it down. And make it official."

So, when it came time for HKO Media and Detroit Public Television to choose a story for our co-production with WXYZ-TV, I jumped at the chance to tell the story of how on March 14, 1968, just three weeks before he was assassinated, a war-weary Dr. Martin Luther King Jr. brought his message of peace and racial tolerance to the house of the hanged.

"I was a student at Grosse Pointe South High School at the time, and when I told my parents I was wanted to hear Dr. King speak," my friend and production cohort Bill Pace told me in the doc, "my father got very angry and told me, 'If you go, don't bother coming back.' When I returned, my father kicked me out of the house."

"We received all kinds of threats," organizer Jude Huetteman told the *Detroit Free Press* of the Grosse Pointe Human Relations Council's decision to invite the country's most revered civil rights leader to Grosse Pointe. "Still, we felt it was important for our community to proceed and hear what Dr. King had to say."

It was a packed house: twenty-seven hundred people crammed into the gymnasium of what was then Grosse Pointe High School, now Grosse Pointe South, to hear Dr. King speak about his vision of what he called the "other America" where white people could confront the truth of their racism and have the courage to do something about it.

When Dr. King appeared on the stage, he appeared gaunt and tired. Still, Jude recalled for the *Free Press*, "the audience came to their feet with a cheer and a roar that could have been heard a mile away. This continued for five minutes and he hasn't even spoken!"

Unfortunately, Dr. King's reception outside the gymnasium was a different story. Two hundred angry demonstrators picketed the event carrying signs and chanting slogans like "America Forever, Communism Never," "King is a Traitor," and "Burn Traitors Not Flags."

"These were not Grosse Pointers," Jude assured me and my co-director, Dennis Carnevale, laying the blame on Breakthrough, a fervently right-wing, anti-communist group whose members prided themselves on their version of patriotism and showed up to embarrass her group and heckle Dr. King. And they almost succeeded, especially when several protestors made their way inside the gym and started shouting at Dr. King during his speech.

It was disturbing to all in attendance, including Dr. King, but the disruption shouldn't have been a surprise. "In those days," journalist Bill McGraw recalled, "Breakthrough didn't just target lefty protestors with its vitriol, but also progressive Catholics, judges, professors, and anyone the group determined were too pink."

"I have to hand it to them," I told Peter Werbe during our *Fifth Estate* days, "they're persistent." Every time we held a demonstration, regardless of the issue, we could count on Breakthrough to show up to protest our protests. We expected that, but for me the most striking thing about the group was that they were even angrier and more strident than we were. And, when they felt like it, more violent. We couldn't prove it, but Peter and I were certain it was Breakthrough that in 1966 shattered the plate glass windows of our *Fifth Estate* offices at 1107 West Warren.

Other than the time I taped President Bush gushing about my socialist father at ECD's United Solar plant, surely the strangest, most out-of-body experience I have ever had was the day I sat down for a one-on-one interview with Breakthrough's leader, the notorious Donald Lobsinger, for *The Night Martin Luther King Jr. Came to Grosse Pointe*.

And I think he felt it, too.

"This must be what it would have felt like," my old nemesis beamed, as amused as he was impressed with the unreality of the situation, "if General Rommel ever had a chance to sit down with Patton."

"Yes, Don," I replied, feeling more than a little uneasy about this awkward disruption in the space-time continuum. And yet I was sickened by his lack of regret for his behavior and the smugness he exuded out of every pore when he spoke with pride of the intense pleasure he felt at having the opportunity to harass Dr. King.

> HARVEY (cont'd)
> But which one of us is Rommel and which one
> of us is Patton?

The interview with Lobsinger was great television and, in addition to excerpts from Dr. King's speech which drove the narrative, provided *The Night Martin*

Luther King Jr. Came to Grosse Pointe with one of the doc's most dramatic and compelling moments. And yet, when it aired, I cringed at my success, reminding myself that despite the shocking impact of his presence in my story, it was precisely the words and actions of racists like Lobsinger and so many others that led to Dr. King's murder in Memphis less than a month after he spoke in Grosse Pointe.

Burn traitors. Not flags.

18

I Hope You Have Stock in Kleenex

"I'm just glad you're on our side," Tammy Boccomino told me after a grueling interview during the taping of *Close to Home: The Tammy Boccomino Story*, HKO Media's co-production with WKBD-TV. "I hope you have stock in Kleenex," the suburban AIDS activist said, after she finished weeping on camera over the guilt she felt for having passed on her undiagnosed HIV virus (from her first husband) to her young son while she was pregnant with him.

"I am tired, I am so tired of doing presentations," she told me. "But I don't care anything about me."

```
            TAMMY (cont'd)
   I don't feel my aches and pains at night. I
   don't feel how tired I am. I'll stay up
   until midnight just to get the laundry done
   so the boys can have an outfit they want to
   wear or get their birthday presents done
   because I don't care about me. I caused
   this. And my family, my children, are my
   whole life. And without my children I don't
   have a life. I don't want a life without my
   boys because they are my dreams. And it's
   something that I did, and I will spend the
   rest of my life making it up to them.
        (beat)
   And I will spend the rest of my life
   changing the world for them.
```

Tammy's story was one of two documentaries HKO Media and its partners produced in the 1980s and 90s about how people infected with HIV and AIDS struggled to live with their disease. And, at the time, with the very real possibility of dying from it.

But here's a surprise, and I've found the best stories always have at least one: as powerful and compelling a speaker as Tammy was, I found myself curiously drawn to Tammy's second husband, Brian Volante. "Did she tell you guys I was an asshole?" he asked my intern Adam Woloszyk and me while we were setting up for his interview.

No, but he sure did.

"It wasn't a good time in our lives," Brian confessed on camera, recalling how he reacted when he found out Tammy had been unknowingly infected with HIV from her first husband and had passed it on to their own son, Michael.

```
            BRIAN (cont'd)
  I definitely had a drinking problem. I didn't
  care about anybody but myself. I went where
  I wanted to go, I did what I wanted to do,
  and I didn't care. I didn't care what Tammy
  thought. I didn't care. I'd leave at six
  o'clock in the morning, and if I wanted
  to come home at midnight, I came home at
  midnight.
```

I suspect my crew, John Ciolino and Gerry Treas, and even my editor, Christine Zampa, were surprised I spent as much time with Brian as I did, but the old writer's adage is true: when you write about a good man, look for the bad in him; if you're writing about a bad man, look for the good in him.

Which is why, in my interviews, even though I burn through more tape than I can often afford, I never mind going fishing; I'm always on the lookout for opportunities that might lead me and viewers to discover the unexpected twists, turns, reveals, and reversals that can help make a good story great.

It's why at the end of *Close to Home*, just before we dipped to black after watching Tammy, as we expected, being embraced by several of the high school students she had been speaking to, viewers had to fight back even more tears as they watched Brian, the self-described asshole, tenderly help his young son brush his teeth and get ready for school, while in voice-over, he recalls how coping with his wife's and Michael's illness has changed him. "We're all working together now," Brian tells us. "[*When*] Michael goes to the doctor, *I* go. I'm 'Doctor Dad.' Michael will only let me take out his IV. Geez, I couldn't imagine doing that myself a year ago!"

I love all my children, but of all my docs, *Close to Home* attracted the most attention, receiving a national Emmy for Community Service, an Iris Award for public affairs programming from the National Association of Television Program Executives (NATPE), the American Film Institute's Robert M. Bennett Award for Excellence, and the George Foster Peabody Award for "informing and educating without sentimentality or sensationalism."

Somebody once asked me what I've learned from telling so many stories that focus on other people's problems and struggles. "Very little," I responded. "Which is why I don't focus on the problems; it's the solutions that bring me to the table."

Suddenly, All These Beepers Started Going Off

Our second "AIDS doc" was *Tony & Friends: A Celebration of Life*, in collaboration with Detroit Public Television and my friends at WXYZ-TV, including my co-director Dennis Carnevale and my intern, Jill Buchanan.

"From the time when you find out that you're infected until the onset of AIDS can be anywhere from a week to fifteen years," Tony Caputo, the director of volunteer wellness services at Detroit's Wellness House told me. "The problem is," he explained, "you can't die for fifteen years."

```
              TONY (cont'd)
Dying actually only takes about thirty
seconds. There's a whole period from the
point of finding out to the point of death
that you can live. At some point I had to say
to myself, "You could die, little kids die,
old people die, people in their forties die,
everybody dies. And although I don't want to
die, I'm not afraid of dying. I'm afraid of
all the stuff in between."
```

The twist, the unexpected surprise in *Tony & Friends,* was not only how wise and compassionate Tony and his staff of volunteers were with their clients and with each other, but also, considering his own painful struggle with the HIV virus, how incredibly *funny* Tony was.

TONY

I was at a funeral just last fall and there was *all* guys, and this man's family was seated up front. And we were all sitting in back. It's seven o'clock and what happens? Suddenly all these beepers started going off. It was like eight guys and six beepers go off! And everyone's reaching for their pockets to see if it's their beepers and like, grabbing for their pills. It was like so weird, just *so* weird.

Riding High

The 1990s were peak years for HKO Media. The money was good, the collaborations rewarding, and we started to receive more and more national attention for our cinematic short stories. I just hope my friend and fellow Detroit filmmaker, Academy Award winner Sue Marx, has forgiven me, considering she passed on one of my next projects. In 1994, HKO Media was the recipient of a duPont-Columbia University Silver Baton for excellence in television and radio journalism for *The Last Hit: Children and Violence*, a half-hour exploration about how kids of all ages and backgrounds manage to cope with the threat or personal experience of violence in their lives.

"I wanted to do it," Sue confessed later. "But I knew I couldn't tell the story with a production budget of only ten thousand dollars."

Our solution? "No visuals," my brilliant co-producer, Char DeWolf, and I agreed. "We won't shoot any B-roll. Except for the opening title sequence, we'll spend all our money on talking heads. Talking, beautiful, and articulate heads."

"Sometimes, simple works best," wrote Mike Duffy in his review for the *Free Press.* "*The Last Hit*'s moments of heartbreaking candor . . . pack an eloquent wallop. No psychologists, no fevered video recreations of bloody moments, just children talking."

And talk they did. "I'm used to violence in my neighborhood," ten-year-old Micah told me, "because I've seen all these killings. It's been going on for years in my life. Ever since I was four, I knew all about it."

The success of *The Last Hit* was particularly satisfying for me because our next doc for Children's Hospital gave me the opportunity, for the first time, to work with Catherine, and to take advantage of her expertise as a nurse therapist on such projects as films about childhood grief, depression, and the struggle many medical professionals face in learning how to deliver bad news to sick children and their families. Our work with Children's Hospital of Michigan taught me a valuable lesson: if you want to know the truth about an event or situation, *any* event or situation, ask a child. In their naïveté and their innocence, in their inability to tell a lie, I have found young people to be among the best experts, the most reliable "third eye" witnesses a documentary director could ask for.

"Did you know," five-year-old Aaron asked me at the beginning of our interview for *The Last Hit*, "Michael Jordan's dad got shot?"

> HARVEY
> How did you feel when he got shot?

> AARON
> Bad.

> HARVEY
> How come? Did you know him?

> AARON
> I never talked to him except I felt bad that
> his own father died.
>   (beat)
> Imagine your own father dying. Would *you*
> feel happy that he died?

Part 4

Impossible Is Hard

19

In Hollywood, I Learn What My Problem Is

My grandson Toby, who likes to scribble with crayons and chalk, has recently discovered finger painting, which makes perfect sense because, like his Nappa, young Toby isn't fussy about which medium he expresses himself in.

Newspapers were fun, but then radio spoke to me. And then television. And then teaching. And then came *P. J. and the Dragon*.

My first screenplay was a painful delivery. Not so much the writing of the script as how long it took for me to pull the trigger and make the decision to engage in the project in the first place. "If you spent half the time writing your movies," Catherine reminded me one morning, "as you do complaining about how you don't have the time to do it, you'd have written half a dozen scripts by now!"

She was right, of course. Catherine generally is about such things.

One of my favorite movies growing up was George Pal's Cinerama production of *The Wonderful World of the Brothers Grimm*. As much as I enjoyed the stop-motion animation, what really struck and has stayed with me ever since was a pivotal scene revealed late in the film.

When Wilhelm Grimm is sick with fever, he's awakened by a late-night visit from a giant peering through his window. The giant is joined by Rumpelstiltskin, Little Red Riding Hood, and so many other beloved Grimm Brothers characters, all urging him not to die. You can't stop now, they implore, because if you die, "who will name us and tell our stories?"

Good question. It's why, in 1984, I finally decided to get off my ass and pull an Elmore Leonard. In his early pulp Western days, Detroit's master novelist and screenwriter forced himself to wake up at five thirty in the morning every day so he could write his books and get his characters and their stories off his chest before going off to his day job at a local advertising agency.

Of Dragons' Wings and Children's Dreams

My father used to say baby steps were for babies, and normally I would agree, but in deciding which story I should tackle for my first screenplay, I realized baby steps were *exactly* the kind I needed to get the job done. Which is why my first movie script was based on a true story. That way, at least I could call on my documentary skills to interview the real-life characters and at least give the *impression* I knew what I was doing.

It was *Detroit Free Press* columnist Jim Fitzgerald who, in his columns, introduced me to the real-life adventures of a "magic dragon" and how it helped a young boy named P. J. Dragan cope during his painful treatments for his newly diagnosed leukemia. P. J.'s dragon wasn't an invisible friend; it was an anonymous benefactor who lived up to their reputation by sending heartfelt cards and letters to P. J. and leaving dragon stickers for the youngster whenever P. J. went to the hospital for his tests and treatments.

Another screenwriter might have focused on the relationship between young P. J. and his secret admirer, and in my magical thinking days I might have considered it, but that was too obvious and on the nose for my taste. In deciding to write *P. J. and the Dragon*, I had bigger fish to fry.

I wanted to write about the parents.

In my script, P. J.'s mother, Sharon, was a Betty Crocker–type mom who eagerly supported her son's belief in his magical friend, but P. J.'s father, Paul Dragan, a hardened Detroit cop, did not.

```
                        PAUL
        You can swallow this crap if you want to,
        Sharon, knock yourself out. But I will not
        allow some stranger to put his happy face on
        my son's cancer.


                       SHARON
        Her.


                        PAUL
        What?
```

```
                    SHARON
    You said "his." You don't know.
        (beat)
    Maybe he's a she.
```

Fortunately, by the end of the movie, Paul comes around just in time to help Sharon and other families from "the cancer clinic" make their own magic by starting a nonprofit childhood cancer research organization they called Leukemia, Research, Life (LRL). Largely due to the publicity generated by news of P. J.'s magic dragon, both in the screenplay and real life, LRL ended up raising over three million dollars, starting with a benefit at the popular Checker Bar in downtown Detroit.

"I suppose chances are good that P. J.'s magic dragon will be at the Checker party," Fitzgerald wrote in one of his columns, "but no one except the dragon will know for sure. All brands of charity and kindness are fine but the giver who refuses to take a bow rates a special seat in heaven."

Not You, Just Your Script

As helpful as Michael Hauge's screenwriting workshop and books like Syd Field's *Screenplay: The Foundations of Screenwriting* are, what most scriptwriting gurus don't tell you is the hardest part for first-time screenwriters: the suffering they will have to endure to find an agent, *any* agent to peddle their masterpiece. It's why in my own screenwriting classes and workshops, I always save that particular dose of reality until the last session.

Which is why I am embarrassed to say how easy it was for me to find an agent for *P. J. and the Dragon.*

Ralph Mann was a co-founder of International Creative Management (ICM), one of the industry's largest and most prestigious talent agencies. In addition to Mort Crim, Ralph represented television news rock stars like Jane Pauley, Tom Brokaw, and *60 Minutes* creator Don Hewitt. "The little people," I once teased Mort.

Whenever he was in town, Ralph was most often seen around WDIV chomping on his cigar. He was always friendly to me when we bumped into each other in the hall, but the one conversation that stands out most in my memory is a remark he whispered to me in the control room on the night of the first *Free4All* taping.

"This," he said excitedly, pointing to the monitor as he watched Mort spar with the panel, "is what we've been waiting for. So, Harvey," Ralph continued as he left the control room to watch Mort from the studio, "if there's ever anything I can do for you . . ."

Weeks later, I took Ralph up on his offer when I wrote to him asking for his help in securing an agent for *P. J. and the Dragon*. He responded almost immediately, saying that, although he knew little about what he called "theatrical properties," he would certainly see what he could do to help me find someone in that department at ICM to help me out.

It turned out that someone was Nancy Josephson, the daughter of his partner, the company's co-founder, Marvin Josephson, who immediately invited me to visit her in New York so we could discuss her plans to represent me.

"Not you," she corrected me. "Just your script."

Months later, when Nancy couldn't find a buyer for what some production companies insisted on calling "the leukemia script," I eventually optioned *P. J.* to my friend and colleague Bill Pace, who had since moved to Los Angeles to start his own production company, Longbow Productions.

Less than a year later, when just about every television actress who was anyone in Hollywood "passed" on the role of Sharon, the hot, up-and-coming Emma Samms stepped up. I wish I could say she was in awe of my prowess as a first-time screenwriter. But that wasn't why Emma said yes.

Oh, she liked my script well enough, but the real reason she agreed to attach herself to the project was that in *P. J. and the Dragon*, she found a script that satisfied a personal need of hers.

Actually, two.

In Emma's newly negotiated contract, ABC was committed to provide her with opportunities to star in several made-for-television movies. And with her *Dynasty* hiatus coming up, she was eager to find a script with her name on it.

But what *really* mattered to her, and why Emma agreed to star in *P. J. and the Dragon*, was the subject matter. Like P. J., her younger brother, Jamie, died at age nine of a deadly blood disease, in his case, aplastic anemia.

Unfortunately, despite Emma's attachment and Michael Gross (*Family Ties*), Tony Danza (*Who's the Boss?*), and fellow Detroiter Max Gail (*Barney Miller*) vying for the part of Paul Dragan, Bill and I never found a network interested in taking up P. J.'s dragon's invitation to soar with him "on dragons' wings and children's dreams and wishes that come true."

"Do you know what your problem is, Harvey?" one producer told me, trying to be helpful after agreeing to read *P. J. and the Dragon*. "Your problem is you write with too much heart. And not enough edge." When I told this to my screenwriter friend and fellow Detroiter Kurt Luedtke (*Out of Africa*, *Absence of Malice*, *Random Hearts*), he was sympathetic but not at all surprised.

"I hope you thanked them for the compliment."

The Pride of Detroit

As much as I loved Leslie Payne's story from one of my last WDIV docs, *Visions in Bubblegum, Canvas & Stone*, it never occurred to me to write a screenplay based on his life. Even before the current hot-potato era of political correctness and cultural appropriation, I knew I had neither the chops nor the interest it would take to get inside the head of Payne, an all-but-illiterate impoverished Northumberland County, Virginia, fisherman with a fourth-grade education.

Besides, I had an even more fantastical tale to tell.

William Faulkner once said, "If a story is in you, it has got to come out." That's how I felt about my need to use my story crush on Leslie Payne as a vehicle to imagine a return, a second chance to resolve, at least on paper, some of the struggles I endured in my childhood.

My first drafts were a bust. I tried writing a movie about missing fathers, broken mothers, and the combined powers of language and magical thinking to help heal and reconcile. But the story ended up being too literal and way too faithful to my own, and it stalled and refused to take off. I should have known; it's what happens when you try to tell a story that's so personal and self-serving that it resists holding anybody's interest and attention other than your own.

So, I pretended I was a writer. And decided to make stuff up.

I started by remembering an incident when my father, while he was still living with us, warned my brothers and me not to, under *any* circumstances, visit or hang out at an old, dilapidated house around the block from us. "The man who lives there is disturbed. You have to promise never to go there."

So naturally we went.

And I stayed because thirty-five years later, in 1988, I sat down and wrote the second draft of my second screenplay, *The Keyman*. I was determined to find out who lived in that mysterious house on Forrer Street. And what could have possibly happened to its occupant that made him so disturbed?

And to find out, I turned to an old Shel Silverstein poem about the whispering what-ifs.

What if, I wondered, a once successful but now recovering alcoholic Hollywood screenwriter finds herself returning to her hometown of Detroit to bury her mother with whom she's been estranged for years? And while she is there, what if Sarah Doner uses the opportunity to visit her old neighborhood, where she recalls and then attempts to resolve a painful and lingering childhood memory?

And *what if* the Leslie Payne–inspired character was the neighborhood's notorious "keyman" who rode around Sarah's neighborhood on a large, adult tricycle, ringing his bell and frantically shouting out offers to sharpen knives and make keys for people, "Fourforadollar! Fourforadollar!"

Only *what if* this ailing, seemingly crazed African American man decked out in a tattered World War II flight jacket and sporting a pair of ancient flight goggles was, in another lifetime, Samuel J. Canfield, a Nobel Prize–winning author whose son was tragically killed in Detroit's 1943 "race riot"?

And, finally, *what if*, by using what he called his "flying words" and a rickety hand-built replica of an old World War I biplane they built together, father and son would travel the world, and in the freedom of their imaginations, find the comfort and refuge from the injustice and racial hatred that confronted them every day in the real world?

EXT. THE KEYMAN'S BACKYARD—DAY

Young Sarah rubs the grime off the side of the Keyman's broken plane and attempts to read the faded letters beneath.

                    YOUNG SARAH
          The Pride of Detroit . . .

                    KEYMAN
          Yes, he was.

                         YOUNG SARAH
I bet it don't work.

                           KEYMAN
Oh, she works all right.
          (stroking the broken propeller)
In her day, the Pride could take you
anywhere you want to go.
          (beat)
If you knew how to ask her right.

But where to start? In the first lesson Mr. Canfield gives Sarah to help her discover her flying words, I decided the Keyman would use a visualization technique similar to the kind I used in the classroom in my early days of teaching creative writing to my fourth and fifth graders at the Grosse Pointe Academy.

INT. THE KEYMAN'S SHED—DAY

Mr. Canfield pulls several blank keys from his
wall and puts one in young Sarah's open palm.

                           KEYMAN
Now close your eyes.

Sarah closes them. And then sneaks a peak with
one eye.

                      KEYMAN (cont'd)
Both of them. No cheating.

Sarah complies.

                      KEYMAN (cont'd)
Now tell me what you see.

                    YOUNG SARAH
It's dark, I don't see anything.

                      KEYMAN
Then use your second sight. What does it
feel like?

                    YOUNG SARAH
This is stupid. It feels like a key.

                      KEYMAN
Then don't just touch it. You have to
listen to the key when it speaks to you.

Sarah closes her eyes even tighter and puts the
key to her ear as if it were as seashell.

                    YOUNG SARAH
Hello, key? Is anybody there? Hello?

                      KEYMAN
This isn't a game, young woman. I'm trying
to teach you something here.

Sarah tries again, this time concentrating,
closing her eyes and clutching her fist as tight
as she can.

                    YOUNG SARAH
I can feel it now. This is a house key. It's
definitely telling me, "I am a house key."

                      KEYMAN
What kind of house key? Is it heavy, is it
light? I can't see it. Be specific, paint me
a picture.

                    YOUNG SARAH
        (clutching her fist, her eyes locked shut)
It's hard to describe. It feels light . . .
like a button off a shirt . . . or a coin, a
new coin . . .

BEGIN FLASHBACK:

It's four years earlier. As her mother looks
on, an excited six-year-old Sarah tears open an
envelope with her name on it, eagerly in search
of what's inside the enclosed card. Meanwhile,
in VOICE-OVER, the lesson continues as she
describes her own version of what Mr. Canfield's
key feels like.

              YOUNG SARAH (VO) (cont'd)
        (beaming)
It's a quarter! A brand-new quarter, like
the ones my grandmother used to send me on
Valentine's Day . . .

Suddenly, we're back in the Keyman's shed. Sarah
opens her eyes not at all understanding what just
happened.

                YOUNG SARAH (cont'd)
. . . before she died.
        (beat)
I really miss her quarters . . .

Carefully, gently, Mr. Canfield removes the key
from Sarah's tight grip and places it in his
jacket pocket for safekeeping.

KEYMAN
Now we're cooking with gas, young woman.
    (beat)
Now, we're going somewhere.

And finally, *what if*, after young Sarah masters her flying words, she convinces herself she can use them and the Pride of Detroit to help rescue the ailing Keyman's teenage son before he was viciously attacked and murdered by the racist mob?

Except it never happened. At the last minute and just before takeoff, Sarah's mother discovers her daughter's relationship with the "mentally disturbed" Keyman and, despite Sarah's desperate pleas, abruptly puts an end to their relationship.

And their plans, real or imaginary, to save the Keyman's son.

"Sorry, Harvey, it'll never happen," a sympathetic producer told me when, shortly after *The Keyman* screenplay won an honorable mention certificate from the New York International Independent Film & Video Festival. "It's a lovely story, I admit, very tender," she said, "but it just won't travel. It's an international market out there, and historical movies about kids and Black people just don't sell."

Still, I've never closed the door on *The Keyman* or given up hope that one day, as adult Sarah does in the last pages of her (my) screenplay, she can be united with her beloved Keyman and finally complete the journey of imagination, hope, and redemption they began so long ago.

And with their flying words, take us with them.

20

Taking Off Is the Hard Part

Before the Seven-Year War, my father would often take me and my brothers to Detroit's old Metropolitan Airport to watch the planes. "Taking off is the hard part, boys," my father the physicist would tell us, sharing his appreciation for the mechanics of flight. "It's the lift, the *energy* it takes to get the plane off the ground that makes it go."

I thought of Dad's physics lesson years later, whenever I found myself resisting beginning a new project. When I was at WXYZ-TV, my interns Barb Koster and Jo-Allison Floyd could always tell I was avoiding lift-off because they could never find me; I'd frequently be off brushing my teeth, schmoozing with Jeanne Findlater's secretary, or hanging out in Studio C offering to help the stagehands move a set or paint a flat—something, *anything* that would delay my taking that first step in the journey.

It's not that I was lazy or felt I wasn't up for the task. Just the opposite: it's because I was smart, I knew what was coming. To this day, whenever my procrastination genie invites me to join him in waiting until the very last minute before starting a new project, we both know he's looking out for my best interest. Because, like me, he knows exactly what's going to happen the moment I stop procrastinating and throw myself into the fire.

And start asking my questions.

And it doesn't help that the work is for a good cause or that I promise the people I interview I'll be gentle with them when I peel their skin and rip their scabs off. Who in their right mind would jump at the chance to go *there*? Which is why, on the days when the work wasn't going well, and the canvas fought back, I came up with a nickname for my angst. "Where's Daddy?" I imagined my children wondering. But really, it was a rhetorical question, because I imagined Sasha and Noah knew perfectly well where to find their father.

I was upstairs in my third-floor home office, locked in the iron grip of my procrastination genie, desperately trying to delay the moment I would have to leave the "turd" floor to go out and earn my living picking away at somebody's fresh wounds.

Children Come to the World with a Thousand Questions

In 1997, when my good friend, the painter and sculptor Arthur Schneider, was dying of cancer, I talked him into letting me, my intern, Alan Bernstein, and my editor, Christa Kindt Newhouse, paint his portrait on film with *Off the Wall: A Creative Journey*, a doc I co-produced with Don Gonyea and his wife, my former intern, Laurie Burdue Gonyea.

It was a tough shoot; Arthur was fighting a losing battle with mesothelioma, a cancer of the lungs resulting from his years of exposure to the toxic chemicals and materials. "I've heard of dying for your art, but this isn't what I had in mind," he told me. "I guess this is the price tag, Harvey. The price tag is that I've been invaded by this malignancy."

Even with his diagnosis, Arthur was one of the most spirited and exuberant artists I have ever known. And unlike me, he *loved* every minute of the creative journey and couldn't wait to get up each morning to begin asking his questions and step into what he called "his light."

At first, Arthur was eager to let me tell his story, but as his health declined and his condition worsened, he began to resent the role reversal of my being the one who was, in his words, "holding the brush" while he "just sat there, playing model." Finally, during our last days of shooting, the dam broke. "Children come to the world with a thousand questions," he told me as he tried to explain his own lifelong passion for art-making and the importance of asking questions on his way to getting to the heart of every one of his magnificent paintings and sculptures.

                    ARTHUR (cont'd)
          You walk as a child, and you say, what is
          this? What is that? I actually did this to
          produce a flower. I went up to the flower and
          I kept asking the flower questions. How many
          petals do you have? How do you grow? What is

In Off the Wall: A Creative Journey, *Ed Kukla, Ron Ayers, Arthur Schneider, and I "step into the light."*
(Photo by Jerome Magid. Courtesy of Harvey Ovshinsky, HKO Media, and Blair Street Productions.)

your architecture? And I think that is part
of the art process. I could have spent the
day asking questions!

                    HARVEY
Are you going to miss the questions, Arthur?

                    ARTHUR
Oh, Harvey . . .
        (breaking down, sobbing)
I weep. I just weep. It's the one thing that
really bothers me. I won't be here to ask
the questions. You got to me, buddy.
        (beat)
That's the great sadness. That's the end.

Once, when I seriously considered ending it all and leaving documentary work for a full-time career in screenwriting, I thought about Arthur, Poletown's Father Maloney, Lawrence from J.O.L.T., Tammy Boccomino, and so many others I've interviewed over the years who trusted me enough to help me help them tell their truths and share their stories.

And then I came to my senses. Although I was a decent enough screenwriter, I realized my fictional work paled in comparison to the stories I encountered whenever I left my "turd floor" to journey below the surface in hot pursuit of what Jean-Luc Godard called "the truth twenty-four frames per second."

21

Think Dory and You Get the Picture

One of the most challenging questions my students at the College for Creative Studies used to ask in their documentary and screenwriting projects was when was the best time to begin a scene, and at what point should they end it? Although there are certainly exceptions, my rule of thumb has always been to start the scene as late as possible in the action, and then, once the point of the scene has been made, get out just as quickly.

But what does that *look* like? What does that even mean?

To demonstrate, I begin the lesson by apologizing for being late. Then, I apologize for not being able to take attendance because, I explain, I left my briefcase in the car. I leave, and upon my return to the classroom, I apologize once again for taking so long to return but I accidentally left my keys in the car.

"So," I ask, "if this was your movie, how many of you would have started your scene by now?"

No hands go up, only yawns. I proceed, this time adding a little tension to the situation by grabbing a thick piece of chalk and hurriedly drawing a long, scraggly line across the surface of the blackboard.

But before I can spell out the words inside the circle below the line, the chalk snaps in my hand.

                    MISTER O
        Shit!
              (beat)
        Not again.

Now we're cooking, I hear the class thinking. *At last, something's happening!*

I thank my students for their keen sense of observation and agree we *could* start the scene here. "But, what if," I ask, staring down at the floor and avoiding all eye contact, "the reason I was late to class today was because I had just come from a doctor's appointment?"

Wait! What?

I look up at them and announce, "It's not good news. She told me I have all the symptoms of early onset Alzheimer's disease."

```
              MISTER O (cont'd)
          (wiping his glasses)
      Which is why the dean and I have agreed
      it would be best if today was my last day
      teaching this class.
          (beat)
      . . . and, really, my last day teaching
      altogether.
```

Silence. Stone-cold, dead silence. I let the news sink in for a few seconds, but once I feel I've made my point, I put my students out of their misery and assure them. It was just a movie, I'm perfectly fine, and I look forward to being their teacher for as long as they'll have me.

And I remind them of the point of this exercise: while my character's irritating bouts of forgetfulness, impatience, and frustration may have, at first glance, *seemed* boring and a complete waste of their time in the telling of my character's story, that really wasn't the case. Because, I continue, picking up the chalk and writing on the chalkboard, the moral of this story is that the moment we decide to enter a scene and when we choose to leave it depends on one thing. And one thing only.

What's this scene *about*? An even more importantly, what's it *really* about?

What I didn't share with my students, and what I never told anyone outside a few friends and my family, was that this painfully bizarre teaching moment was inspired by an actual event in my life.

Kaboom

Although creatively HKO Media was a dream job, keeping the lights on in the face of growing competition from young producers starting their own one-man-band production companies, and with so many of my corporate clients thinking they could shoot and edit their stories in-house or on their cell phones, iPads, and laptops, the stress eventually took its toll, and the pressure became overwhelming.

Kaboom.

Baby boomers and Generation Xers know what I'm talking about. It's the sound of the other shoe dropping, when, in what's left of this fragmented gig economy of ours, we're told our own gig is up and worse, we're too old to get hired. And too young to retire.

But these days you don't have to be a kaboomer to be one, you just have to *look* like one. Hugh Wilson, who created *WKRP in Cincinnati* and *Police Academy*, suffered the same fate when, after retiring from Hollywood, moving to Virginia to teach, and then returning to Los Angeles to pitch a new project, he found himself facing rejection at every turn. "I shouldn't have been surprised," he said. "When I was working on *KRP* or *Bob Newhart*, if some *I Love Lucy* writers came in and wanted a job, we'd go, 'Please; you're so done.'"

I knew the feeling well.

I don't know how I'm going to pull it off this time, I wrote in so many of my hundreds of pages of diaries, journals, and war dances. *What if Blue Cross doesn't renew my contract? What happens if WDET doesn't accept my proposal for their new morning show? I still dream about* The Keyman, *maybe I should rewrite it as a play? Jesus, I hate chasing my tail!*

And then, in 2002, it happened, something that made me take stock and stop my whining in its tracks.

Transient global amnesia (TGA) is a strange, mysterious neurological condition characterized by a "sudden onset of memory loss and confusion," according to the National Center for Advancing Translational Sciences. "The person may be disoriented in regard to time and place but can remember who they are and can recognize family members. During an episode of TGA, a person is not able to make new memories."

Think Dory, the royal-blue tang fish voiced by Ellen DeGeneres in *Finding Nemo*, and you get the picture. "I forget things almost instantly," she explains to Nemo's father. "It runs in my family . . . well, at least I *think* it does."

But the loss of short-term memory is only one of TGA's horrific symptoms. When it strikes and the brain short circuits, it gives new meaning to *Star Trek's* notion of a "rift in the space-time continuum." You know *who* you are, that's not the problem. But you have no idea *where* you are.

Or why?

"It's as if the brain is on overload and takes a break to recharge," Dr. Carolyn Brockington, a vascular neurologist, told the *New York Times*'s personal health columnist, Jane Brody, who likened a TGA episode to "rebooting a computer to eradicate an unexplainable glitch."

In my case, it's very likely one of my glitches stemmed from the tension and the stress I was feeling in fighting my losing battle to try to keep HKO Media afloat. The irony for me was that, until the moment I was struck by this asteroid, Catherine and I were enjoying a pitch-perfect visit with our son, Noah, gorging on the Windy City's fine food, Chicago's Lyric Opera's production of Sondheim's *Sweeney Todd*, and the Chicago Shakespeare Theater's magnificent, intimate staging of his *Sunday in the Park with George*. I was in heaven.

Until the sky fell.

We were back at the hotel when suddenly my mind went blank. And that was just for starters. Within minutes, my brain felt like a planet whose atmosphere was suddenly burned away. Where did it go? What happened to my planet's protective surface, my soul's *skin*? Without it, I felt naked and exposed to even the slightest sights and sounds cascading from within the infinite universe that was once my immediate environment.

"It could be a stroke," Bloom told Catherine when, in a panic, she called from the hotel to ask my old therapist what she should do. I couldn't help because I couldn't remember where I was. Or what we were doing there in the first place. When I refused to get out of the shower, Bloom stepped on the gas. "Get him dressed and take him to the ER. You're in Chicago, so Northwestern is your best bet."

He was right. The temptation might have been to medicate me right away, just in case it was a stroke, but one of the attending physicians recognized the symptoms immediately. Although I don't remember any of this, after seeing the results of my MRI, he assured my wife and son that my bewildered condition was very much a temporary one and that I would most likely recover fully within 24–48 hours.

Most *likely*? Part of the collateral damage from TGA is that the person inflicted isn't the only causality. Because I had no ability to hold my thoughts or retain any short-term memory for more than a few seconds, Catherine and Noah had to endure my endless questioning and need for reassurance. "Is it a good hospital?" I asked dozens, if not hundreds of times. They assured me it was.

Over and over again.

Where did it come from? How could this have happened? It depends on who you talk to. Transient global amnesia (TGA) is one of those confounding but increasingly more familiar boutique disorders, perhaps genetic in origin, but also triggered by emotional stress and/or exacerbated by bouts of physical exertion. Which, according to the textbooks, is a polite way of saying my episode could also have been caused by shoveling too much heavy snow, diving into bracing-cold water, or making love. Modesty prevents me from admitting which was my culprit.

For me, the great absurdity was that, for someone who prided himself on earning a living asking deep, penetrating, probing questions, I had to suffer the hell of repeating the same painfully banal ones dozens, if not hundreds, of times. What time is it? What *day* is it?

Is this a good hospital?

With TGA, "the desire to know is there," reported the *New York Times*, but sadly, "the ability to hold onto the answer is not."

And I missed my answers.

I Was Hoping I Was Wrong

One of the challenges of surviving a full-blown TGA episode is getting out of the hospital. Once the shock begins to dissipate and the brain's atmosphere begins the work of healing and reconstructing itself, the medical team won't release a patient unless they can correctly answer a series of key questions as part of what's called a Mini-Mental State Exam (MMSE). My doctor at Northwestern was a good sport, and because he shared my desire to see me discharged, he gave me the questions to the exam in advance. And, not unaware of the irony of the situation, he urged Catherine and Noah to help me memorize them.

Fortunately, I passed with flying colors. Although later Catherine admitted I gave her a scare when I balked at naming the then president of the United States. That was a tough one. Not because I didn't remember the answer, but because I did. "George W. Bush," I finally stated, confidently.

"Very good," the doctor said, smiling. "But why did you hesitate?"

"Because," I said, relieved that I had recovered my sense of humor as well as my memory, "I was hoping I was wrong."

22

In Sweden, They Have a Name for It

In 2001, the year before my TGA episode, my creative partners, Sesame Workshop consultant Sheri Perelli and my former WDIV intern Bob Kernen, and I were invited to pitch a new multimedia literacy series for children to the newly created Noggin television network, a partnership between Nickelodeon and Sesame Workshop.

Please Don't Eat the Books imagined the adventures of a twenty-first-century team of live-action preteen "Guardians" pledged to protect the last of the world's books buried in an ancient depository we called Aesop's Tomb. The original library, according to legend, was destroyed eons ago by a horde of book-eating, page-chewing gargoyles, trolls, and gremlins led by the evil golem Cursiff and his ravenous minions, Koogle and Spew.

And now they're back, hungrier than ever.

Noggin appreciated the concept, especially the interactive web component, which invited television viewers and web users to join the Guardians and "secretly" replenish a new Aesop's Tomb with their own favorite books.

But the network passed. We never found out what the problem was, but I suspect, like *Your Body Knows Best*, the all-singing, all-dancing anti-drug/pro-healthy living series I proposed to Detroit Public Television thirteen years earlier, *Please Don't Eat the Books* may have been "too rich" for Noggin's blood.

At least, that's what I told myself. "Research and development" was how I used to write off such rejections. In Sweden, they have another name for it.

There's a museum in Helsingborg that celebrates the world's most famous flops. The exhibitions are no joke, insists Dr. Samuel West, director of the Museum of Failure. "The risky business of innovation requires failure," he told the *New York Times*. "Our goal is to encourage organizations to be better at learning from failures—not just ignoring them and pretending they never happened."

That was never my problem.

Although, I have to confess, in 2017 it was hard for me to read news reports that David Oyelowo and Russell Crowe were set to star in the movie version of *Arc of Justice*, Detroit native Kevin Boyle's National Book Award–winning account of how famed civil rights attorney Clarence Darrow came out of retirement to defend Ossian Sweet, a Black physician who was tried for murder in 1925. His and his family's crime was allegedly shooting one of his white neighbors while defending his Detroit home from an attack by an angry, rock-throwing crowd.

Of all my collaborations with Bill Pace, the Darrow/Sweet story has always held a special place in our hearts. In 1989, we were *this* close to going into production on our own Darrow-Sweet project, first for HBO and then ABC, until a hot up-and-coming actor named Denzel Washington decided not to play Sweet after all (to Burt Lancaster's Darrow) because he was weary of playing "one more" victim. For us, it was déjà vu all over again because it reminded us of when *Mork and Mindy's* Pam Dawber passed on playing Sharon Dragan in *P. J. and the Dragon* because, we were told, she felt the part was "too sad." (Not unlike Pam's role later that year, as the wife in *Quiet Victory: The Charlie Wedemeyer Story*, "a real-life story of a high school teacher and football coach diagnosed with Lou Gehrig's disease.")

There are many reasons why so many of our creative efforts succeed, and others do not, why our back burners brim with so many unfulfilled, unrealized projects. I believe one of the biggest culprits is our own vanity; it's what happens when we swallow our own propaganda and can't imagine anyone not adoring our precious darlings as much as we do. But it's a slippery slope. After all, if we don't believe our work is magnificent and a gift from the gods, how could we ever muster the courage to even begin to create let alone complete a project? Not to mention have the nerve and the self-confidence necessary to try and peddle our wares.

Even when it feels like no one is buying.

The Seed Beneath the Snow

Another occupational hazard is when we insist on putting our eggs in one basket, and after our first pitch, presentation, or proposal is rejected, we run out of steam, lose all interest, and move on to another project, one which, we convince ourselves, is sure to be even more exciting and *so* much more successful.

But, of course, it doesn't work that way.

On our way to a development deal with Fred Rogers Productions for *The Playful Universe of the Mighty Hubble*, Bill and I burned through more than a half-dozen ideas. Each one, we felt at the time, was more brilliant than the other.

We started with a series we affectionately called *Mister Rogers' Play Shop*, centered around the adventures of a group of preschool friends learning about themselves and the world within an entirely renovated and refurbished version of the original television home of Fred Rogers. Fred's people were tempted, and while they welcomed the legacy aspect of *Mister Rogers' Play Shop*, the concept was rejected. "It's too soon," we were told. "Better to start with a clean slate."

Next came *Aggie's Farm*, an animated series that we imagined took place in a foster home for lost or discarded balloon animals. When that didn't fly, we came up with *The Really Big Adventures of Little Marmalade*, about a little girl who lives with her father in a downtown warehouse, home to one of the oldest parade companies in the country. Inspired by the parade company's fantastical array of floats created by her father, Marmalade and her friends create all kinds of fun and educational adventures with the magical creatures she and her friends bring to life with their imaginations.

Close but no cigar.

The feedback we received for this latest proposal was encouraging but not unconditional. While Fred's team enjoyed the feisty, imaginative character of Marmalade, we were cautioned not to, under *any* circumstances, call her by that name. Apparently, we were informed, in addition to being another name for jam or jelly, *marmalade* was once a derogatory term for Black people.

Who knew?

This was a revelation! Not only because Bill and I had no clue, but because here we were, two fifty-something white guys, trying to come up with ideas for a new national educational TV series for children, and we were the ones getting the education!

Fred Rogers was right. "To get somewhere new," he wrote in his posthumously published book, *Life's Journey According to Mister Rogers*, "we may have to leave someone else behind."

So goodbye Aggie, goodbye Little Marmalade. And hello the Mighty Hubble. For a while, anyway.

"You have to accept not everyone is going to see the light through your heat, Harvey," Dad reminded me when, not long after Fred Rogers Productions accepted our proposal, we were told PBS rejected Hubble and his playful universe. "One has to struggle to be able to express innovation. You have to be patient and not easily discouraged," my father told a class of eager middle-school scientists in Winnebago, Manitoba, just weeks before he died in 2012. "It is like the seed beneath the snow, or worse, the seed beneath the concrete."

Or, in my case, I thought, licking my wounds and recalling my childhood misadventure with my brother's poor carrot sprout, the seed in the Styrofoam cup.

23

Where the Heat Comes From

In all the hundreds of hours of conversations and interviews Dad and I had with each other, the subject of his dying only came up once. "It doesn't interest me," he once told me. "I'd rather talk about living." And then he changed the subject.

Until he couldn't anymore.

Dad always said he wanted to die with his boots on, and on October 17, 2012, he got his wish. "Freya, get me the summary!" he shouted to his loyal assistant, who was nowhere in the room during a painful recurrence of his prostate cancer that had metastasized to his bones.

While he was dying, I never heard any discussion of Dad wanting to "let go" or head for the light; in my experience, that was the last thing he'd ever want to do. Still, a week before he died, surrounded by several of the hundreds of people who knew and loved him, I couldn't resist attempting at least one visualization exercise. While he was unconscious, I kissed his hand and suggested he imagine swimming in the lake on his property, on his way to meet his beloved Iris on the other side, even though, six years earlier, poor Iris had died tragically while swimming with him there.

I'd like to think Dad bought it, but I doubt it. As much as my father loved to swim and though he cared deeply for Iris, all he really wanted to do now was to continue the struggle and live to fight another day.

After his death a week later, I was grateful my father was no longer in pain, and I wanted to think, after enduring the excruciating loss of Iris and later the takeover of Energy Conversion Devices after a bloody revolt by the board of directors, his death might actually have been a respite for him, even a relief.

But of course, that was my movie. Not his. Dad was a swashbuckler, a brilliant, trailblazing adventurer who loved every minute of his charmed life of creativity, science, and invention. Unlike me, my father not only accepted but *embraced* the years of sacrifice and struggle that were required—*demanded*—for the effort. "You're the only person I know," I once told him, "who, on his death-bed, will wish he spent *more* time at the office."

He laughed heartily. But he also did not disagree.

Of Singing Birds and Gilded Butterflies

As a nurse psychotherapist with a doctorate in clinical psychology, Catherine taught hospice and palliative studies to nursing, spiritual care, and social work students, reminding them of the five most important conversations dying persons can have with their families. One of the most important is about forgiveness. I forgive you; do you forgive me?

That never happened between Dad and me. For one thing, it wasn't nec-essary. Over the years there was really very little unsaid or unspoken between us. Although, truthfully, some conversations were more painful than others. For both of us.

"No, Dad, your grandchildren are not going to call you Stan. That's not going to happen."

"No, Noah may appear to be delayed in his walking, but we're *not* going to have him evaluated at Johns Hopkins to validate your theory about how devel-opmentally delayed lab rats need extra stimulation and exercise to help them advance their range of lower-body motion."

"Oh, and by the way, I've changed my middle name from Eugene (after his hero, the early twentieth-century socialist presidential candidate Eugene Victor Debs) to Kurek, the maiden name of my own hero, Catherine." *That* must have really hurt him terribly, and in retrospect, I regret not being gentler in its handling.

But at the time I didn't care. I was in the throes of therapy and, in my mind, making up for lost time.

It was not the first time we butted heads. The problem with living with a genius is that so much of Dad's thought process and decision-making was instinc-tive. "I just have a feel for such things," he would say about his dependency on gut feelings and what he called his "physical intuition."

I pride myself on my own share of instinct and intuition, but in my father's case, there was also a shadow side to his gift. How can you dispute or win an argument with such a person? And even if I did ever manage to change Dad's mind, which was a rare occasion, you couldn't change his feelings about the subject, which, in the end, drove his every decision.

Still, it didn't keep me from trying.

"I'm sorry you feel that way, Harvey," he once told me when I informed him how hurt and disappointed I was at whatever he said or did at the time that offended me. "But did it ever occur to you that disappointment between fathers and sons is a two-way road?"

What? *Well, no,* my inner voice fought back.

```
              BAD HARVEY (cont'd)
       That thought never occurred to me.
          (beat)
       I thought disappointment was your job.
```

To be clear, I've always known my father loved me; he made no secret of that. But feeling desired and *needed* is another story. It's one reason why I jumped at the chance to work with him at ECD. Growing up, how many times had I watched him conduct his "meetings" with his circle of friends, comrades, and collaborators? Embedded on the family leather coach in the living room of his and Iris's Bloomfield Hills home, engaged in passionate discussions about science and politics, these living room salons always struck me as being tender, almost romantic, in my young adulthood, reminding me of the pivotal moment near the end of *King Lear* when, as prisoners, the fallen monarch invites his beloved daughter Cordelia away to prison: "We two alone will sing like birds . . . we'll live, and pray, and sing, and tell old tales, and laugh at gilded butterflies."

I loved my father deeply, probably more than he ever knew, but singing birds and gilded butterflies were never a part of our story. Our relationship was unlike his relationship with his own father and what he demanded from Iris and so many others in his life. I didn't worship him.

I didn't know how.

In the end, what I *could* do for my father was what I did so often when we worked together: I helped Stan Ovshinsky tell his story. During the last stages of his dying, I threw myself into producing mode, with input from the family, feverishly writing a press release and in one particularly vigorous war dance imagining how, with support from my friends in the media—Don Gonyea, *Metro Times* columnist Jack Lessenberry, Reuters's Paul Lienert, and the *Wall Street Journal*'s Dale Buss—we could create a rigorous campaign to help spread the word about Dad's death.

And his remarkable life.

We were more than successful, with dozens of national and international newspapers and radio stations reporting on his passing, describing Dad as "a hero for the planet," "the modern world's most important energy visionary," "the Edison of our age," and "the most important inventor you never heard of." I was especially proud of the coverage by *Forbes* magazine, which nine years earlier had famously described Stan Ovshinsky as a tireless, self-aggrandizing promoter, "a great pretender" and a "puppet master," but now that he was dead, the magazine mourned him as the "battery genius behind smartphones and hybrids."

But perhaps the best tribute of all came three years after his death, when, for his "dramatic improvements in . . . electronics, and solar power, with special recognition for his invention of the first working nickel-metal hydride battery," Dad, along with thirteen other people described as among "the world's greatest inventors," was inducted into the National Inventors Hall of Fame.

In the posthumous Washington, DC, induction ceremony, Stan Ovshinsky was described as a self-taught physicist committed to using his more than four hundred patents in science and technology to "solve social problems with the goal of bettering the world and the quality of life for humanity."

The word *maverick* never came up.

It's Complicated

As satisfying as it was in his last days to promote my father and his work, Catherine was not impressed. "I know this is important work for you," she said, choosing her words carefully, "and all this writing, planning, and organizing is helping you get through. But he's your father, and feelings are important, too."

I understood what she was saying. Knowing how complex my relationship with Dad was, she cautioned me to at least consider the *possibility* that unless I stopped spinning and hit the pause button to shed some tears, I may later experience what they called in her trade "complicated grief."

Maybe, probably, I insisted, but some griefs are more complicated than others. Although I loved my father, I was surprised not to feel any suffering from his death, complicated or otherwise. In fact, just the opposite. "Death not merely ends life," wrote Hannah Arendt, "it also bestows upon it a silent completeness."

The irony is my tears eventually did flow, albeit six years later when I completed the later drafts of this chapter and discovered an undated note written on ECD stationery buried among Dad's personal files. It was addressed to me.

"I would fly anywhere to have seen and heard Harvey tonight," it read. "He not only has great talent but true depth and *menschkeit* [Yiddish for admirable, noble, or dignified characteristics]. I am proud of him, not only as a son, but as a person. I was moved—I am happy to have lived to see him—with his wisdom and his maturity."

So, here's what I know, a lesson learned about my father only after I put this chapter to rest:

For as long as I can remember, in both my real and imagined lives, I have always preferred, even craved, the sweet sounds of harmony over discordance, peace and quiet over noise, compliance over conflict. But in thinking about the convoluted, lifelong push/pull I felt for my parents, my mother included, I'm reminded of an incident, a rare, tender middle moment from my early childhood.

(Photo courtesy of Harvey Ovshinsky.)

It happened one Saturday afternoon when Dad took my brothers and me to work with him at his lab. After punching holes in a scrap shard of plexiglass, I burned my fingers touching a hot drill bit too soon.

He was sorry it happened but didn't appear surprised or fazed by the accident. "It's called friction, Harvey," my father tried to explain, blowing on the bit to help cool it.

"It's where the heat comes from."

24

The Great Gusto

I never wanted to be a teacher. The thought never occurred. For the longest time, all I ever wanted to do was tell my own stories; I never imagined I would have the opportunity, let alone the interest, to help others tell theirs. But then, like Pole-town's Father Maloney, I fell in love. I fell in love with my students' energy, their passion, and their need to speak their truths and share their Good Stuff with others.

Looking back more than thirty years ago, how brave Sid DuPont was when, despite my lack of training and experience in the classroom, the academy's head-master at the Grosse Pointe Academy agreed to hire me to help me work off my kids' tuition by teaching classes in creative writing. Still, I wasn't worried about my lack of credentials.

Starting from scratch is what I do best.

"Breathing his fire wasn't Pendleton's problem," I told my fourth and fifth graders, reading from a story I had written for them. In "Have You Seen Pendrag-on's Fire?" Pendleton Pendragon didn't mind the breathing part, it was *showing* and *sharing* his fire with anyone that frightened him more than anything.

So far, so good, but when I asked my young Pendragons to draw the color of their own fire and demonstrate the sound of their roar, a fellow teacher was not amused. "Mr. O, we are testing next door," Mrs. F wrote in a note she asked one of her students to deliver to me. "Could you be a bit more quiet?"

As satisfying as it was to stretch these new muscles, there was a brief moment in time when I had just a tinge of self-doubt about my work in the classroom. After the unexpected deaths of both her husband and brother, singer, poet, and Grosse Pointe Academy parent Patti Smith was curious about how her son Jack-son and daughter Jesse were doing in my class. I was always of two minds dur-ing my parent-teacher conversations with Patti. I always felt I had to be specific,

Playing with Pendragon's fire in Mister O's classroom.
(Photo by Mike Shamus, montage by Christa Kindt Newhouse and Steve Kruk.
Courtesy of Harvey Ovshinsky and HKO Media.)

careful not to glaze over or in any way be generic in my answers to her questions about her children's progress.

But it was hard, too. What could I *possibly* say to Patti Smith about creative writing?

And anyway, what I *really* wanted to do was gush and remind her we'd actually met years earlier during a taping of ABX's *Tubeworks* TV show, and how before that, during my *Fifth Estate* years, I'd met her late husband, guitarist Fred "Sonic" Smith, when he and his band, the MC5, used to rehearse in the paper's basement.

With a Little Help from My Friends

They say you can't teach creativity, and they may be right, but I'm with educational psychologist and author Jane Healy, who insisted there's no reason why we can't at least *model* creative thinking. Which is why I always showed up in class accompanied by my teaching assistants, a gaggle of imaginary animal spirit guides I conjured up to help my students visualize what the creative process looks like. And how it feels.

Wanda the Wild Goose was my go-to muse of choice, a master brainstormer, who was as brave and fearless as she was wild and wacky, a high-flying bird who was unafraid to stick her neck out and dive headfirst into any problem-solving or creative situation. "No worries," she would comfort my young writers, flapping her wings with great gusto and encouraging them to do the same. "After all," Wanda reminded us at every turn, "it's about the going, not the gone!"

On the other hand, her partner in creativity, Ponder the Polar Bear, was never in a hurry to complete anything. Our ever-present incubator, the big fellow relished preparing, planning, organizing, *structuring* his time, and unlike Wanda, he preferred to look before he leaped and aim before he fired. Options and choices didn't scare this lug of a polar bear; Ponder actually looked forward to being stumped during the creative process because it gave him the opportunity to ask his questions and examine his problems from every angle.

My students were never sure what Shredder looked like because all we ever saw of the creature were its tiny claws clutching the outside of our classroom's wastepaper basket. Still, it didn't take long for my students to feel comfortable embracing every writer's best friend and, once the hugging was over, look forward to shooting hoops in Shredder's direction with what was left of their crumpled-up rough drafts and sloppy copies.

And finally, there was Yezzbutt, our resident idea douser, representing every creative person's worst nightmare. My students *loved* to hate Yezzbutt because she was so scary. And familiar. After all, who would dare to be open, vulnerable, and willing to speak their minds only to have Yezzbutt, their very own inner judge, jury, critic, and executioner, standing by ready to pass her judgments and lower her boom.

"That's very interesting, Harvey," I can hear her saying even now, whispering to me over my shoulder as I write this. "Yezzbutt, you're not going to actually hand that in, are you?"

When Someone Tells You Something You've Done Is So Gay

As much fun as we had playing with words, what I remember most about the eighteen years I spent teaching creative writing at the Grosse Pointe Academy wasn't the laughter. And really, there were times it wasn't even the writing.

Once, after what I thought was an otherwise successful field trip to WDIV's downtown television studios, I heard one of my sixth graders, who was white, repeatedly refer to Detroit as a ghetto. Class was in session! His remarks prompted a heated, impromptu conversation about the meaning of the G word and the harmful consequences of using negative stereotypes to describe places or situations that young people had little, if any, personal contact with.

"Can anyone give another example of how words can be used to deride and disrespect?" I asked. James (not his real name) raised his hand. He was someone whose name I always had to force myself to remember because he was one of those deadeyes, an apparently disinterested student who rarely spoke up or participated in class.

JAMES

```
Mister O, when someone tells you something
you've done is so gay, that's not a compliment.
     (beat)
Is it?
```

As educational as these conversations were, it was the death of a parent that provided the most powerful learning experiences, for me as well as my students, especially when they needed help coping with the fact that this parent had died by suicide.

When Carol's (not her real name) father locked himself in his garage and hanged himself, no one in our class knew what to say to her or how to find the words to say it. So, we scrapped the day's planned activity and instead talked about love and how each of us chose to express it. "The question is," I asked several days later when Carol returned to school, "how do we know someone loves us? How can we tell?" That led to an energetic discussion about the meaning of the concept "show, don't tell" and how in life, as well as our writing, our actions speak so much louder than our words.

Which is why I asked my students to take the next few minutes to write about a memory they had about one of their parents and how they might have demonstrated, not so much by their words but by their deeds and actions, their love for their children.

Carol was stuck. A perfectionist to the nth degree, she was just too traumatized to even pick up her pen. I handed her a pencil with a particularly thick eraser and suggested this time not to worry about making any mistakes.

Of course, several of my rock stars wanted to read their assignments first, and that was fine; it helped warm us all up for what we knew was coming, when a tearful Carol stood up and proceeded to break our hearts with her tearful recitation of how, knowing how much she loved baseball, her father once took her to see a Detroit Tigers opening game.

On a school day.

When Carol began to sob, I offered to finish reading her reflection aloud; she considered it for a moment, then demurred, reaching out to accept my hand to hold as she finished reading her assignment. Teachers could get away with such behavior in those days.

It's been a long while since my academy days, but the lessons still linger, especially when, once a year, during Black History Month, my daughter, Sasha Ovshinsky Murphy, the intermediate and middle school dean of students, honors the memory of Dr. Martin Luther King Jr. by showing her students *The Night Dr. Martin Luther King Jr. Came to Grosse Pointe* and discussing with them her father's story about what happened in their community.

25

Kintsugi

"What's this?" I would ask my students whenever I introduced the second part of my two-part Scratching the Surface exercises. Turning away from the scraggly lines, arrows, and circles on the chalkboard, I face the class and, rolling up one of my sleeves, proceed to give my bare arm an exaggerated pinch.

"Skin" was the obvious answer, the largest organ in our body and the sole protector of our muscles, soft tissues, and internal organs.

"So, can you imagine," I continued, "what would happen if we woke up one morning and, metaphorically speaking, decided to shed our surface and expose to the world all the Good Stuff we normally keep inside? What do you think would happen to our precious truths, our private, innermost thoughts and feelings, our most intimate secrets we dare not tell anyone? Can you imagine what they would *do* to us?"

My kids knew; they got it. They always do.

"Splat," my young Pendragons shouted with glee, as they eagerly leaped from their chairs to join me in crushing our spilled guts with the heels of our shoes.

Skin. Don't leave home without it.

Unless, of course, you can't help yourself. And that's the point. Because, despite the risk, real or imagined, the only thing more difficult and more painful than opening ourselves up and sharing the best part of ourselves with others is how it feels when we don't even try.

The Japanese know what I'm talking about. While the nation's celebrated ceramic makers are grateful for and revel in the success of their achievements, the ancient art of *kintsugi*, or "the golden repair," has also taught them to appreciate the outcome of their efforts and accept and even embrace their missteps, disappointments, and what others might call their "failures" along the way.

Cracks and crevices in their pottery don't scare these artisans, who honor and show respect for their work's flaws and imperfections by creating what they call a "precious scar" for each one, consisting of carefully concocted portions of liquid or powdered silver or gold.

I liked the sound of that, which is why, in time, I eventually changed the name of my own failure museum to Harvey's Golden Repair Shop. And although I don't linger, I sometimes allow myself the luxury of engaging in a little kintsugi of my own. And when that happens, and when in the distance I hear the sound of a phone ringing or a text pinging, I imagine it might be a former student of mine, or a hot new up-and-coming independent filmmaker wondering, considering the country's current efforts to balance the scales and confront its history of racial injustice and inequality, if the rights to *The Keyman* might still be available? Or it's PBS calling to say that, after learning about the growing number of educators clamoring for more playtime and recess in the schools, they've had a change of heart, and well, maybe, it's time, once students recover from their Covid-induced staycations, to take another look at *The Playful Universe of the Mighty Hubble*.

But then I snap out of it, and when visiting hours are over, I remind myself, though I would certainly welcome such news, I'm not sitting on my hands waiting for the call. Like the Mighty Hubble, I'm just burstin' to dig in, get my hands dirty, and join my guerrilla army of shoemaker's elves in storming the barricades of my keyboard in hot pursuit of my next story.

And my next surface to scratch.

I have no idea what my next project is or where the work will take me, but not knowing no longer bothers; for me, it's all part of the great mystery, what my fellow Detroiter and Mumford Mustang Gilda Radner called life's "delicious ambiguity." And although I may not know what questions might stump me along the way, I do know with absolute certainty what my answers will be.

"Yes!"

Acknowledgments

(Photo by Edda Pacifico.)

One of my all-time favorite teaching exercises was when I would give my younger students "the treatment" by inviting them to read their work aloud while standing on a swatch of red carpet. We had only one rule: you had to work for it; only revisions and rewrites got the treatment. No sloppy copies on Mister O's red carpet!

So thanks Kathryn Wildfong, Annie Martin, Carrie Downes Teefey, Kristin Harpster, Lindsey Alexander, my peer reviewers, and the rest of the talented editorial, design, marketing, and production team at Wayne State University Press for keeping my red carpet warm for me whenever I was tempted to bolt during this, my maiden journey as an author. Also thanks to the brilliant Brad Norr for designing a cover I never saw coming. And to my developmental editor, Ronit Wagman, who, whenever I felt like pulling my punches, helped me dig deeper and scratch harder than I ever imagined possible. "Butt naked" was our battle cry, recalling how my gym teacher corrected me when I asked if it was true the boys at Mumford swam in the nude.

Many thanks to my friends and colleagues, among them Bill Pace, Bill McGraw, Jack Lessenberry, Mike Kerman, Peter Werbe, Paul Lienert, Matt Zacharias, Jay Nelson, Tony Kovner, Peter Garrett, Lillian Hoddeson, Chris Cook, Herb Ovshinsky, and especially my wife and life partner, Catherine Kurek-Ovshinsky, who read my chapters and told me what worked. And what didn't.

In my next life, I want to be Don Gonyea, who interrupted his reporting on the grueling 2020 presidential election to pitch in and, in his foreword, help me properly frame my picture. Thanks, Don, I can't wait to read *your* adventures in storytelling.

I'd like to acknowledge the debt I owe Detroit's television stations, WXYZ-TV/Channel 7, WDIV-Local 4/Graham Media Group, CW50 Detroit, and Detroit Public Television, as well as two now defunct area production and post-production houses, Grace & Wild and General Television Network. Without the generous creative and production support I received from collaborators like Ginny Hart, Steve Wild, Ron Herman, Christa Kindt Newhouse, and so many others, many of my most passionate of passion projects never would have materialized.

A special shout-out to my support staff over the years, especially Shannon Verklan, Matt Prested, Melissa Kufel Heath, Cindy Yee, Barbara Hayes, Bev Wood, Mike Hoffstrom, Oliver Thornton, Alex Wright, Bob Kernen, Bob Rossbach, et al, whose creativity, talent, loyalty, and commitment to the work allowed me the freedom to have my fun and make my dreams come true.

Game of Thrones creator George R. R. Martin once said of his version of paradise, "They can keep their heaven, when I die, I'd sooner go to Middle Earth." That's how I have always felt when my good friends and collaborators Dana Newhouse and Joe LoDuca (*The Evil Dead, Hercules: The Legendary Journeys, Xena: Warrior Princess*) created original scores for my films and videos and, in the process, managed to find their own stories in mine.

I am grateful to the University of Michigan's Bentley Historical Library for facilitating my access to its collection, the Harvey Kurek Ovshinsky Papers, processed by Daina Andries and digitized by Melissa Hernández-Durán. A special shout-out to Olga Virakhovskaya, lead archivist for Collections Management, and Malgosia Myc, assistant director and archivist for Reference and Academic Programs, who went out of their way to accommodate my somewhat disordered and embarrassingly sloppy research habits. I REALLY missed my interns on this project!

Thanks also to Wendy Rose Bice, who in 2016 helped me test the waters of memoir writing by publishing two articles recalling my early days with the *Fifth Estate* in the Jewish Historical Society of Michigan's journal, *Michigan Jewish History*. And to Tracy Irwin and the staff of the Detroit Historical Museum for welcoming Tim Kiska, Peter Werbe, and me as curators of the museum's 2015 exhibition, *Start the Presses: 50 Years of the Fifth Estate*. Also to Peter and Tim for contributing to my chapter on my *Fifth Estate* years. Ditto for Michael Jackman and the *Detroit Metro Times* for use of several excerpts of Peter's and my memories of the Detroit "riots," originally published in its July 19, 2017, cover story "A Radical's Oral History of Detroit in 1967."

And above all, thanks to Anne Serling for giving me permission to reprint her father's letter to me. Her own book, *As I Knew Him: My Dad, Rod Serling*, was an especially inspiring read as I attempted to recall my adventures with my own father.

"Here's a gift you may not have expected," Fred Rogers wrote in *Life's Journey According to Mister Rogers*, published two years after his death. That's how Bill Pace and I felt about Chief Operating Officer Kevin Morrison and his team at Family Communications, Inc. (later renamed Fred Rogers Productions) when they invited us to submit our proposals for a new series to replace *Mister Rogers' Neighborhood*. Thanks, Kevin, for sticking with us on our way to finding *The Mighty Hubble*.

No story is complete without sidekicks and supporting characters, so I'd like to acknowledge mine: the hundreds of interns, production assistants, and associate producers who, over the years, invited me to share with them what I was taught and learned about telling stories. A recent note from Joe Phillips was especially satisfying. My former HKO Media intern and production assistant was "in the soup" (as we used to call it), producing and directing a series of all-new training videos for a hospital struggling to keep up with the latest Covid-19 protocols. "It's as exhilarating as it is exhausting," Joe wrote, "but I do miss craft services. We ate VERY well at HKO Media."

Special thanks to all the participants in my weekend screenwriting workshops and monthly support groups. And especially to Jeanette Keramedjian, my good friend and collaborator, who helped me get the ball rolling so many years ago when she invited me to conduct my first writing workshop at Cranbrook PM, once part of the Continuing Education and Outreach program at the Cranbrook Educational Community. Ah, Cranbrook! We go WAY back.

And to my students at Wayne State University, the College for Creative Studies, Madonna University, and Washtenaw Community College, you know how I feel about you. As do my hundreds of talented young Pendragons who raised their voices and fearlessly showed me their fire in our creative writing classes at the Grosse Pointe Academy.

And finally, a special nod to Leonard Bernstein, whose book *The Unanswered Question: Six Talks at Harvard* inspired the closing line of this book. Although we never played in the same league, the maestro and I shared a common thread when it came to surface scratching. "Is it because you're short of breath?" the French novelist Alphonse Daudet once wrote of a bird who was frequently asked why he sang such short songs.

"No," the bird replied. "It is chiefly that I have many songs, and I would wish to tell them all."